Workbook/Lab Manual/Video Manual

Third Edition

Plazas

LUGAR DE ENCUENTROS

JILL PELLETTIERI
Santa Clara University

SILVIA ROLLE-RISSETTO
California State University, San Marcos

VERÓNICA AÑOVER
California State University, San Marcos

THOMSON
HEINLE

Australia Brazil Canada Mexico Singapore Spain United Kingdom United States

Plazas
Third Edition
Workbook/Lab Manual/Video Manual
Pellettieri | Rolle-Risetto | Añover

Editor-in-Chief: PJ Boardman
Senior Acquisitions Editor: Helen Richardson Greenlea
Development and Media Editor: Heather M. Bradley
Senior Content Project Manager: Esther Marshall
Senior Marketing Manager: Lindsey Richardson
Marketing Assistant: Denise Bousquet
Managing Technology Project Manager: Wendy Constantine

Manufacturing Manager: Marcia Locke
Composition & Project Management: Pre-Press PMG
Senior Art Director: Cate Rickard Barr
Cover Designer: Monti Lewis
Text & Cover Printer: West Group

Cover image: Front cover photos:Arch© iStockphoto.com; Plaza:©Photographer's Choice/David Norton/Getty Images

Printed in the United States of America
1 2 3 4 5 6 7   10 09 08 07

ISBN 1-4282-0598-5

Thomson Higher Education
25 Thomson Place
Boston, MA 02210-1202
USA

For more information about our products, contact us at:
Thomson Learning Academic Resource Center
1-800-423-0563
For permission to use material from this text or product, submit a request online at **http://www.thomson-rights.com**
Any additional questions about permissions can be submitted by e-mail to
thomsonrights@thomson.com

Table of Contents

WORKBOOK

LAB MANUAL

Preface

Workbook

The **Plazas** Workbook has been written and designed to accompany the **Plazas** textbook. Through a tightly structured instructional sequence that closely parallels the main text, the workbook leads students first through a set of highly contextualized form-focused activities and then through more open-ended contextualized activities that foster the development of skills for creative expression in Spanish.

Each chapter of the **Plazas** Workbook contains activities targeted at vocabulary and grammar building, as well as at the development of critical skills and strategies necessary for the comprehension and production of written texts. Following are some suggestions for the use of each of the chapters' sections:

Vocabulary and grammar exercises parallel each vocabulary and grammar section of the main text and can be assigned as homework as these sections are covered in class. They are designed to help students memorize and comprehend the words, phrases, and structures as well as to practice their application in context. This type of work will support students' active comprehension and production in their more open-ended and creative classroom oral activities.

Bienvenidos a... This section is designed to help students view and comprehend the Bienvenidos a... video segments that accompany each chapter. These activities include pre-viewing activities that lead students to recognize cognates they will hear in the video narration and post-viewing activities to check their comprehension of key cultural points made in the video. These activities can be assigned as stand-alone homework or as support to a class session in which the video will be presented.

¡A escribir! This writing section mirrors the strategies and task presented in the main text. The section's *pasos* guide students through the process of composing and editing in Spanish.

Autoprueba This section provides a short set of exercises that allow students to check their mastery of the target vocabulary and structures of a chapter. Students should complete these exercises prior to a review session or an exam. The answer key is located in the back of the Workbook/Lab Manual/Video Manual.

Laboratory Manual

The **Plazas** Laboratory Manual and Audio program have been written and designed to accompany the **Plazas** textbook. Each chapter is designed to help students improve their listening and speaking skills through vocabulary-based and form-based activities that parallel the analogous presentations in the main text. Listening tasks have been carefully written to allow practice of the material presented in the main text. They were crafted to target the appropriate proficiency level.

In the third edition, we are very excited to present our students with new and exciting activities. In the *Ritmos y música* section, the first-year university student is exposed to a vast representation of Hispanic music and in the *¡A ver!* section students are encouraged to work independently with the video segments that they may have viewed in class. We are confident that you will enjoy the new content in the Lab Manual!

Like all of the components of **Plazas**, the Laboratory Manual embeds culture and provides examples of authentic oral expressions. The audio recordings feature native speakers and, where possible, speakers that exhibit accents typical of the countries featured in the main text.

The following sections appear in a typical Laboratory Manual chapter:

Vocabulario checks the core of the lexicon presented in each chapter of the main text with enhanced listening comprehension and pronunciation activities.

Estructuras and Así se dice parallel each grammatical structure and function presented in the main text. The activities in this section reinforce listening comprehension, as well as the handling of structures, forms and expressions from the aural perspective.

Pronunciación provides a complete review of sounds of the Spanish language. This section is comprised of pronunciation and listening activities targeting difficult sounds and pronunciation rules. This section has been expanded from previous editions.

Ritmos y música exposes students to Hispanic songs from the countries featured in the main text. The activities that are included in this section ask students to express their opinions about the music they hear, and give them an opportunity to explore the song's lyrics and its message.

¡A ver! allows students to expand their comprehension of the video clips featured in the *Plazas* video program. The Real World-inspired video presents the target vocabulary and structures in the context of an engaging storyline.

All sections in the Laboratory Manual follow the same format, and are composed of three activities per section, with the exception of the two brand new sections which appear at the end of each chapter. In each activity, students are asked to provide a set number of answers. This will allow students to more easily gauge both the length and time it will take them to complete their work.

Acknowledgments:

I would like to thank my husband, Bruce Storms, for all his love and support throughout the completion of this project. I would also like to thank my dear friends and coauthors, Dr. Silvia Rolle-Rissetto and Dr. Verónica Añover, for their expertise, inspiration, collaboration, love, and humor. Without them, this third edition would not be the excellent pedagogical tool that it is. Finally, I would like to thank all of the Heinle team for their support and good spirit throughout the production of this project.

Dr. Jill Pellettieri

I would like to send my heart-felt thank you to everyone on the Heinle team involved in this project. I am grateful to my partner and my family for their unfaltering love and support throughout this long process of recreation, revision, and completion. And last but certainly not least, I extend my gratitude to my two dear Musketeers/*Mousquetaires*, my co-authors, Dr. Jill Pellettieri and Dr. Verónica Añover. Their unparalleled expertise, diligent work, and friendship have made this revision a sheer joy.

Dr. Silvia Rolle-Rissetto

I would like to thank all the members at Heinle involved in this new edition of *Plazas*. I am very grateful to my husband and son for allowing *Plazas* to steal away my presence, and for always supporting my work. I would like to express my most sincere gratitude to my two co-authors and dear friends Dr. Silvia Rolle-Rissetto and Dr. Jill Pellettieri for forming a great team, and for working so smoothly together.

Dr. Verónica Añover

¡Mucho gusto!

VOCABULARIO Saludos y despedidas

WB P-1 | Saludos y despedidas For each picture, circle or select the most appropriate of the three salutations or responses.

WB P-2 | Presentaciones Your roommate wants to practice meeting and greeting people in Spanish. Help her by selecting the appropriate response from the first column to each expression in the second column. **¡OJO!** Some expressions may have more than one response.

_D_ 1. ¡Encantada!   **a.** Bien, gracias.

_B_ 2. ¡Hola! ¿Qué tal?   **b.** Muy bien, ¿y Ud.?

_D_ 3. ¡Mucho gusto!   **c.** Soy de San Diego.

_G_ 4. ¿Cómo se llama?   **d.** El gusto es mío.

_H,E_ 5. ¡Buenas noches, Carolyn!   **e.** Nos vemos.

_A,B,F_ 6. ¿Cómo está Ud.?   **f.** Bastante bien, ¿y tú?

_C_ 7. ¿De dónde eres tú?   **g.** Felicia. Y Ud., ¿cómo se llama?

_H_ 8. ¡Hasta luego!   **h.** ¡Buenas noches, señor Guzmán!

WB P-3 | En una fiesta At a party you overhear a conversation between two new students, Tomás, from Puerto Rico, and Carlos, from the Dominican Republic. Based on the answer, write out the question that was asked. **¡OJO!** Remember that students would probably use the informal form of address.

Modelo   CARLOS: *Hola*.
          TOMÁS: Hola.

1. CARLOS: Me llamo Carlos, ¿ _Cómo te llamas_ ?

   TOMÁS: Mucho gusto, me llamo Tomás.

2. TOMÁS: ¿ _Cómo estás_ ?

   CARLOS: Bastante bien, gracias.

3. CARLOS: ¿ _Y tu, Que tal_ ?

   TOMÁS: Muy bien.

4. TOMÁS: ¿ _De dónde eres_ ?

   CARLOS: Soy de la República Dominicana.

ESTRUCTURA I   Talking about yourself and others: Subject pronouns and the present tense of the verb *ser*

WB P-4 | ¿Qué pronombre? Which pronouns would Alberto Yáñez, a professor from Spain, use to address or talk about the following people? In the spaces provided below, write the most appropriate pronoun. **¡OJO!** Remember that Alberto is from Spain, which affects the pronouns he selects in certain situations.

1. Referring to students Alicia and Cristina _ellas son_

2. Talking to Mr. Gutiérrez _usted es_

3. Referring to his brother Carlos _~~yo tu eres~~ él_

4. Talking to Mr. and Mrs. Morán _ustedes son_

5. Talking to his two sons _~~vosotros~~ sois_ ^(ustedes)

6. Referring to himself _Yo soy_

Nombre _____ Fecha _____

7. Talking to his wife _tú eres_
8. Referring to his wife _ella es_
9. Referring to himself and three friends ~~los~~ _nosotros somos_
10. Talking to his two daughters ~~vosotras~~ _sois_
   ustedes

WB P-5 | ¿Qué piensas? What do you think? Give your opinion by forming sentences with the words provided. Following the model, use the appropriate form of the verb **ser.**

   Modelo   el presidente Clinton / sincero
             El presidente Clinton es sincero.
          o *El presidente Clinton no es sincero.*

1. Jerry Seinfeld/cómico
   Jerry Seinfeld es cómico
2. Richard Simmons/energético
   Richard Simmons es energético
3. yo/inteligente
   Yo soy inteligente
4. Julia Roberts/atractiva
   Julia Roberts es atractiva
5. mis amigos (friends) y yo/interesantes
   Mis amigos y yo ~~es~~ somos interesantes

ASÍ SE DICE Identifying quantities: *Hay* and numbers 0–30

WB P-6 | El sabelotodo Juan Carlos is a **sabelotodo** (know-it-all) who doesn't always know it all. Mark each of Juan Carlos's sayings with **cierto** (true) or **falso** (false). If they are false, rewrite the sentence correcting Juan Carlos's error. **¡OJO!** Use the verb form **hay** as well as numbers. Follow the model.

   Modelo   En el mes de septiembre hay 28 días (days).
             Falso. En el mes de septiembre hay treinta días.

1. En una semana (week) hay siete días.

   _____

2. Hay trece huevos (eggs) en una docena.

   _____

3. Hay nueve números en un número de teléfono en los Estados Unidos.

   _____

4. En un año (year) hay doce meses (months).

   _____

5. Hay quince pulgadas (inches) en un pie (foot).

WB P-7 | Problemas de matemáticas Test your mathematical ability by completing the following equations. **¡OJO!** Write out the numbers, not the numerals. Follow the model.

Modelo   Treinta menos dos son *veintiocho*.

1. Once más tres son _____ .

2. Ocho menos ocho son _____ .

3. Siete más tres son _____ .

4. Catorce más quince son _____ .

5. Veintiséis menos dos son _____ .

6. Dieciocho más cuatro son _____ .

WB P-8 | Guía telefónica Laura's new "user-friendly" handheld computer won't let her input numerals! She can only store friends' and family's telephone numbers by answering the software's questions and spelling out these telephone numbers. Help Laura by writing out the numerals in words as they are displayed.

1. ¿Cuál es el número de teléfono de tu mejor amiga *(best female friend)*?

   4-0-8-26-5-15-17

   _____

2. ¿Cuál es el número de teléfono de tus padres?

   3-21-2-19-13-29

   _____

3. ¿Cuál es tu número de teléfono?

   9-19-7-10-14-28

   _____

VOCABULARIO Palabras interrogativas

 To learn more about **Question Words**, go to Heinle iRadio at www.thomsonedu.com/spanish.

WB P-9 | Más preguntas Look at the following pictures and choose which questions are likely being asked.

1. **a.** ¿Qué es?

   b. ¿De dónde eres?

   c. ¿Cuál es su número de teléfono?

2. **a.** ¿Quién es tu profesora de español?

   b. ¿Cuándo tienes clase?

   c. ¿Cuál es tu número de teléfono?

3. **a.** ¿Cuántos libros tienes?

   b. ¿Por qué preguntas?

   c. ¿Cómo estás?

WB P-10 | ¿Cuál es correcto? Fill in the blanks with the appropriate question word.

1. ¿_____ se llama usted?

2. ¿_____ estudiantes hay en su clase?

3. ¿_____ estudias español?

4. ¿_____ es tu cumpleaños *(birthday)*?

WB P-11 | Tantas preguntas You are meeting your date at his/her house, and your date's mother has many questions for you. Complete her questions by supplying the appropriate question words below.

1. ¿_____ estás?

2. ¿De _____ eres?

3. ¿_____ años tienes?

4. ¿_____ es tu número de teléfono?

5. ¿_____ son tus padres?

6. ¿_____ personas hay en tu familia?

EL MUNDO HISPANO

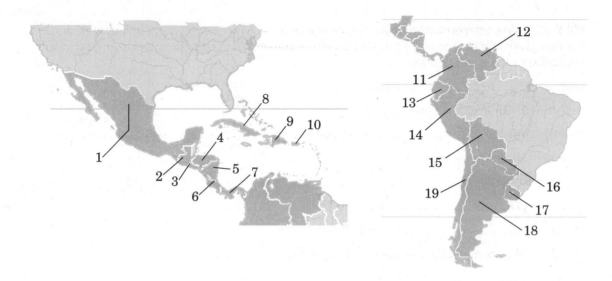

Study the maps of Latin America in your textbook and then name each of the numbered countries on the maps.

1. _____
2. _____
3. _____
4. _____
5. _____
6. _____
7. _____
8. _____
9. _____
10. _____
11. _____
12. _____
13. _____
14. _____
15. _____
16. _____
17. _____
18. _____
19. _____

Autoprueba

WB P-12 | Una conversación típica Below is a typical conversation likely to be heard during the first days of a new school year. Complete the conversation by supplying the appropriate vocabulary words or phrases.

MIGUEL: _____, Tomás. ¿_____ tal?

TOMÁS: Bien, Miguel. Tanto tiempo *(It's been awhile)*. ¿Y cómo _____ tú?

MIGUEL: Bien, _____. Tomás, ésta es mi novia *(this is my girlfriend)*, Elena.

TOMÁS: Hola, Elena, mucho _____.

ELENA: El gusto _____ _____.

TOMÁS: ¿De _____ eres, Elena?

ELENA: _____ de Puerto Rico.

TOMÁS: Muy bien. Bueno, ya me voy *(I've got to go)*. _____.

ELENA: _____, Tomás.

MIGUEL: _____ vemos, Tomás.

WB P-13 | Números Write out each of the numerals indicated below, as well as the numeral that precedes it. Follow the model.

Modelo   28
            veintiocho / veintisiete

1. 15 _____

2. 1 _____

3. 30 _____

4. 17 _____

5. 25 _____

WB P-14 | Presentaciones Complete the following conversation with the appropriate form of the verb **ser.**

PILAR: Me llamo Pilar. ¿Quién _____ tú?

LOLA: _____ Lola Araña Téllez. Y éste *(this)* _____ mi amigo, Carlos.

PILAR: Encantada. ¿De dónde _____ Uds.?

LOLA: Nosotros _____ de Cuba.

WB P-15 | **¿Sois de España?** Ramón has come from Spain to the University of California to study engineering. Complete one of his campus conversations by supplying the appropriate subject pronoun. **¡OJO!** Remember the difference between formal and informal subject pronouns, as well as the differences between Peninsular and Latin American Spanish with respect to pronoun usage.

RAMÓN: Perdón, ¿ _____ sois de España?

DIANA (Y DIEGO):   No, _____ somos de México. _____ soy de

                     Guanajuato y _____ es de Morelia.

DIEGO: El profesor Carrazco es de España. ¿De qué parte de España *(From*

                     what part of Spain) es _____, profesor?

PROFESOR CARRAZCO: _____ soy de Galicia.

RAMÓN: Mi mamá es de Galicia. _____ es de Vigo.

DIEGO: ¿De qué parte eres _____, Ramón?

RAMÓN: _____ soy de Toledo.

DIANA: Bueno, profesor y Ramón, _____ son compatriotas y van a ser

                     (are going to be) buenos amigos.

PROFESOR CARRAZCO: ¡Seguro!

Nombre _____ Fecha _____

 1 | *En una clase de español: Los Estados Unidos*

VOCABULARIO En la clase

WB 1-1 | Colores revueltos *(scrambled)* Unscramble the letters to reveal each color.

1. ojor _____
2. conlab _____
3. ramnór _____
4. lamirola _____

WB 1-2 | Una de estas cosas no es como las otras. *(One of these things isn't like the others.)* For each series, indicate the word that does not form a set with the others.

1. el lápiz, la tiza, la pluma, la pizarra

2. la clase, el diccionario, la lección

3. la silla, el escritorio, el lápiz

4. la pizarra, el borrador, la lección

WB 1-3 | Asociaciones Write in Spanish the color you usually associate with the following items.

Modelo   snow   *blanco*

1. a crow _____
2. an orange _____
3. grass _____
4. cherries _____
5. paper _____
6. chocolate _____
7. a banana _____
8. the sky _____
9. an eggplant _____

WB 1-4 | En mi clase Joaquín, a pen pal from Quito, Ecuador, is interested in how college classes in the United States are different from college classes in Ecuador. Choose the most appropriate response to his questions.

1. ¿Cuántos estudiantes hay en tu clase de español?

   a. Hay veintitrés.   **b.** Hay tres exámenes.   **c.** El diccionario.

2. ¿Cómo se llama tu libro de texto de español?

   a. El libro.   **b.** *Plazas*   **c.** Mucho dinero

3. ¿Cómo se llama tu profesor(a) de español?

   a. Se llama la profesora Muñoz.   **b.** Bien, ¿y tú?   **c.** Está aquí.

4. ¿Cuántos bolígrafos tienes *(do you have)*?

   a. No hay muchos estudiantes.   **b.** Tres.   **c.** Dos novias.

5. ¿Tienes computadora? ¿De qué marca *(What brand)* es?

   a. Sí, es un Mac.   **b.** El Dell no tiene pantalla.   **c.** Hay muchos PCs.

WB 1-5 | Amigos raros *(Strange friends)* Norma Vayaloca is a strange woman who likes to name every object that she owns with human names! Help Norma determine whether she needs to give the following items feminine or masculine names. For each of the nouns listed below, select **F** for **femenino** or **M** for **masculino.** Then write the appropriate definite article needed to accompany the noun. **¡OJO!** Be sure that the definite articles agree with the nouns in number as well as in gender. Follow the model.

Modelo   **a.** F *la* calculadora

1. **a.** F / **b.** M _____ diccionarios

2. **a.** F / **b.** M _____ lápiz

3. **a.** F / **b.** M _____ luces

4. **a.** F / **b.** M _____ escritorio

5. **a.** F / **b.** M _____ mapa

6. **a.** F / **b.** M _____ computadoras

7. **a.** F / **b.** M _____ calendario

8. **a.** F / **b.** M _____ mesas

9. **a.** F / **b.** M _____ relojes

10. **a.** F / **b.** M _____ pizarra

WB 1-6 | ¡Qué exagerada! *(How exaggerated!)* Mari Bocazas is one of those people who often exaggerates. Whatever you do, she says she does it better, and whatever you have, she says she has more. What would Mari say if you were to tell her that you had each of the following?

Modelo   una mochila
             dos mochilas

1. un(a) novio(a)

   _____

2. una computadora Mac

   _____

3. una clase de español

   _____

4. una pluma Cartier

   _____

5. un reloj Rolex

   _____

WB 1-7 | Inventario Your roommate works at the college bookstore and is taking inventory on school supplies. How many of each item are there? Follow the model.

> **Modelo**   cuaderno (18)
> *dieciocho cuadernos*

1. bolígrafo (15)

_____

2. diccionario (1)

_____

3. lápiz (12)

_____

4. mochila (29)

_____

5. calendario (14)

_____

6. computadora (1)

_____

VOCABULARIO Lenguas extranjeras, otras materias y lugares universitarios

WB 1-8 | Internacional Below is a list of the countries available for next year's Study Abroad programs. For each country indicate the language in which interested applicants must be minimally fluent. **¡OJO!** In Spanish, country names are capitalized, but the names of languages are not. Follow the model.

> **Modelo**   Alemania: *el alemán*

1. Japón: _____

5. España: _____

2. China: _____

6. Francia: _____

3. Portugal: _____

7. Rusia: _____

4. Italia: _____

8. Los Estados Unidos: _____

WB 1-9 | Cursos The following is a course list for the Universidad de Buenos Aires Semester Abroad Program. Write the name of the major to which each course would normally pertain. Follow the model.

> **Modelo**   genética y evolución: *la biología*

1. anatomía: _____

2. análisis de mapas: _____

3. legislación ambiental: _____

4. teoría literaria: _____

5. programación de computadoras _____

6. cálulo _____

7. filosofía del derecho: _____

8. literatura española: _____

WB 1-10 | **Lugares universitarios** Where on campus are you most likely to do each of the following activities? Use a different location in each sentence.

> **Modelo**   practicar deportes *en el gimnasio*

1. comprar *(to buy)* un sándwich _____

2. hablar con mi profesor _____

3. estudiar _____

4. comprar libros _____

5. dormir *(to sleep)* _____

6. hablar *(to talk)* con mis amigos _____

ESTRUCTURA II Describing everyday activities: Present tense of regular -*ar* verbs

WB 1-11 | **Actividades** Jorge and his friends talk about some of their more common activities during the school year. Complete their sentences with the appropriate present-tense verb form.

1. Yo _____ (tocar) mis instrumentos.

2. Noelia y yo _____ (bailar) en la discoteca.

3. Tú _____ (practicar) español con Noelia.

4. Amanda _____ (estudiar) mucho en la biblioteca.

5. Jaime y Teresa _____ (mirar) la televisión toda la noche.

WB 1-12 | **Conversando** Manu is an exchange student from Spain studying at the University of Massachusetts. Below is one of the conversations he has with Alicia and Tomás, two Mexican-American students. Complete their conversation by supplying the appropriate form of the verb in parentheses.

ALICIA: ¡Hola, Manu! ¿Qué tal? ¿Cómo está todo?

MANU: Muy bien, pero *(but)* **1.** _____ (tomar) muchas clases y

2. _____ (estudiar) mucho.

TOMÁS: ¿Cuántas clases **3.** _____ (tomar) tú?

MANU: Seis. ¿Y vosotros? ¿Cuántos cursos **4.** _____ (llevar) este semestre?

TOMÁS: Nosotros... solamente dos. Alicia y yo **5.** _____ (tomar) las

mismas *(the same)* clases. **6.** _____ (Estudiar) fisiología y química.

ALICIA: Manu, ¿**7.** (Tú) _____ (trabajar) en la biblioteca?

MANU: No, mi compañero de cuarto **8.** _____ (trabajar) allí *(there)*.

Yo no **9.** _____ (necesitar) trabajar.

ALICIA: Sí, entiendo *(I understand)*. Tú compañero... se llama Juan, ¿no? ¿Cómo es él? ¿Es

simpático *(nice)*?

MANU: Sí, es muy simpático. Nosotros **10.** _____ (hablar) mucho y

siempre **11.** _____ (mirar) «Baywatch» juntos *(together)* en

nuestra casa. Y después del *(after the)* programa, nosotros **12.** _____

(practicar) inglés.

ALICIA: ¡Manu! ¿Uds. **13.** _____ (mirar) «Baywatch»? ¡Ese programa

es horrible!

MANU: ¿Horrible? ¿Cómo que horrible *(What do you mean it's horrible)*? ¿Vosotros aquí en

los Estados Unidos no **14.** _____ (mirar) «Baywatch»?

ALICIA: ¿Yo? ¡Ni modo *(Not a chance)*!

TOMÁS: Pues *(Well)*...

ASÍ SE DICE   Telling time and talking about the days of the week: *La hora y los días de la semana*

WB 1-13 | ¿Qué hora es? Write out the time indicated in twelve hour format.

1. 12:15 _____

2. 1:30 _____

3. 6:45 _____

4. 12:50 _____

5. 5:20 _____

WB 1-14 | ¿Qué clases tomo? Roberto Torres, an exchange student, is having trouble reading the new course catalog for next semester. Help him by writing out in Spanish the time the course begins and the days of the week the course meets. Follow the model.

Modelo la clase de psicología
Es a las dos de la tarde los sábados.

Course code	Course title	Units	Time	Days	Instructor
55940	Art 120	4	0900–1000	T/Th	Paredes
24965	Biology 10A	4	1730–1945	W	Smith
84804	Computer Science 101	3	1500–1600	M/W	Richardson
48997	Chemistry 7C	5	0700–0845	MWF	Nelson
94942	English 205	4	1400–1630	T	Hershberger
40900	Geography 10	3	0900–1000	Th/F	Cox
28817	Literature (US) 1A	3	1000–1150	T/Th	Rolle
38822	Mathematics 6C	4	1300–1400	MWF	Añover
99944	Music Appreciation 20	2	1120–1350	Sa	Frail
19902	Psychology 1C	4	1200–1445	T/Th	Von Son
53229	Zoology 167	4	0900–1045	W/F	Clark

1. la clase de biología

_____

2. la clase de química

_____

3. la clase de geografía

_____

4. la clase de literatura

_____

5. la clase de matemáticas

_____

BIENVENIDOS A LOS ESTADOS UNIDOS

 In this video segment, you will learn about Latinos in the United States with regard to the following topics:

- population
- countries of origin of Latino immigrants
- Latino centers in the U.S.

Nombre _____ Fecha _____

WB 1-15 In the video segment, you will hear a number of Spanish words that are cognates of English words, that is they look and sound like English words and have similar meanings. Identifying these words and their meanings will help you to understand the Spanish used in the video. Try to pronounce each of the following Spanish words, and then try to match each with their meaning in English.

1. _____ presencia hispana   **a.** Puerto Rican

2. _____ arquitectura colonial   **b.** colonial architecture

3. _____ mexicano   **c.** percent

4. _____ Sudamérica   **d.** Mexican

5. _____ puertorriqueño   **e.** Hispanic presence

6. _____ centro turístico   **f.** Central America

7. _____ cubano   **g.** tourist center

8. _____ Centroamérica   **h.** South America

9. _____ por ciento   **i.** Cuban

WB 1-16 Watch the video segment, and listen for the following sentences, in which the cognates you just identified in activity **WB 1-15** will appear. Fill in the blank with the correct cognate.

1. La _____ en los Estados Unidos aumenta cada día.

2. La mayoría es de origen _____, _____ o _____.

3. En los últimos años muchos inmigrantes vienen también de _____ y _____.

4. En Los Ángeles, el 40 _____ de la población es hispano.

WB 1-17 Watch the video again and determine whether the following sentences are true (T) or false (F).

1. _____ In San Antonio, Texas it is still easy to see its Mexican roots.

2. _____ The majority of the Latinos living in Los Angeles, CA are of Mexican and South American origin.

3. _____ Los Angeles, CA has many murals that represent the Latin pride in the city.

4. _____ Many of the Latinos in New York are of Puerto Rican origin.

¡A ESCRIBIR!

El mundo verdadero The Spanish language television network **Telemundo** has just announced on the local Spanish TV station that they are going to produce a new show and are looking for participants. This show will bring together five people who have never met to live for six months in a house in Miami's South Beach. For your application to be considered, you must submit a paragraph in which you introduce yourself and describe your daily routine.

> ### Strategy: Organizing your ideas
> A good way to improve your writing is to organize the ideas you want to express before you begin composing your document.

 To learn more about **Ser** and **Estar**, and **Tener** and **Tener Expressions,** go to Heinle iRadio at www.thomsonedu.com/spanish.

Paso 1 Start the paragraph that you would send by organizing your ideas before writing your first draft. Some of the following questions may help you do so:

- What will you say about yourself? your name? where you are from? how old you are? what you study in school?
- What will you say about your daily routine? what days of the week you attend classes? what times of the day you study? where you study?

Paso 2 Now that you have all the ideas organized, write a first draft on a separate sheet of paper. Then, review it and write the draft of your paragraph below.

_____

_____

_____

_____

_____

_____

_____

_____

_____

_____

 **ATAJO 4.0**

Functions: Describing people; Introducing; Talking about the present

Vocabulary: Countries; Languages; Studies; Arts

Grammar: Verbs: **ser, tener;** Prepositions: **de;** Personal pronouns: **él, ella;** Articles: indefinite: **un, una;** Articles: definite: **el, la, los, las**

Autoprueba

WB 1-18 | **Los cursos** Select the course that does not belong in the category.

1. Letras: **a.** literatura   **b.** matemáticas   **c.** filosofía

2. Lenguas: **a.** alemán   **b.** inglés   **c.** historia

3. Ciencias sociales: **a.** biología   **b.** sicología   **c.** economía

4. Arte: **a.** música   **b.** pintura   **c.** biología

WB 1-19 | **¿Qué hora es?** What time is indicated on each digital display below? Use the twelve hour format.

1. 2:45 PM   _____
2. 1:22 PM   _____
3. 12:31 PM   _____
4. 5:15 AM   _____
5. 9:30 AM   _____

WB 1-20 | **Está muy ocupada.** Roberto wants to get to know Nancy and wants you to find out when she is available to go out with him. Look at Nancy's busy study schedule below and explain to Roberto how busy she is. Tell him in Spanish what language she studies on each day of the week and at what time she studies. Follow the model.

Nancy's Study Schedule						
Monday	Tuesday	Wednesday	Thursday	Friday	Saturday	Sunday
Spanish 9:00 AM	German 3:45 PM	Chinese 12:45 PM	Russian 1:30 PM	Italian 5:15 PM	Portuguese 7:30 PM	Japanese 10:00 AM

Modelo   Los lunes Nancy estudia español a las nueve de la mañana.

1. _____
2. _____
3. _____
4. _____
5. _____
6. _____

WB 1-21 | Los colores Write in Spanish the color that you associate with the following items.

1. a lemon _____

2. night _____

3. blood _____

4. dirt _____

5. a snowman _____

6. a U.S. dollar bill _____

WB 1-22 | Lupe y Lalo To learn about Lupe's and Lalo's lives at the university, complete the following paragraphs with either a definite or an indefinite article. **¡OJO!** Remember that these articles must agree in number and gender with the nouns they modify.

Lupe Zarzuela es **1.** _____ persona inteligente. Ella estudia turismo, sicología y dos

lenguas en **2.** _____ UNAM, que es **3.** _____ universidad enorme de **4.** _____

Ciudad de México.

Para Lupe, **5.** _____ lenguas son fáciles, especialmente **6.** _____ inglés y

7. _____ alemán. Uno de **8.** _____ compañeros de clase de Lupe se llama Lalo

Rodríguez, y es estudiante de ingeniería nuclear. Para Lalo, **9.** _____ inglés es

10. _____ lengua muy difícil.

11. _____ clase de inglés de Lupe y Lalo es a **12.** _____ nueve de **13.** _____

mañana todos **14.** _____ días de **15.** _____ semana, excepto **16.** _____ sábados y

domingos.

WB 1-23 | Las actividades del día Everyone who lives in Ramón's dorm has many activities and interests. Form sentences with the words provided to find out what everyone does each day.

1. Ramón / trabajar / todos los días

_____

2. Teresa y Evelia / estudiar / matemáticas / por la tarde

_____

3. yo / practicar / deportes / por la mañana

_____

4. nosotros / descansar / a las cuatro de la tarde

_____

5. tú / enseñar / ejercicios aeróbicos / por la noche

_____

6. Uds. / regresar / a la casa / a las seis de la tarde

_____

Nombre _____   Fecha _____

 2 | *En una reunión familiar: México*

VOCABULARIO La familia

WB 2-1 | Familiares Unscramble the letters to reveal each family-related term.

1. neory: _____
2. soirbno: _____
3. otag: _____

4. jaropá: _____
5. georsu: _____

WB 2-2 | Buscapalabras Below are clues to six Spanish words you will find embedded in this word search. Can you find them? Can you find others? Circle the words that you find, and inside the circle write the number of the clue to which the word corresponds.

1. La madre de tu padre
2. El hijo de tu hermana
3. El nombre de la familia

4. Los hijos de tus hijos
5. La hermana de tu madre
6. Can you find other family-related vocabulary? Other Spanish words?

```
T  O  D  A  D  A  Ñ  C  R  E  O  J  E  D
A  L  O  I  N  I  A  S  O  L  T  E  R  O
N  O  Ñ  O  V  S  E  Ñ  E  I  I  T  I  E
U  T  A  H  A  O  C  U  Ñ  A  D  O  A  N
E  D  U  D  O  B  R  I  A  Z  E  G  P  E
R  I  O  C  T  R  E  C  U  U  F  A  E  R
A  V  E  S  T  I  A  S  I  N  P  E  L  O
L  A  P  A  C  N  R  T  R  A  A  L  L  A
E  N  I  E  T  O  S  B  E  U  D  U  I  T
U  H  E  R  M  A  N  A  S  T  R  O  D  A
B  O  R  J  E  S  O  T  T  O  I  B  O  M
A  R  A  Ñ  A  T  N  Y  E  R  N  O  F  A
J  O  B  A  R  U  A  R  B  I  O  D  I  O
O  R  T  E  R  A  S  U  O  P  S  A  R  A
```

WB 2-3 | La familia de Mariana Mariana is telling her coworkers all about her family members. Complete her story by supplying the appropriate words from the list below.

sobrinos   hermana   perro   esposo   hija   hijos

En mi casa somos cinco personas y un animal. Mi 1. _____ se llama Paco.

Tenemos dos 2. _____, se llaman Tomás y Miguelito y tenemos una

3. _____, que se llama Carolina. El 4. _____ se llama Popeye.

Yo tengo una 5. _____, Claudia. Su esposo se llama Jaime. Ellos tienen tres hijos,

Carlos, Jesús y Mateo. Ellos son mis 6. _____. Paco no tiene hermanos.

WB 2-4 | La familia Herrera Castellanos Carlos Herrera Castellanos has just finished researching the paternal side of his family tree. Answer the following questions about his family members.

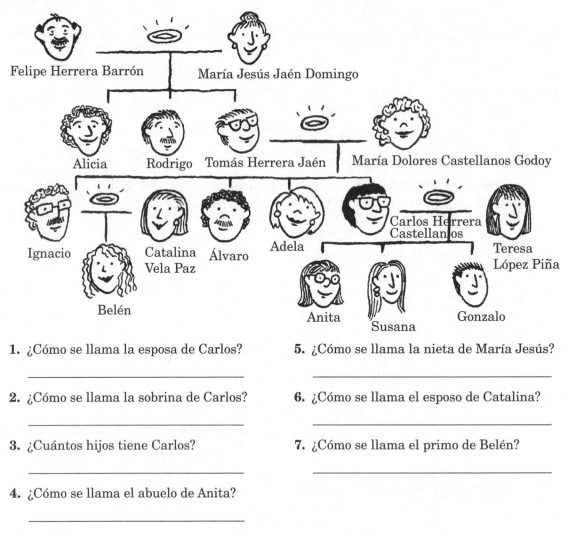

Felipe Herrera Barrón   María Jesús Jaén Domingo

Alicia   Rodrigo   Tomás Herrera Jaén   María Dolores Castellanos Godoy

Ignacio   Catalina Vela Paz   Álvaro   Adela   Carlos Herrera Castellanos   Teresa López Piña

Belén   Anita   Susana   Gonzalo

1. ¿Cómo se llama la esposa de Carlos?

_____

2. ¿Cómo se llama la sobrina de Carlos?

_____

3. ¿Cuántos hijos tiene Carlos?

_____

4. ¿Cómo se llama el abuelo de Anita?

_____

5. ¿Cómo se llama la nieta de María Jesús?

_____

6. ¿Cómo se llama el esposo de Catalina?

_____

7. ¿Cómo se llama el primo de Belén?

_____

| ASÍ SE DICE | Indicating ownership and possession: Possession with *de(l)* and possessive adjectives |

WB 2-5 | Nuestras familias Francisco and his sister, Linda, are discussing families with their new friend, Antonio. Complete their conversation with the appropriate possessive forms. **¡OJO!** Pay attention to who is speaking to whom so that you will know which possessive form is necessary.

FRANCISCO: ¿Es grande **1.** _____ familia, Antonio?

ANTONIO: Sí, **2.** _____ familia es muy grande. Somos ocho personas. Y Uds., ¿es grande **3.** _____ familia?

FRANCISCO: No, **4.** _____ familia no es muy grande. Somos cinco.

LINDA: Pero **5.** _____ padres tienen familias grandes. Nuestra madre tiene seis hermanas y **6.** _____ padre tiene cuatro hermanos.

ANTONIO: Muy interesante. Linda, ¿de dónde es **7.** _____ madre?

LINDA: **8.** _____ madre es de México, de Zacatecas. Y tú, ¿de dónde son

9. _____ padres?

ANTONIO: **10.** _____ padres son de Canadá, pero **11.** _____ padres (mis abuelos)

son de España.

WB 2-6 | Compañeros You and your roommates clean house and find all kinds of things. Identify the owner of each of the following items. Follow the model.

Modelo   ¿De quién son las fotos de Ricky Martin? (Mariana)
Son de Mariana. *Son sus* fotos.
¿De quién es esta mochila? (yo)
Es *mi* mochila.

1. ¿De quién es el disco compacto de los Red Hot Chili Peppers? (Juan)

_____ Juan. _____ disco.

2. ¿De quién es la computadora? (ustedes)

_____ ustedes. _____ computadora.

3. ¿De quién es el dinero? (nosotros)

_____ dinero.

4. ¿De quién son las bicicletas? (Mariana)

_____ Mariana. _____ bicicletas.

6. ¿De quién es la radio? (yo)

_____ radio.

ESTRUCTURA I	Describing people and things: Common uses of the verb *ser*

WB 2-7 | ¡Mucho gusto! Aníbal and Jaime, two exchange students from Spain, are trying to get to know all the other Spanish speakers on their floor. Fill in the blanks with the appropriate form of the verb **ser** in their conversation.

ANÍBAL: ¿De dónde **1.** _____ vosotros?

CELIA: Nosotros **2.** _____ de Latinoamérica. Jesús **3.** _____ de Nicaragua. Felipe,

Mabel y yo **4.** _____ de Cuba. Y tú, Aníbal, ¿de dónde **5.** _____?

ANÍBAL: Yo **6.** _____ de España, de Burgos.

MABEL: Y tú, Jaime, ¿de dónde **7.** _____?

JAIME: De España también, **8.** _____ de Córdoba.

CELIA: ¡Qué bueno! Y, ¿Uds. **9.** _____ hermanos?

JAIME: No, no **10.** _____ hermanos; **11.** _____ buenos amigos.

WB 2-8 | La vida de Elena Your pen pal from Guanajuato, Elena, has sent you the following letter telling you a little about her and her family and friends. Fill in the blanks with the appropriate form of the verb **ser** to read her letter.

Hola,

Yo **1.** _____ Helena. **2.** _____ de Guanajuato, México. En mi familia nosotros

3. _____ cinco. Tengo dos padres, una hermana y un hermano. Mis padres **4.** _____

profesores en la universidad. Los dos **5.** _____ muy trabajadores. Mis hermanos

6. _____ estudiantes. Mi hermana Jaime **7.** _____ alto y guapo, pero **8.** _____

un poco tímido. Mi hermana Linda **9.** _____ morena y muy bonita. Ella no

10. _____ tímida, al contrario **11.** _____ súper extrovertida. También tengo

diez tíos y veinticinco primos. Nosotros **12.** _____ una familia grande, pero feliz.

¿Y tú?, ¿cómo **13.** _____ tu familia? ¿Cómo **14.** _____ tú?

ASÍ SE DICE Describing people and things: Agreement with descriptive adjectives

To learn more about **Adjectives,** go to Heinle iRadio at www.thomsonedu.com/spanish.

WB 2-9 | ¡Qué familia tiene! Ángel has a large family with very different relatives. Write out complete sentences to describe each of these relatives shown below. Use the appropriate possessive form, as well as the adjective that best describes each person. Make sure the adjective agrees with the person/persons. Follow the model.

la mamá

Modelo   *Su mamá es artística.*

1. el padre   2. las hermanás, Marcela y Vanesa   3. el hermano, Raúl   4. los primos, Fabián, Anaís y Aldo   5. la abuela

1. _____

2. _____

3. _____

4. _____

5. _____

WB 2-10 | ¿Cómo son? Describe each of the people listed by providing the correct form of the verb **ser** and an appropriate form of the adjective indicated.

    Modelo   Antonio Villaraigosa, alcalde *(mayor)* de Los Ángeles (liberal)
                Antonio Villaraigosa *es liberal*.

1. Eric Chavez, jugador de béisbol profesional en Estados Unidos (atlético)

    Eric Chavez _____ _____.

2. Gael García Bernal y Salma Hayek, actores (guapo)

    Gael García Bernal y Salma Hayek _____ _____.

3. Dolores Huerta, cofundadora de los United Farm Workers (trabajador)

    Dolores Huerta _____ _____.

4. Elena Poniatowska y Sandra Cisneros, escritoras (listo)

    Elena Poniatowska y Sandra Cisneros _____ _____.

VOCABULARIO Las nacionalidades

WB 2-11 | ¿De dónde son y qué lengua hablan? Describe each of the following people's nationality and native language. ¡OJO! Nationalities agree with the number and gender of the person or people being described. Follow the model.

    Modelo   Alicia Ramos / España
                Es española. / Habla español.

1. Teresita Sedillo / Honduras

    _____ / _____

2. Tomás Romero / Puerto Rico

    _____ / _____

3. Beatriz y Nancy Ruiz / Costa Rica

    _____ / _____

4. Helmut Schmidig / Alemania

    _____ / _____

5. Steven Ensley / Canadá

    _____ / _____

6. Madeline Depuy / Francia

    _____ / _____

7. Alejandro y Luis Villegas / Paraguay

    _____ / _____

WB 2-12 | Cosas del mundo Test you worldliness. Write the origin of each of the items listed below. Choose from the list of countries. Follow the model.

Guatemala   Argentina   Cuba   Rusia   Puerto Rico   Egipto   Japón

Modelo   Los gauchos *son argentinos*.

1. El reggaetón *(type of music)* _____ _____.

2. Las chicas Harajuku _____ _____.

3. El vodka _____ _____.

4. La esfinge *(sphynx)* _____ _____.

5. Los cigarros Cohiba _____ _____.

ESTRUCTURA II Describing daily activities at home or at school: Present tense of *-er* and *-ir* verbs

WB 2-13 | La vida universitaria David is a Mexican college student studying at the Universidad La Salle, a Catholic university in Mexico City. To find out how his life compares to yours, complete the sentences with the appropriate form of the verb in the present tense.

1. Mis amigos y yo _____ (asistir) a la universidad.

2. Todos nosotros _____ (vivir) con nuestros padres.

3. Ahora estudio ciencias religiosas *(religious)* y _____ (aprender) sobre la historia de los franciscanos en México.

4. Yo _____ (creer) en Dios y _____ (asistir) a la misa *(Mass)* con mis padres los domingos.

5. Mi novia _____ (vivir) en Aguascalientes y no me visita mucho. Por eso yo _____ (escribir) muchas cartas.

6. _____ (beber) un café con mis amigos en el centro todos los días.

WB 2-14 | Dos amigos Tomás and Estela are students at the Universidad de Guadalajara. See how similar their lives are to yours by writing the appropriate form of the verb provided.

Estela y su familia **1.** _____ (vivir) en México, D.F. Estela es estudiante y

2. _____ (aprender) mucho en sus clases de la UNAM. Ella **3.** _____

(comprender), **4.** _____ (leer) y **5.** _____ (escribir) tres lenguas:

español, japonés e inglés. Estela trabaja mucho en sus clases porque quiere ser intérprete.

Tomás no **6.** _____ (vivir) con su familia. Sus padres, sus dos hermanas y

su hermano **7.** _____ (vivir) en Mérida, la capital del Yucatán. Carlos le

8. _____ (escribir) a su familia *(writes to his family)* frecuentemente y él

9. _____ (recibir) muchas cartas de ellos. Tomás y Estela **10.** _____

(aprender) inglés por la mañana. Él **11.** _____ (deber) estudiar más porque el

inglés es difícil. Por la tarde Tomás y Estela **12.** _____ (comer) en la cafetería de

la UNAM. Ellos **13.** _____ (comer) sándwiches y **14.** _____

(beber) refrescos *(sodas)*. Después de comer, ellos toman un café.

WB 2-15 | Actividades diarias To create a schedule of chores, you and your roommates need to know who is available at what time. Make a chart of everyone's routines by using one element from each of the categories below and writing logical sentences that describe what each roommate does on a regular basis. Follow the model and conjugate each verb properly in the present tense.

> **Modelo**   Magaly (beber café)
> *Magaly bebe café en el Café Roma por la mañana.*

¿Dónde?	¿Cuándo?
en un restaurante	por la mañana
en café Roma	los domingos
en casa	todos los días
en el centro universitario	por la tarde
en la universidad	por la noche
en la biblioteca	los lunes
en la librería	los fines de semana

1. Mi familia y yo (comer) _____

2. Teresa (deber estudiar) _____

3. Yo (asistir a clases) _____

4. Esteban (escribir cartas) _____

5. Tú (leer libros) _____

6. Nancy (vender libros) _____

WB 2-16 | Una clase diferente Lorenzo's class is a bit strange today. To find out what is happening, fill in the blanks with the appropriate form of one of the verbs listed below. **¡OJO!** Not all verbs are used, but no verb is used twice.

abrir   aprender   asistir   beber   comprender   creer

deber   escribir   leer   recibir   vender   vivir

La profesora **1.** _____ la puerta y entra en la sala de clase. Carlos y Héctor

2. _____ un libro cómico pero *(but)* ahora la profesora dice que ellos

3. _____ abrir su libro de texto. La profesora **4.** _____ en la

pizarra. Ahora Antonia y Mónica **5.** _____ Coca-Cola y **6.** _____

un burrito loco. ¡Y Javier! Él habla por teléfono y **7.** _____ su computadora.

Yo no **8.** _____ esta clase hoy.

ASÍ SE DICE	Expressing possession, age, and physical states: Common uses of the verb *tener*

To learn more about **Tener** and **Tener Expressions,** go to www.thomsonedu.com/spanish.

WB 2-17 | ¡Algo tienen! Alicia is talking about how strange her family is. Match each of her statements with the corresponding picture of a family member.

A.

B.

C.

D.

_____ **1.** Siempre tenemos mucha hambre.

_____ **2.** Mi hermano siempre tiene prisa.

_____ **3.** Mi hermanita siempre tiene sueño.

_____ **4.** Mi abuela siempre tiene sed.

WB 2-18 | Una conversación Javier and Silvia are classmates who are getting to know each other better. Complete their conversation by using the appropriate form of the verb **tener**. **¡OJO!** Remember that Javier and Silvia are classmates and would use the **tú** form.

JAVIER: ¿Cuántos años **1.** _____, Silvia?

SILVIA: **2.** _____ diecinueve años. ¿Y tú?

JAVIER: Yo **3.** _____ veinticuatro.

SILVIA: ¿Cuántos hermanos **4.** _____?

JAVIER: **5.** _____ seis: tres hermanas y tres hermanos.

SILVIA: ¡Qué bueno! Yo no **6.** _____ hermanos. Pero mi mamá

7. _____ un pájaro.

JAVIER: Pues, en mi casa nosotros no **8.** _____ mascotas. Pero mis abuelos

9. _____ tres gatos.

WB 2-19 | Arte mexicano Form sentences with the following elements. Conjugate the verbs in the present tense.

1. María y Tomás / tener / la famosa película *(movie)* mexicana *Como agua para chocolate*

_____

2. Yo quiero ver esa película pero / yo / tener / sueño

_____

3. Los suegros de mi hermano / tener / una colección grande de arte de Diego Rivera

_____

4. Mi familia y yo / tener / solamente un cuadro de Frida Kahlo

_____

ASÍ SE DICE Counting to 100: Numbers 30 to 100

WB 2-20 | Números Write the numerals that correspond to the following written numbers.

Modelo   treinta y cinco

35

1. treinta y dos _____

2. cincuenta y cinco _____

3. cuarenta y nueve _____

4. noventa y nueve _____

5. ochenta y uno _____

6. setenta y siete _____

7. sesenta y ocho _____

8. cien _____

WB 2-21 | Más números Write out the words represented by the following numerals.

1. 66 _____

2. 44 _____

3. 83 _____

4. 91 _____

5. 37 _____

WB 2-22 | Los gastos del mes How much did Jorge spend this month on the items listed? Write the numeric value of the prices written below.

1. café: treinta y tres dólares $ _____

2. comida: noventa y seis dólares $ _____

3. discos compactos: cuarenta y dos dólares $ _____

4. videojuegos: ochenta y cinco dólares $ _____

5. teléfono celular: setenta y cuatro dólares $ _____

BIENVENIDOS A MÉXICO

DVD In this video segment, you will learn about the following topics in Mexico:

- economy
- geography
- government
- population
- tourist attractions

WB 2-23 | In the video segment, you will hear a number of Spanish words that are cognates of English words. Try to pronounce each of the following Spanish words, and then match each with its meaning in English.

1. _____ contrastes

2. _____ futuro

3. _____ exporta

4. _____ origen

5. _____ república federal

6. _____ sitios arqueológicos

7. _____ zonas industriales

8. _____ régimen democrático

9. _____ prósperas

a. Federal Republic

b. future

c. prosperous

d. archeological sites

e. exports (verb)

f. industrial zones

g. origin

h. democratic regime

i. contrasts

WB 2-24 | Watch the video segment, and listen for the following sentences, in which the cognates you just identified in activity **WB 2-23** appear. Fill in the blank with the cognate that you hear.

1. México es un país grande, rico, lleno de _____.

2. México es una _____.

3. Tiene _____ excepcionales como los de Uxmal, Tula y Teotihuacan.

4. México tiene un _____ y una de las economías

   más sólidas y _____ de Latinoamérica.

WB 2-25 | View the video segment again, and then answer the following questions.

1. ¿Cuáles son los dos países vecinos *(neighboring)* al sur de México?

   _____ y _____

2. ¿Qué es el Distrito Federal? *(Choose the best answer.)*

   _____ **a.** El centro petrolero más grande de México.

   _____ **b.** La capital de México.

   _____ **c.** La capital de España.

   _____ **d.** La capital de Guatemala.

3. ¿Dónde están dos de las playas más famosas de México? *(Choose the best answer.)*

   _____ **a.** Acapulco y Zacatecas

   _____ **b.** Cancún y Aguascalientes

   _____ **c.** Monterrey y el Distrito Federal

   _____ **d.** Acapulco y Cancún

¡A ESCRIBIR!

Anuncios personales One of your good friends has been having trouble in the romance department lately and has asked you to help write a personal ad. He/She is very interested in meeting Spanish-speaking people and wants you to write the ad in Spanish. Write the personal ad that will help your friend meet the **amor de sus sueños** *(love of her / his dreams)*.

Strategy: Learning Spanish word order

Word order refers to the meaningful sequence of words in a sentence. The order of words in Spanish sentences differs somewhat from that in English. Some common rules of Spanish word order that were presented to you in the textbook are these:

- Definite and indefinite articles precede nouns.
  Los gatos y **los perros** son animales.
  Tengo **un gato** y **un perro**.
- Subjects usually precede their verbs in statements.
  Mi gato es negro.
- Subjects usually follow their verbs in questions.
  ¿**Tiene usted** animales en casa?
- Adjectives of quantity usually precede nouns.
  ¿**Cuántos animales** tienes en casa?
- Adjectives of description usually follow nouns.
  El **perro pardo** *(brown)* se llama Bandido.
- Possession is often expressed by using **de** with a noun.
  Tigre es **el gato de Sara**.

Paso 1 Unscramble the words in the following sentences and then rewrite them in their correct sequence. Be sure to capitalize the first word of every sentence and to use a period or question marks where appropriate.

ATAJO 4.0

Functions: Introducing; Describing people

Vocabulary: Nationality; Numbers; University

Grammar: Verbs: **ser, tener**; Possession with **de**; Adjectives: agreement, position

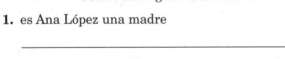

Modelo   es Carlos Rodríguez de México
Carlos Rodríguez es de México.

1. es Ana López una madre

   _____

2. años tiene cuántos ella ¿?

   _____

3. chino es padre su

   _____

Paso 2 Now think of your ideas for your ad and write a first draft on a separate sheet of paper. Then, review it and write the draft of your paragraph below. Remember to check for correct word order.

_____

_____

_____

_____

_____

Nombre _____ Fecha _____

Autoprueba

WB 2-26 | Los miembros de la familia Read the following statements and fill in the blanks with a family-related vocabulary word.

1. Mi mamá es la _____ de mi papá.

2. El hijo de mi tío es mi _____.

3. Me llamo Antonio Casagrande. Casagrande es mi _____.

4. La hija de mi hermano es mi _____.

5. Los hijos de mi hija son mis _____.

WB 2-27 | Descripciones Describe the following people by completing each sentence with the appropriate form of the verb **ser** and the appropriate form of the adjective in parentheses. Make any changes necessary so that the adjectives agree in number and gender with the person they are describing.

1. Salma Hayek _____ una actriz _____ (mexicano).

2. Michael Jordan y yo _____ personas _____ (simpático).

3. Ace Ventura y Austin Powers _____ hombres _____ (tonto).

4. Tú _____ una persona _____ (atlético).

5. Hillary Rodham Clinton _____ una mujer bastante _____ (paciente).

WB 2-28 | Probablemente son... Your new friend, Andrés, is describing different friends and family members. Read his descriptions and then write the adjective that best matches each description. **¡OJO!** Do not use the same adjective more than once.

1. Iliana y Rafael trabajan diez horas al día. Probablemente son _____.

2. Eva estudia la filosofía de la ciencia. Estudia y lee libros todo el día. Probablemente es

   _____.

3. Carlos tiene mucho dinero, pero nunca gasta dinero. Probablemente es

   _____.

4. Belén usa mucho su tarjeta de crédito, pero nunca paga sus facturas (pays her bills). Probablemente es _____.

5. Mi hija nunca limpia su cuarto y nunca estudia. Probablemente es

   _____.

6. Adán y Lupe comen mucho y nunca hacen ejercicios (exercise). Probablemente son

   _____.

WB 2-29 | Los números Write out the numbers that correspond to the following numerals.

1. 32 _____   5. 15 _____

2. 99 _____   6. 17 _____

3. 24 _____   7. 46 _____

4. 12 _____   8. 79 _____

WB 2-30 | **Una conversación** Complete the following conversation with the appropriate forms of the verb **tener** and the appropriate possessive pronouns.

PILAR: ¿ **1.** _tienes_ tú una familia pequeña o grande, Lola?

LOLA: **2.** _Tengo Mi_ familia es grande. Yo **3.** _Tengo_ cuatro hermanas.

PILAR: ¿No **4.** _tienes_ hermanos?

LOLA: No, **5.** _tengo mis_ padres **6.** _tienen_ cinco hijas.

PILAR: Pues, tus padres también **7.** _tienen_ un gato. ¿Cómo se llama **8.** _tiene su_ gato?

LOLA: **9.** _Tiene Mi_ gato se llama Pipo.

PILAR: ¡Pipo! **10.** _tienes_ razón. ¡Qué gato más lindo!

LOLA: Oye, Pilar. Yo **11.** _tengo_ hambre. Vamos a (*Let's go*) comer algo. ¿**12.** _Tienes_ hambre tú?

PILAR: No, pero **13.** _tengo_ sed. Yo voy contigo (*I will go with you*).

WB 2-31 | **En la universidad** Complete the following conversation between Diana and Tomás with the appropriate verb form. Some verbs will be used more than once.

creer   deber   escribir   recibir   tener   vivir

TOMÁS: ¿Dónde **1.** _____, Diana?

DIANA: Yo **2.** _____ con mi tía aquí en D.F. pero mi familia

3. _____ en Guadalajara.

TOMÁS: ¿**4.** _____ muchas cartas para tus padres?

DIANA: Sí, de vez en cuando (*once in a while*). Y tú, Tomás, ¿**5.** _____

muchas cartas para tus padres?

TOMÁS: No, pero yo **6.** _____ muchas cartas de mis padres. Yo

7. _____ escribir más.

DIANA: Tú **8.** _____ razón. ¡Yo **9.** _____ en la

importancia de la correspondencia escrita!

Nombre _____ Fecha _____

3 | *El tiempo libre: Colombia*

VOCABULARIO Los deportes y los pasatiempos

WB 3-1 | **Juanjo el increíble** Juanjo likes to do it all. Look at the pictures of Juanjo doing many of his favorite activities and write the letter of the picture that corresponds to each description.

_____ **1.** Le gusta patinar en línea.

_____ **2.** Le gusta montar a caballo.

_____ **3.** Le gusta ir a la discoteca.

_____ **4.** Le gusta esquiar.

_____ **5.** Le gusta el ciclismo.

_____ **6.** Le gusta caminar por las montañas.

_____ **7.** Le gusta jugar al golf.

_____ **8.** Le gusta hacer ejercicios.

_____ **9.** Le gusta visitar el museo.

_____ **10.** Le gusta ir de compras.

A	C	A	T	B	E	D	T	O	F	U	C
C	E	A	R	A	Q	U	E	T	A	D	A
A	I	H	E	P	U	P	A	L	O	S	N
M	I	N	I	A	T	E	P	I	E	U	T
P	A	O	E	T	E	S	N	U	A	P	A
O	D	G	U	I	T	A	R	R	A	E	J
B	E	T	E	N	I	S	U	U	I	R	U
I	T	A	F	A	A	B	F	M	R	I	E
G	A	F	A	R	E	T	A	O	E	L	R
O	R	D	E	N	A	R	A	R	T	E	G
R	D	I	S	C	O	T	E	C	A	O	A
N	A	T	A	C	I	O	N	D	I	Y	S
O	K	L	O	B	T	U	F	A	R	O	X
N	O	T	R	R	I	C	N	O	C	I	N

Pistas:

1. Me gusta nadar; mi deporte favorito es la _____.

2. Tocar la _____.

3. Para *(In order to)* bailar, voy *(I go)* a la _____.

4. Juegas al golf en un _____ de golf.

5. Anna Kournicova juega al _____.

6. Los 49ers son un equipo de _____.

7. Arnold Schwartzenegger levanta _____ americano.

8. El fotógrafo saca _____.

9. Para *(In order to)* escuchar música, voy a un _____.

10. Necesitas patines para _____.

11. Me gustan las películas; me gusta ir al _____.

WB 3-3 | **Actividades** Amelia and her friends are always busy. Form sentences from the items below and then indicate if these activities are likely done indoors (**adentro**) or outdoors (**al aire libre**).

1. Amelia y sus amigos / mirar la tele / todas las noches.

   _____

2. Nosotros / andar en bicicleta / los sábados.

   _____

3. Nancy y Pedro / levantar pesas / todas las mañanas.

   _____

4. Amelia / visitar el museo / los domingos.

   _____

Nombre _____ Fecha _____

ESTRUCTURA I *Gustar* + infinitive and *gustar* + nouns

WB 3-4 | ¿Qué les gusta? Colombian born, U.S. cycling champion Freddy Rodríguez discusses how he and his friends and family spend their free time. To find out what he says, form sentences by matching appropriate elements from each column.

1. A mí

2. A mi esposa y a mí

3. A su hijo

4. A mis amigos

a. nos gusta hacer un picnic.

b. les gusta el ciclismo.

c. me gusta andar en bicicleta por las montañas.

d. le gusta correr por la casa.

e. te gusta correr.

WB 3-5 | Gustos famosos Alex Villalobos, manager for an exclusive hotel for the rich and famous, discusses the likes and dislikes of some of his most notorious guests. Use **me, te, le, nos, os,** or **les** to find out what he has to say.

Nuestro hotel sí es popular con la gente más conocida *(best known)* del mundo. A todos los famosos **1.** _____ gusta pasar por lo menos *(at least)* una semana aquí. Tenemos clientes políticos, como el vice presidente. A él **2.** _____ gusta bailar en la discoteca toda la noche. Pero él no es el único cliente político. El expresidente Clinton nos visita *(visits us)* también. A él no **3.** _____ gusta bailar en la discoteca, pues prefiere practicar los deportes. Por ejemplo, a Bill **4.** _____ gusta jugar al tenis.

A mí **5.** _____ gustan los clientes políticos, pero prefiero las estrellas de cine. A ellas **6.** _____ gusta hacer muchas actividades divertidas conmigo *(with me)*. Por ejemplo, a Madonna y a mí **7.** _____ gusta montar a caballo, andar en bicicleta, patinar en línea y pescar.

WB 3-6 | Mis preferencias Ignacio Casaverde is looking for a Spanish-speaking sports partner and has posted the following message to your gym billboard. Complete his message by selecting the correct verb form.

Hola, soy Iggi. En general me **1.** (gusta / gustan) los deportes como el tenis y el baloncesto, pero me **2.** (gusta / gustan) más el ciclismo y el hockey. No me **3.** (gusta / gustan) la pesca porque es aburrida *(boring)*. Los viernes por la mañana a mi hermano y a mí nos **4.** (gusta / gustan) ir al gimnasio a levantar pesas. Los sábados por la mañana nos **5.** (gusta / gustan) jugar al fútbol. Por la tarde a mí me **6.** (gusta / gustan) jugar al billar *(billards, pool)*. A mi hermano le **7.** (gusta / gustan) más las cartas *(cards)* y no juega conmigo. Los domingos no me **8.** (gusta / gustan) practicar ningún deporte porque a mi esposa le **9.** (gusta / gustan) ir de compras y no hay tiempo para jugar. ¿Qué te **10.** (gusta / gustan) hacer?

VOCABULARIO Los lugares

WB 3-7 | Lugares revueltos Unscramble the letters to reveal different places in the city.

1. el emorcda: _____

2. la ientda: _____

3. la slegiai: _____

4. la cpisian: _____

5. el enic: _____

6. el suemo: _____

WB 3-8 | ¿Adónde va para... ? Where in the city does one go to do the following activities? Choose the answers from the list provided. **¡OJO!** Use each response only once.

al museo	al centro comercial
al parque	a la discoteca
a la piscina	al supermercado
al café	al restaurante
al cine	al banco

1. Para ver una película: _____

2. Para nadar: _____

3. Para hacer las compras, hablar con amigos o tomar algo: _____

4. Para depositar dinero: _____

5. Para ver arte: _____

6. Para bailar: _____

7. Para comprar comida: _____

8. Para jugar al fútbol: _____

9. Para tomar café: _____

10. Para cenar con amigos: _____

ESTRUCTURA II — Expressing plans with *ir, ir a* + destination, and *ir a* + infinitive

WB 3-9 | Entre amigos Gilberto and his girlfriend, Alejandra, run into Lola, Gilberto's ex-girlfriend. Does Gilberto still have a crush on her? Find out by filling in the banks with the correct form of the verb **ir.**

GILBERTO: Hola Lola, ¿Cómo estás? ¿Qué tal el viaje *(How was the trip)*?

LOLA: Ay, muy bien, gracias. Bueno, ustedes, ¿qué **1.** _____ a hacer aquí hoy?

GILBERTO: Nosotros **2.** _____ al gimnasio aquí en el campus. Y tú, ¿adónde

3. _____ tan guapa *(looking so cute)*?

ALEJANDRA: ¡Gilberto!

LOLA: Yo **4.** _____ a ver a mi compañero de clase, Cali Caretas. Nosotros

5. _____ a sacar fotos juntos *(together)*.

GILBERTO: ¿Con Cali? ¡Él no saca buenas fotos!

ALEJANDRA: ¡Gilberto! Yo me **6.** _____ a ir de aquí *(I am getting out of here)*.

Mira Lola, Gilberto **7.** _____ a hacer ejercicio ahora. Nos vemos.

LOLA: Pues, ¡hasta luego!

GILBERTO: ¡Hasta pronto!

ALEJANDRA: ¡Gilberto!

WB 3-10 | Compañeros de cuarto You and your roommates have busy lives. Based on the following calendar page, describe in complete sentences what everyone is going to do and when (day and time) they are going to do it. Follow the model.

Modelo   Eugenia y Cati
Eugenia y Cati van a ir al cine el lunes a las tres de la tarde.

lunes 17	jueves 20	sábado 22
Eugenia y Cati: cine, 3 PM Carlos: sacar fotos con Silvia, 11 AM	Ángel: iglesia, 9 AM–1 PM	Carlos y yo: cenar y bailar, 9 PM
martes 18	viernes 21	domingo 23
Alberto: plaza, 8 PM	Eugenia: mercado al aire libre, 5 PM	Ángel, Carlos y Eugenia: jugar al tenis, 2 PM
miércoles 19		
Yo: comer con mis padres, 1 PM		

1. Carlos y Silvia

_____

2. Alberto

_____

3. Carlos y yo

_____

4. Ángel, Carlos y Eugenia

_____

5. Eugenia

_____

6. Ángel

_____

7. Yo

_____

ESTRUCTURA III Describing leisure-time activities: Verbs with irregular *yo* forms

WB 3-11 | Conjugaciones Select the appropriate verb form for the persons listed.

1. yo / estar
   a. esta   **b.** esté   **c.** estoy   **d.** estamos

2. Mario y Elena / poner
   a. pones   **b.** pongo   **c.** ponen   **d.** pongan

3. nosotros / salir
   a. salimos   **b.** salgamos   **c.** salen   **d.** sabemos

4. Julio / dar
   a. dan   **b.** de   **c.** da   **d.** doy

5. Teresa y yo / hacer
   a. hagamos   **b.** hacemos   **c.** hacen   **d.** hago

6. tú / conocer
   a. conozcas   **b.** conoce   **c.** conoces   **d.** conocen

7. yo / saber
   a. salen   **b.** sabe   **c.** saber   **d.** sé

8. Antonio, Jimena y su madre / ver
   a. ven   **b.** ves   **c.** vemos   **d.** vean

9. yo / traer
   a. trae   **b.** traen   **c.** traes   **d.** traigo

WB 3-12 | El profesor excéntrico Paco Empacanueces is the Colombian "Nutty Professor." Find out his strange habits by building sentences from the words below. ¡**OJO!** Be careful to add prepositions where necessary. Follow the model.

Modelo   yo / traer / comida / mis clases
Yo traigo comida a mis clases.

1. Todos los días / yo / salir de la casa / cuatro de la mañana

_____

2. yo / hacer ejercicio / el parque

_____

3. allí *(there)* / yo / ver / a mis amigos

_____

4. yo / traer / discos compactos / universidad

_____

5. yo / poner / música de Metallica / mi oficina

_____

6. yo / dar fiestas / por la mañana

_____

7. yo / conocer / a todos mis colegas / la universidad

_____

8. pero / yo / no saber / su nombre

_____

WB 3-13 | Los sábados Mercedes likes to spend her Saturdays with friends. Complete the following paragraph with the appropriate form of the verb in parentheses to find out what she does.

Los sábados por la mañana me gusta pasear por la ciudad. Normalmente yo

1. _____ (salir) de mi casa temprano para ir al mercado al aire libre. Allí

2. _____ (ver) a mis amigos y todos 3. _____ (hacer)

las compras juntos. Mi amiga Lilián siempre 4. _____ (traer) a sus

hermanos, Fabián y Santi. Ellos 5. _____ (conocer) a todos los

vendedores *(vendors)* del mercado y por eso nosotros compramos a muy buenos precios.

Después de ir al mercado mis amigos y yo 6. _____ (dar) una vuelta

(go around) por el centro. Muchas veces vamos al museo de arte. Mi amiga Silvia

7. _____ (saber) mucho del arte y me gusta ir con ella. Otras veces

vamos a un café muy especial que yo 8. _____ (conocer). En este café, el

dueño *(owner)* siempre 9. _____ (poner) música reggae y todos bailamos.

ASÍ SE DICE — Expressing knowledge and familiarity: *Saber, conocer,* and the personal *a*

 To learn more about **Saber** and **Conocer,** go to Heinle iRadio at www.thomsonedu.com/spanish.

WB 3-14 | ¿Cierto o falso? Read the following statements and indicate whether each is true by writing **cierto**, or false by writing **falso.** If you are not familiar with some of the people mentioned, look them up on the Internet.

_____ **1.** Shakira sabe jugar al golf muy bien.

_____ **2.** Carlos Vives conoce la ciudad de Bogotá.

_____ **3.** Gabriel García Márquez conoce a muchos escritores.

_____ **4.** Juanes sabe tocar la guitarra.

_____ **5.** Fernando Botero sabe cantar bien.

WB 3-15 | Y ahora... You are interviewing a future Spanish-speaking roommate from Colombia. Complete the following questions with the correct form of the verb **saber** or **conocer.** ¡OJO! In many parts of Colombia the **usted** form is used instead of **tú.**

1. ¿_____ a muchas personas aquí?

2. ¿_____ jugar al tenis?

3. ¿_____ cocinar bien?

4. ¿_____ a los dueños del apartamento?

5. ¿_____ qué tiendas están cerca *(close by)*?

WB 3-16 | Los abuelos de Camila To find out what Camila's grandparents are like, complete the phrases with the correct form of **saber** or **conocer.**

CAMILA: Diego, usted **1.** _____ tocar muy bien la guitarra.

DIEGO: Gracias, Camila, pero también usted **2.** _____ tocar el piano y cantar muy bien.

CAMILA: ¡Gracias! Oye, quiere **3.** _____ a mis abuelos? Mi abuela toca el tambor en una banda de rock metálico y mi abuelo canta con un grupo de música punk.

DIEGO: Sí, con mucho gusto. Yo **4.** _____ que ellos tienen como ochenta años, ¿no?

CAMILA: Sí, es cierto, ¡pero todavía *(still)* **5.** _____ vivir!

DIEGO: Bueno, quiero **6.** _____ a tus abuelos. ¡Voy a aprender mucho de ellos!

ASÍ SE DICE Talking about the months, seasons, and the weather

WB 3-17 | Estaciones y meses Write the season, the months of that season (in the Northern Hemisphere), and the weather that each drawing represents.

1. Estación: _____

   Meses de la estación:

   _____

   El tiempo: _____

   _____

2. Estación: _____

   Meses de la estación:

   _____

   El tiempo: _____

   _____

3. Estación: _____

   Meses de la estación:

   _____

   El tiempo: _____

   _____

4. Estación: _____

   Meses de la estación:

   _____

   El tiempo: _____

   _____

WB 3-18 | Las condiciones en El Tolima Consult the following weather report for El Tolima, Colombia and answer the questions in complete sentences.

CONDICIONES ACTUALES: EL TOLIMA, COLOMBIA	
Temperatura	77° F
Humedad	84%
Viento	0–6 mph
Condiciones	Neblina
Visibilidad	6 millas

1. ¿Qué tiempo hace hoy en El Tolima?

_____

_____

2. ¿Hace mucho viento hoy en El Tolima?

_____

3. ¿Es un buen día para esquiar? ¿Por qué sí o por qué no?

_____

WB 3-19 | ¿Cuando...? Provide the appropriate information about when the following events occur. Follow the model.

Modelo   Es el primer día de primavera en Santa Fé, Nuevo México. ¿En qué mes estamos?
        Estamos en marzo.

1. El 25 de diciembre en Nueva York. ¿Qué estación es?

_____

2. Es el 4 de julio en la Patagonia, Argentina. ¿Qué estación es?

_____

3. Es el 15 de octubre en Madrid. ¿Qué estación es?

_____

4. La gente esquía en el agua en Minnesota. ¿Qué estación es?

_____

5. Es el primer día de verano en Ohio. ¿En qué mes estamos?

_____

BIENVENIDOS A COLOMBIA

In this video segment, you will learn about the following topics in Colombia:

- geography
- nature
- agriculture
- main cities

WB 3-20 | In the video segment, you will hear a number of Spanish words that are cognates of English words. Try to pronounce each of the following Spanish words, and then match each with its meaning in English.

1. _____ climas
2. _____ cultivan
3. _____ banano
4. _____ caña
5. _____ carbón
6. _____ valles

a. carbon / coal
b. climates
c. valleys
d. banana
e. cultivate / grow
f. cane

WB 3-21 | Watch the video segment and listen for the following sentences, in which the cognates you just identified in activity **WB 3-20** appear. Fill in the blank with the appropriate cognate.

1. Colombia es el país de América Latina más rico en variedades de _____, fauna y flora.

2. En sus montañas se _____ el maíz, las flores, el

   _____ y café.

3. Y en sus valles hay variedad de frutas y _____ de azúcar.

WB 3-22 | View the video segment again, and then answer the following questions.

1. ¿Qué se cultiva *(is grown)* en las montañas de Colombia? *(Select all that apply.)*

   a. maíz   **c.** flores

   b. banano   **d.** lechuga

2. ¿Cuáles son algunas de las ciudades de Colombia?

   a. Buenos Aires   **c.** Cartagena

   b. Cali   **d.** Medellín

¡A ESCRIBIR!

Mis planes para el verano Your friend Carlos wrote to tell you about his summer vacation plans, and he wants to know what you are doing. Write him back and tell him about your summer plans.

Strategy: Combining sentences

Learning to combine simple sentences into more complex ones can help you improve your writing style immensely. In Spanish, there are several words you can use as connectors to combine sentences and phrases.

y	and (**y** becomes **e** before **i** or **hi**)
que	that, which, who
pero	but
o	or (**o** becomes **u** before **o** or **ho**)
porque	because

Before you begin to write, follow these steps.

Paso 1 Write a few basic sentences about your plans for summer. Follow the model.

> Modelo   Este verano (yo) ir a
> *Este verano voy a ir a Nueva York.*
>
> Este verano (yo) querer
> *Este verano quiero visitar a mis abuelos.*

1. Este verano (yo) ir a

   _____

2. Este verano (yo) no ir a

   _____

3. Este verano (yo) querer

   _____

4. Este verano (yo) no querer

   _____

Paso 2 Connect some of these phrases you have just written with **y**, **o**, **pero**, or **porque** to form more complex, logical sentences. Follow the model.

> Modelo   *Este verano voy a ir a Nueva York porque quiero visitar a mis abuelos.*

1. _____
2. _____
3. _____
4. _____
5. _____

Paso 3 Now that you have your ideas organized, write a first draft on a separate sheet of paper. Then, review it and write the final draft of your letter with complete sentences. You can begin with **Querido Carlos.**

ATAJO 4.0

Functions: Writing a letter (informal); Describing people; Talking about the present

Vocabulary: Sport; Leisure; Board games; Family members; Domestic;University

Grammar: Verbs: **ser**, **tener**, **concocer**, and **saber**; Verbs: Future with **ir**; article: contractions **al**,**del**

Autoprueba

WB 3-23 | Los meses y las estaciones In the first column, write the Spanish names for the months in which the following U.S. holidays are celebrated. In the second column, write the season in which the holiday falls.

	Mes	Estación
1. Christmas	_____	_____
2. Valentine's Day	_____	_____
3. New Year's Day	_____	_____
4. Halloween	_____	_____
5. Memorial Day	_____	_____
6. Thanksgiving	_____	_____

WB 3-24 | En la ciudad Place the letter of the description next to the place where you would most likely do that activity.

_____ 1. un museo

_____ 2. una plaza

_____ 3. el mercado

_____ 4. un banco

_____ 5. la oficina de correos

_____ 6. la piscina

_____ 7. el restaurante

a. aprender historia

b. comprar comida

c. mandar una carta

d. sacar dinero

e. comer algo

f. nadar

g. hablar con los amigos

WB 3-25 | Los pasatiempos State your pastimes by matching a verb with an appropriate phrase in the second column and forming a complete sentence. Follow the model.

Modelo   hacer + ejercicio
Me gusta hacer ejercicio.

1. ver   fotos

2. sacar   la guitarra

3. jugar   al tenis

4. tocar   mis abuelos

5. bailar con   la música rock

6. visitar   películas en video

1. _____

2. _____

3. _____

4. _____

5. _____

6. _____

WB 3-26 | **Entre amigos** Complete the following conversation with the appropriate forms of the verb **ir.**

IRENE: ¿Adónde **1.** _____ tú este fin de semana?

CARLOS: **2.** _____ al parque para estudiar. ¿Por qué no **3.** _____ conmigo?

IRENE: No, gracias. Mi mamá y yo **4.** _____ de compras.

CARLOS: ¿No **5.** _____ tu papá con Uds.?

IRENE: No, porque mi papá, Raúl y Sara **6.** _____ al cine.

WB 3-27 | **Un joven contento** Complete the paragraph with the **yo** form of the appropriate verb from the list.

conocer   saber   ver   dar   salir   estar   hacer   ir   poner

Yo **1.** _____ con mis amigos frecuentemente. **2.** _____ muchas

cosas con ellos, y normalmente yo **3.** _____ a fiestas con estos amigos.

También a veces **4.** _____ fiestas en mi casa con ellos. **5.** _____

mucha música rock y todo el mundo baila. **6.** _____ a muchas personas y

7. _____ que a todos les gusta estar en mis fiestas. Los domingos

8. _____ a mis abuelos y comemos juntos. La verdad es que *(the truth is that)*

9. _____ muy contento.

WB 3-28 | **¿Qué vas a hacer?** Match the verb with an appropriate phrase from the list to form complete sentences with **ir** + **a** + infinitive. Follow the model.

Modelo   visitar   un museo
           Voy a visitar un museo.

practicar   al tenis
jugar   a caballo
nadar   en la piscina
montar   pesas
levantar   deportes

1. _____

2. _____

3. _____

4. _____

5. _____

WB 3-29 | ¿Qué tiempo hace? Describe the weather depicted in each of the following scenes.

1. _____

2. _____

3. _____

4. _____

5. _____

6. _____

4 *En la casa: España*

VOCABULARIO La casa

WB 4-1 | Sopa *(Soup)* de letras Unscramble the letters to reveal the name of a household item. Then write where in the house that item is typically found. Follow the model.

Modelo   MACA

Palabra	**Lugar de la casa**
cama	*dormitorio/habitación*

	Palabra	**Lugar de la casa**
1. MRRAIOA	_____	_____
2. ORDONIO	_____	_____
3. SEMA	_____	_____
4. ÁFSO	_____	_____
5. REBAÑA	_____	_____
6. NÓLISL	_____	_____
7. DAHUC	_____	_____
8. AMÓDOC	_____	_____

WB 4-2 | En la agencia de bienes raíces *(real estate)* Which house will you rent? Match the letter of each picture with its description. Then, in each drawing write the names of the items mentioned in its description.

A.

B.

C.

_____ **1.** Esta casa tiene tres habitaciones, un baño y una sala que están en el segundo piso. La sala tiene un sofá y un estante para libros. En el primer piso, hay una cocina grande con una puerta muy elegante que da a un patio pequeño. La casa también tiene un jardín pequeño que está al lado del garaje.

_____ **2.** Esta casa de dos pisos tiene tres habitaciones, un baño, una cocina y una sala. La sala está en el primer piso. Tiene dos sillones, un sofá, una lámpara y una alfombra. Una de las paredes de la sala tiene un espejo pequeño. También en la sala hay una escalera elegante para llegar al segundo piso. Las habitaciones y el cuarto de baño están en el segundo piso. La casa no tiene garaje, pero tiene un patio pequeño.

_____ **3.** Esta casa tiene tres habitaciones, una cocina y un cuarto de baño con inodoro y lavabo. La casa también tiene una sala grande con tres sillones y una lámpara. Esta casa tiene muchas ventanas que dan al *(look out on the)* patio. Al lado del *(Next to the)* patio hay un jardín grande con muchas flores. La casa también tiene sótano y un garaje pequeño.

WB 4-3 | ¿Para qué es esto? Select the name of the appliance described in each statement.

_____ **1.** Es para preparar la comida rápidamente.

    a. la estufa   **b.** el horno microondas   **c.** la tostadora

_____ **2.** Es para limpiar la alfombra.

    a. la aspiradora   **b.** la plancha   **c.** la secadora

_____ **3.** Es para quitar arrugas *(wrinkles)* de la ropa.

    a. el despertador   **b.** la nevera   **c.** la plancha

_____ **4.** Es necesario usarla después de lavar la ropa.

    a. el lavaplatos   **b.** el horno mircroondas   **c.** la secadora

WB 4-4 | Una venta Stella and José are moving in together and trying to organize their things. Help them organize by writing the name of the items under the appropriate category. They will sell what they have two of. Follow the model.

Cosas que tienen...

para la cocina

_____

_____

para la habitación

_____

_____

para la limpieza *(cleaning)*

_____

_____

Cosas que tienen que vender...

para la cocina

una tostadora

_____

para la habitación

_____

_____

para la limpieza

una aspiradora

_____

WB 4-5 | ¿Dónde? Where in the home do you usually find the following items? Follow the model.

> Modelo   el horno microondas
> *En la cocina*

1. el lavabo

_____

2. el lavaplatos

_____

3. la alfombra

_____

4. la cama

_____

5. el inodoro

_____

ESTRUCTURA I   Describing household chores and other activities: Present tense of stem-changing verbs ($e \rightarrow ie$; $o \rightarrow ue$; $u \rightarrow ue$; $e \rightarrow i$)

WB 4-6 | Una nueva casa Teresa wants to move to a bigger house and is talking with her real estate agent about what she is looking for. To find out what they discuss, fill in the spaces with the appropriate verb form.

AGENTE: ¿Qué tipo de casa **1.** _____ (preferir) usted?

TERESA: Ay, por favor, trátame de tú. *(Use the **tú** form with me.)*

AGENTE: Vale *(Ok)*. Pues ¿qué **2.** _____ (querer) tú en una casa?

TERESA: Bueno, yo **3.** _____ (querer) una casa con tres habitaciones porque tengo un hijo y una hija y todos nosotros **4.** _____ (querer) nuestra propia *(own)* habitación. La casa que yo **5.** _____ (tener) ahora, solamente **6.** _____ (tener) dos habitaciones. Pues, es demasiado *(too)* pequeña.

AGENTE: Vale, yo **7.** _____ (entender) tu situación. ¿**8.** _____ (preferir) vosotros vivir en el centro o fuera de la cuidad?

TERESA: Nosotros no **9.** _____ (tener) coche y por eso *(for that reason)* nosotros **10.** _____ (pensar) que es mejor vivir en el centro.

AGENTE: Y, ¿cuándo **11.** _____ (pensar) vosotros mudaros *(move)*?

TERESA: Bueno, mis hijos **12.** _____ (preferir) mudarse *(move)* cuanto antes *(as soon as possible)*, y yo también **13.** _____ (tener) prisa.

AGENTE: Vale, yo **14.** _____ (empezar) a buscar casas para vosotros mañana.

TERESA: Muchísimas gracias.

AGENTE: De nada.

WB 4-7 | **¡Qué compañeros!** Paqui lives in a **colegio mayor** *(dorm)* in Madrid and is always complaining about her roommates. To find out what she says, complete the following sentences with an appropriate form of a verb from the list below.

cerrar   comenzar   pedir   perder   regar   venir

1. Tomás siempre _____ favores.

2. El día de Santi _____ a las tres de la mañana.

3. Lola y Eva siempre _____ sus llaves *(keys)*.

4. Carlos nunca _____ las plantas.

5. Los amigos de Amparo _____ a visitar muy tarde.

6. Belén nunca _____ la boca *(mouth)*.

WB 4-8 | **Los Adanes** The Adanes are the Spanish version of the Addams family—a little creepy and kooky. Today the daughter, Miércoles, is giving an oral report on her family life. Form complete sentences with the words below to find out what she says.

1. mi papá / siempre / jugar / con una espada *(sword)*

_____

2. mi tío Fester / dormir / en una cama de clavos *(nails)*

_____

3. mi madre Morticia / siempre / volver a casa / con plantas muertas *(dead)*

_____

4. nosotros / almorzar / a las dos de la mañana

_____

5. mi hermano Pugilio / poder / dormir con los ojos abiertos

_____

ASÍ SE DICE   Expressing physical conditions, desires, and obligations: Expressions with the verb *tener*

To learn more about **tener** and **tener** expressions, go to Heinle iRadio at www.thomsonedu.com/spanish

WB 4-9 | **¡Muy ocupados!** Tomás is talking to his girlfriend about how busy he and his roommates are. Complete his sentences with the appropriate form of **tener** to find out what they have to do this weekend. Follow the model.

Modelo   yo / limpiar / mi cuarto
Yo tengo que limpiar mi cuarto.

1. Carlos / almorzar / con sus padres

_____

2. Arturo y Ramón / regar / todas sus plantas

_____

3. Tú / comenzar / tus clases de baile

_____

4. Yo / jugar / baloncesto con mi hermanito

_____

5. Nosotros / ver / la nueva película de Almodóvar

_____

WB 4-10 | **La familia Ortega** To learn more about the Ortega family, complete the following sentences with the correct form of an appropriate **tener** expression.

1. María Elena _____. Ella va a descansar en el sofá por media hora.

2. Chús está enferma, pero su mamá no sabe qué hacer. Ella _____.

3. Beti y Tomás son jóvenes. Ella _____ catorce _____ y él

   _____ dieciocho _____.

4. Juanjo _____ porque son las ocho y cuarenta y cinco y él debe llegar

   a su trabajo a las nueve.

5. Esta noche Elena va a salir a comer con Eduardo, un viejo amigo del colegio. Ahora el

   novio de Elena _____ de Eduardo.

6. Carlos es un travieso _(rascal)_, pero su mamá _____ mucha _____ con él.

7. Silvia va al cine. _____ de ver la nueva película de Almodóvar.

WB 4-11 | **Estados** Based on the pictures, describe each person's state using an expression with **tener.**

1.

Alicia _____.

2.

Alex y Alberto _____.

3.

Jorgito

Juanito

Jorgito _____.

4.

Carmen _____.

5.

María y Verónica _____ estudiar.

VOCABULARIO Los quehaceres domésticos

WB 4-12 | Entrevista Mariana is talking to her friend about her chores. Look at her answers and write the question that Mariana most likely asked. **¡OJO!** Remember some question words you have already learned. Follow the model.

Modelo   *¿Cuándo te gusta barrer el piso?*
         Me gusta barrer el piso por la mañana.

1. ¿_____?

   Sí, pongo la mesa todos los días.

2. ¿_____?

   No, no me gusta planchar la ropa.

3. ¿_____?

   Mi hermano riega las plantas.

4. ¿_____?

   No, no tenemos que lavar las ventanas.

5. ¿_____?

   Sí, hago la cama todos los días.

WB 4-13. | ¿Qué hacen? Find out what the **Servicio de limpieza** can do for you. Form sentences with the elements listed. Follow the model.

Modelo   Ana María / lavar / los platos
         Ana María lava los platos.

1. Juan Carlos y Ana María / pasar la aspiradora

   _____

2. Yo / regar / las plantas

   _____

3. Todos nosotros / lavar / las ventanas

   _____

4. Juan Carlos / barrer / el piso

   _____

5. Ana María / hacer / las camas

   _____

WB 4-14 | De vacaciones Pedro asked you to house-sit for him while he's on vacation, but he left you with an incomplete list of chores. Complete the list with the chores that he most likely wants you to do in each place indicated. Follow the model.

En la cocina

barrer el piso

_____

En la habitación

_____

_____

En toda la casa

_____

_____

En el jardín

_____

_____

ESTRUCTURA II Expressing preferences and giving advice:
Affirmative *tú* commands

WB 4-15 | Las reglas Ana has just moved into the sorority house, and her house mother is telling her the rules of the house. To find out what she says, make **tú** commands with the following phrases.

Modelo   Llegar a casa antes de las once de la noche.
          Llega a casa antes de las once de la noche.

1. Leer los anuncios del día.

   _____

2. Limpiar tu habitación una vez a la semana.

   _____

3. Hablar con tus hermanas.

   _____

4. Regar las plantas del jardín todos los lunes.

   _____

5. Cantar nuestra canción con tus hermanas.

   _____

WB4-16 | Mari Mandona Mari Mandona always has advice for all of her friends. For each of her friend's problems listed in the first column write the letter of Mari's advice listed in the second column.

_____ 1. Tengo que limpiar toda la casa hoy.

_____ 2. No me gusta estar en casa.

_____ 3. No me gusta mi nuevo compañero de casa.

_____ 4. No tengo comida en la casa.

_____ 5. Quiero visitarte.

_____ 6. Soy muy mala.

_____ 7. La universidad ya no tiene habitaciones disponibles *(available)* en la residencia.

_____ 8. Tengo un secreto.

a. Ven a mi casa.

b. Dime.

c. Haz un buen trabajo.

d. Pon tu nombre en la lista de espera *(waiting list)*.

e. Sé buena.

f. Sal de la casa.

g. Ve al supermercado.

h. Ten paciencia con él.

WB4-17 | Y tú, ¿qué dices? You have just been hired to write the advice column of your university's newspaper. What advice will you give to the following people? For each situation, write a different **tú** command. Follow the model.

Modelo   Una mujer mayor que quiere conocer a hombres jóvenes.
Ve a muchos partidos de fútbol.

1. Una chica que quiere vivir en la residencia estudiantil.

_____

2. Un chico que quiere vivir en Argentina.

_____

3. Un chico que quiere saber cómo sacar buenas notas.

_____

4. Una chica que no sabe qué llevar a una fiesta latina.

_____

5. Un chico que nunca dice la verdad.

_____

ESTRUCTURA III — Talking about location, emotional and physical states, and actions in progress: The verb *estar*.

WB4-18 | ¿Dónde está? Based on the pictures below, state where the indicated items are located by supplying the appropriate prepositional phrase from the list. Do not use the same phrase more than once. Follow the model.

Modelo El sillón está *al lado de* la mesa.

al lado de	debajo de	en	lejos de
cerca de	delante de	encima de	sobre
con	detrás de	entre	

1. La aspiradora está _____ los estantes.

2. El baño está _____ la habitación y la sala.

3. El espejo está _____ la mesa.

4. La cómoda está _____ de la sala.

5. La lámpara está _____ la mesa.

6. Los estantes están _____ la aspiradora.

WB4-19 | Pobre Antonio Antonio Banderas is in Spain to film a movie without his wife, Melanie Griffith. Help Antonio complete the following letter to Melanie by filling in the blanks with the appropriate form of the verb **estar**.

Muy querida Melanie:

¿Cómo 1. _____ tú? ¿Cómo 2. _____ mi hija, Stella? Yo, pues,

3. _____ muy triste porque tú no 4. _____ aquí. Ahora

5. _____ en las islas Canarias para filmar una escena de mi película, «Dos

noches de amor». Penélope Cruz 6. _____ aquí también y nosotros dos

7. _____ muy ocupados. Nosotros 8. _____ en la playa para

filmar nuestra escena. Mañana voy a 9. _____ en las Islas Baleares con

Victoria Abril. Ella 10. _____ muy guapa estos días. Como puedes notar, yo

11. _____ muy ocupado. Bueno, me tengo que ir (have to run), pero espero verte

a ti (see you) y a Stella muy pronto. Cuando vosotras no 12. _____ conmigo

no puedo vivir.

Un beso, Antonio

WB4-20 | Todos están trabajando When you arrive at your friend's house you find that everyone but one person is working. Describe what each person is doing in the pictures. Use the verb **estar** + the progressive form.

1. Patricio _____.

2. Paula _____.

3. Angelita _____.

4. Esteban _____.

5. Carlos _____.

6. Francisco y Stella _____.

WB4-21 | ¡Sólo en sueños (dreams)! Imagine that you are watching a movie of your ideal life. Write complete sentences to describe what is happening in this movie. Use an appropriate form of the present progressive. Follow the model.

Modelo   Mis amigos *están bailando en un club famoso.*

1. Yo _____.

2. Mis padres _____.

3. Mis amigos y yo _____.

4. Mis profesores _____.

ASÍ SE DICE | Counting from 100 and higher: Numbers from 100 to 1,000,000

WB 4-22 | Matemáticas Solve the following math problems. Write out the numbers in words. Follow the model.

> **Modelo**   doscientos cincuenta + tres = *doscientos cincuenta y tres*

1. trescientos cuarenta y ocho + quinientos setenta y nueve = _____

2. doscientos cincuenta y ocho + mil cuatrocientos y tres = _____

3. mil ochocientos catorce + cinco mil noventa y siete = _____

WB4-23 | Pagando las facturas Luis Ángel, an exchange student from Burgos, Spain, is leaving for a long vacation. Because he is such a shopaholic he's got a lot of big bills that will come due and needs you to help him keep current with them. Following the notes he left for you, write out the checks to pay his bills.

Hola.
¡Gracias por ayudarme!
         Luis Ángel

El Corte Inglés:
€536.000 euros

Coches SEAT:
€1.117.000 euros

Luis Ángel Martín Elordieta   **102**
c/ Altamirano 9
Burgos, España   Fecha _____

Páguese por este cheque a: _____

_____euros.

002659870002687 6698 9897598 7889   *Luis Ángel Martín Elordieta*

Luis Ángel Martín Elordieta   **103**
c/ Altamirano 9
Burgos, España   Fecha _____

Páguese por este cheque a: _____

_____euros.

002659870002687 6698 9897598 7889   *Luis Ángel Martín Elordieta*

Nombre _____ Fecha _____

WB 4-24 | El costo de la vida Your Spanish pen pal wants to know how much it costs to be a university student in the United States. Answer his questions using words in place of numerals.

1. ¿Cuánto es la matrícula universitaria, al trimestre o al semestre, en tu universidad?

_____

2. ¿Cuánto gastas *(do you spend)* en libros al trimestre o al semestre?

_____

3. ¿Cuánto es el alquiler *(rent)* por un piso en tu ciudad?

_____

4. ¿Cuánto gastas en comida al mes?

_____

BIENVENIDOS A ESPAÑA

In this video segment, you will learn about the following topics in Spain:

- geography and autonomous communities
- languages of Spain
- Madrid and Barcelona, two principle cities

WB 4-25 | ¿Dónde está ubicada España?
Which countries does Spain border?

MAR CANTÁBRICO

MAR MEDITERRÁNEO

OCÉANO ATLÁNTICO

WB 4-26 | In the video segment, you will hear a number of Spanish words that are English cognates. Try to pronounce each of the following Spanish words, and then match each with its meaning in English.

_____ 1. océano   **a.** historic monuments

_____ 2. avenidas   **b.** cultural diversity

_____ 3. diversidad cultural   **c.** ocean

_____ 4. monumentos históricos   **d.** region

_____ 5. Mediterráneo   **e.** financial center

_____ 6. región   **f.** avenues

_____ 7. cosmopolita   **g.** cosmopolitan

_____ 8. centro financiero   **h.** dynamic

_____ 9. dinámica   **i.** Mediterranean

WB 4-27 | Watch the video segment and listen for the following sentences, in which some of the cognates you just identified in activity **WB 4-26** appear. Write the appropriate cognate in the blank.

1. Tiene modernas _____ y edificios que se combinan con grandes monumentos históricos.

2. Esta _____ es debida a los numerosos pueblos y etnias que habitaron en España.

3. Sevilla es la capital de la comunidad y Granada, Córdoba y Cádiz son otras de las ciudades importantes de esta histórica _____.

4. Valencia es la capital, una ciudad _____ con gran tradición cultural.

WB4-28 | Watch the video segment again and then match the phrases on the left to the place names on the right. You may use the same answer more than once.

1. El flamenco	**a.** Madrid
2. El centro geográfico del país	**b.** Andalucía
3. San Sebastián	**c.** Cataluña
4. El idioma catalán	**d.** Castilla la Mancha
5. Don Quijote	**e.** Toledo
6. El idioma gallego	**f.** Galicia
7. Barcelona	**g.** El País Vasco
8. Sevilla	
9. Mucha diversidad cultural en su arquitectura	

WB4-29 | Fill in the blanks with the appropriate answer in Spanish.

1. España está situada en la Península _____.

2. España está formada por _____ comunidades autónomas.

3. La comunidad autónoma de Valencia está situada al lado del mar _____ y tiene muchas playas bonitas.

4. Galicia está al lado del océano _____.

¡A ESCRIBIR!

Las viviendas estudiantiles You have been asked to write a short article on student residences in the United States for a magazine for international students. Before you begin to write, reflect on the writing strategy you learned in your text.

> ### Strategy: Writing topic sentences
> The first step in writing a well-structured paragraph is to formulate a clear, concise topic sentence. A good topic sentence has the following characteristics.
>
> - It comes at the beginning of a paragraph.
> - It states the main idea of the paragraph.
> - It focuses on only one topic of interest.
> - It makes a factual or personal statement.
> - It is neither too general nor too specific.
> - It attracts the attention of the reader.

Nombre _____ Fecha _____

Paso 1 Think about the types of questions you might answer in this article. For example:

- Where do the majority of students choose to live?
- What options are available for students?
- How much does each type of living arrangement cost?

Paso 2 On a separate piece of paper write a sentence about the most important idea you would want to communicate to international students about student living arrangements in the United States. This will be your topic sentence. Then, write several sentences that support the point you make in your topic sentence. Organize these sentences and complete the first draft of your brief article.

Paso 3 Check over your paragraph, focusing on the characteristics of a good topic sentence and its relationship to the rest of the paragraph. You may use the following checklist questions as a guide. Does the topic sentence . . .

1. come at the beginning of the paragraph?   _____ yes   _____ no

2. state the main idea of the paragraph?   _____ yes   _____ no

3. focus on only one topic of interest?   _____ yes   _____ no

4. make a factual or personal statement?   _____ yes   _____ no

5. seem neither too general nor too specific?   _____ yes   _____ no

6. attract the attention of the reader?   _____ yes   _____ no

Paso 4 Make any necessary changes to your paragraph and write the final version below.

_____

_____

_____

_____

_____

_____

_____

_____

_____

_____

_____

_____

_____

_____

_____

_____

ATAJO 4.0

Functions: Writing an introduction; Describing objects
Vocabulary: House: bathroom, bedroom, furniture, kitchen, living room
Grammar: Verbs: **estar, tener;** Progressive tenses; Position of adjectives

Autoprueba

VOCABULARIO

WB 4-30 | **Los muebles** Complete the sentences with the names of the appropriate household items from the following list.

un armario   mi cama   un escritorio   el inodoro   el jardín

1. Escribo mis cartas en _____.

2. Pongo toda la ropa en _____.

3. Duermo bastante bien en _____.

4. En el baño limpio _____.

5. Riego las plantas en _____.

WB 4-31 | **Los electrodomésticos** Complete the sentences with the names of the appropriate appliances from the following list.

un despertador   un horno   un horno microondas   la nevera   una lavadora   una aspiradora

1. Siempre lavo mi ropa en _____.

2. Preparo la comida rápida en _____.

3. Limpio las alfombras con _____.

4. Para llegar a clase a tiempo uso _____.

5. Para mantenerla fría, pongo la comida en _____.

WB 4-32 | **Los quehaceres** Complete the following sentences with the names of the places where the chores described are normally done.

la cocina   el comedor   el jardín   la sala

1. Pongo la mesa en _____.

2. Lavo los platos en _____.

3. Corto el césped en _____.

4. Paso la aspiradora en _____.

ESTRUCTURAS

WB 4-33 | **Entre novios** Complete the following conversation with the appropriate present-tense form of the verbs listed. **¡OJO!** You must use each of the verbs at least once.

comenzar   pensar   preferir   querer   tener

TOMÁS: ¿Qué **1.** _____ ganas de hacer hoy, Ceci?

CECI: **2.** _____ ganas de ir al cine. ¿Qué **3.** _____ hacer tú?

TOMÁS: Yo no **4.** _____ ir al cine. **5.** _____ ver videos en casa esta noche. Pero, dime *(tell me)*, ¿a qué hora **6.** _____ la película en el cine?

CECI: **7.** _____ a las seis. Mi hermana y yo no **8.** _____ ver videos en casa, **9.** _____ ir al cine.

TOMÁS: ¿Tú hermana va con nosotros? Yo **10.** _____ que no voy con Uds.

WB 4-34 | La hora del almuerzo Complete the following paragraph with an appropriate present-tense form of the verbs listed.

almorzar   decir   dormir   jugar   servir   volver

Normalmente, yo **1.** _____ con mi familia a las dos durante la semana. Mis

padres preparan la comida, luego mi padre **2.** _____ la comida. Siempre como

dos porciones y mi padre siempre **3.** _____ que voy a estar gordo. Después de

4. _____, yo **5.** _____ la siesta por media hora. Después, mis

padres **6.** _____ a su trabajo y yo **7.** _____ a la universidad.

A veces, mis amigos y yo **8.** _____ al fútbol después de nuestras clases. Yo no

9. _____ muy bien, pero me gusta mucho practicar ese deporte.

WB 4-35 | En otras palabras Change the verb phrases in the sentences, using an expression with the verb **tener.** Some suggestions appear below. Follow the model.

Modelo   Quiero dormir.
Tengo sueño.

tener celos   tener paciencia   tener ganas de   tener prisa
tener hambre   tener sueño   tener miedo

1. Quiero salir a bailar esta noche.

_____.

2. No puedo dormir por la noche.

_____.

3. No me gusta el nuevo novio de mi novia.

_____.

4. No me gusta estar en la casa solo.

_____.

WB 4-36 | ¿Qué hago? Tell your friend how to get along better with his roommates. Use the following verb phrases to form **tú** commands.

1. hacer tu cama todos los días

_____

2. quitar la mesa después de comer

_____

3. sacar la basura todos los días

_____

4. ir al supermercado todos los sábados

_____

WB 4-37 | ¿Cómo están todos? You are baby-sitting, and the children's mother calls to find out how everyone is and what everyone is doing. Tell her, using the verb **estar** + *adjective* or the *present progressive*. Follow the model.

> Modelo   Tomás / furioso / pasando la aspiradora
> *Tomás está furioso. Está pasando la aspiradora.*

1. Lolita / emocionada / jugar en el patio

   _____

2. Teresita y Javi / ocupado / regar las plantas

   _____

3. Miguelín / aburrido / leer un libro

   _____

4. Ángel y yo / sucios / preparar un pastel

   _____

WB 4-38 | ¿Cuántos son? Solve these mathematical problems using words, not numerals.

1. doscientos treinta y cinco + mil quinientos tres =

   _____

2. seiscientos setenta y nueve + cuatrocientos ochenta y uno =

   _____

3. dos mil trescientos cincuenta y dos – novecientos treinta y seis =

   _____

Nombre _____   Fecha _____

 5 | *La salud: Bolivia y Paraguay*

VOCABULARIO El cuerpo humano

WB 5-1 | El cuerpo humano Escribe los nombres de las partes del cuerpo del dibujo *(drawing)*.

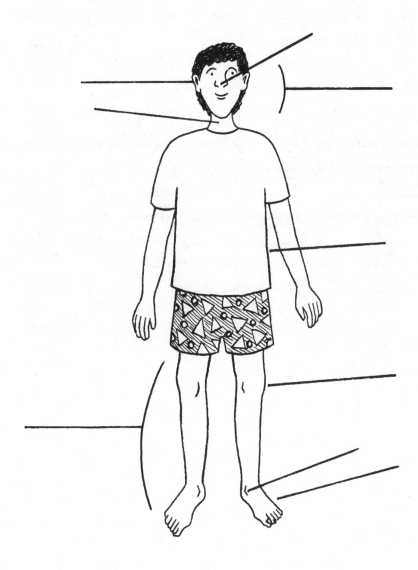

WB 5-2 | Crucigrama Soluciona el siguiente crucigrama rellenando los espacios en blanco con la palabra indicada en cada pista *(clue)*. Todas las palabras son partes del cuerpo humano.

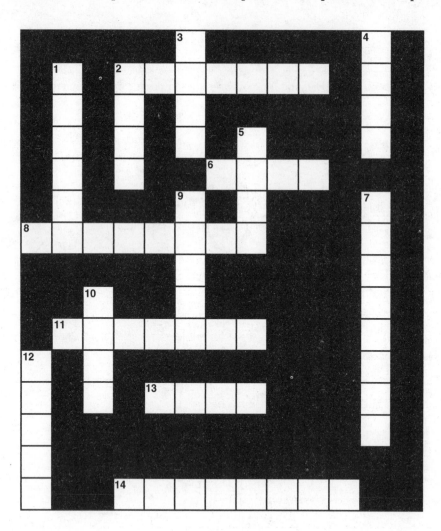

Vertical

1. Dumbo tiene _____ muy grandes.
2. Señalas *(You point)* con el _____.
3. Michael Jordan no tiene _____.
4. Ves con los _____.
5. La _____ tiene cinco dedos.
7. Cuando tomas algo, el líquido pasa por la _____.
9. La _____ es parte de la cara.
10. Comes con la _____.
12. El _____ está conectado con la mano.

Horizontal

2. Tienes _____ en la boca.
6. Jennifer López tiene una _____ muy bonita.
8. Si comes mucho te duele *(hurts)* el _____.
11. El _____ es el símbolo del amor.
13. En medio del brazo está el _____.
14. Respiras con los _____.

WB 5-3 | El cuerpo revuelto Estas palabras son partes del cuerpo. Pon las letras en orden para revelar *(reveal)* qué parte es. Sigue el modelo.

> Modelo   gualen: *lengua*

1. anreip: _____

2. sodde: _____

3. rizan: _____

4. dooc: _____

5. ózarnoc: _____

ESTRUCTURA I — Talking about routine activities: Reflexive pronouns and present tense of reflexive verbs

WB 5-4 | La familia Soriana La casa Soriana es un lugar de mucha actividad. Todos los miembros tienen una rutina distinta. ¿Cómo son? Para saberlo *(To find out)* forma oraciones completas con los elementos dados *(given)*. Sigue el modelo.

> Modelo   MariPepa / acostarse / las 6:30 / la mañana
> *MariPepa se acuesta a las seis y media de la mañana.*

1. Carmen / despertarse / 6:30 / la mañana

_____

2. don Carlos y Miguel / afeitarse / por la noche

_____

3. yo / lavarse / y después / cepillarse / los dientes

_____

4. los niños / bañarse / por la mañana

_____

5. doña Lucía y Luisita / maquillarse / y después / peinarse

_____

6. Miguel / quitarse / la ropa / y acostarse / las 8:00 de la noche

_____

WB 5-5 | ¿Compañeros? Jerry piensa compartir *(share)* su apartamento con tres estudiantes hispanos: Elena de Bolivia, Jorge de España y Lola de Miami. Ahora están hablando de su rutina diaria para ver si van a poder compartir el apartamento pequeño de Jerry. Para saberlo, rellena los espacios en blanco con la forma apropiada del verbo. **¡OJO!** Jorge es español y usa la forma **vosotros**.

JERRY: Debemos hablar de cómo vamos a compartir el apartamento, ¿no?

JORGE: Pues, yo **1.** _____ (despertarse) a las cinco de la mañana porque

trabajo muy temprano. **2.** _____ (Bañarse) en seguida *(right*

away) y después **3.** _____ (secarme) y **4.** _____

(ponerme) la ropa. ¿Y vosotras? ¿A qué hora **5.** _____

(levantarse)?

ELENA: Yo aunque *(although)* **6.** _____ (dormirse) tarde,

7. _____ (despertarse) a las siete de la mañana porque tengo

clase a las ocho. ¿Y tú, Lola? **8.** ¿_____ (acostarse)

tarde y **9.** _____ (despertarse) temprano también, ¿no?

LOLA: Sí. Y **10.** _____ (ducharse), **11.** _____

(vestirse) y **12.** _____ (maquillarse) en el baño, así que paso

mucho tiempo allí por la mañana.

ELENA: Ah, ¡no te preocupes! A mí me gusta **13.** _____ (pintarse)

en mi cuarto. No paso mucho tiempo en el baño por la mañana. Parece que todo está

bien entonces, ¿no?

JERRY: Un momento, por favor. Yo también **14.** _____ (levantarse)

temprano, a las siete y media. Necesito **15.** _____ (bañarse)

inmediatamente para **16.** _____ (despertarse).

Después **17.** _____ (cepillarse) los dientes,

18. _____ (peinarse) y **19.** _____

(afeitarse). Finalmente, **20.** _____ (ponerse) la ropa y salgo del

baño a las 8:30.

JORGE: Este hombre **21.** _____ (cuidarse) bien, ¿no?

WB 5-6 | ¿Qué está pasando? ¿Qué va a pasar? Mira los dibujos y contesta las preguntas. Escoge *(Choose)* un verbo apropiado de la lista y escribe las dos posibles maneras de contestar. **¡OJO!** No todos los verbos son necesarios. Sigue el modelo.

peinarse	dormirse	lavarse	quitarse	cepillarse
vestirse	ducharse	levantarse	maquillarse	

Modelo ¿Qué está haciendo Nuria?
Nuria está cepillándose el pelo /
Nuria se está cepillando el pelo.

1. ¿Qué está haciendo José María?

   _____

   _____

2. ¿Qué está haciendo Carlos?

   _____

   _____

3. ¿Qué va a hacer Pablo?

   _____

   _____

4. ¿Qué va a hacer Susana?

   _____

   _____

ASÍ SE DICE | Talking about things you have just finished doing: *Acabar de* + infinitive

WB 5-7 | ¡Hecho! Forma oraciones con la estructura ***acabar de + infinitivo.*** Sigue el modelo.

　　Modelo　　Tú / bañarse: *Acabas de bañarte.*

1. Yo / maquillarse: _____.

2. Elio / cepillarse los dientes: _____.

3. Miguel / dar un paseo: _____.

4. Belen / sacar fotos: _____.

WB 5-8 | La vida sana El doctor Ruiz, un médico de España, está conversando con la familia Bodega sobre una vida sana. Les hace *(He asks them)* varias preguntas sobre su estilo de vida. Escribe sus respuestas usando la construcción ***acabar + de + el infinitivo.*** Sigue el modelo.

　　Modelo　　A los niños: ¿Os cepilláis los dientes todos los días?
　　　　　　　　Sí, acabamos de cepillarnos los dientes.

1. A toda la familia: ¿Se desayunan todos los días?

_____

2. A la señora Bodega: ¿Descansa Ud. durante el día?

_____

3. A Juanito: ¿Te bañas todos los días?

_____

4. A la señora Bodega: ¿Toman mucha agua los niños?

_____

WB 5-9 | ¿Qué acaban de hacer? Escribe lo que estas personas acaban de hacer en cada situación. Escoge los verbos de la lista. Sigue el modelo.

　　　　andar　despertarse　maquillarse　comer　levantarse　acostarse
　　　　　　dibujar　comprar　quitarse　secarse　dormirse

　　Modelo　　Silvia y Gabriela / Son las seis y media de la mañana.
　　　　　　　　Silvia y Gabriela acaban de despertarse.

1. Nosotros / No tenemos hambre.

_____

2. Tú / Estás seco.

_____

3. Antonio / Se va a dormir.

_____

4. Yo / No llevo ropa.

_____

VOCABULARIO La salud

WB 5-10 | Bienvenidos Dolores Castellanos les da un tour de la clínica a unos voluntarios de la Clínica de Salud Rural Andina. Completa su descripción de la clínica con una palabra apropiada de la lista. **¡OJO!** No vas a usar todas las palabras, y no puedes usar la misma palabra más de una vez.

> ambulancia enfermero(a) mareado receta antibiótico farmacia médico
> sala de emergencia catarro gripe pacientes sala de espera
> enfermedad jarabe pastillas síntomas

Empezamos en la **1.** _____ donde los **2.** _____

esperan su cita *(appointment)* con el **3.** _____. Antes de ver al doctor

Dardo Chávez, ellos comentan sus síntomas con el (la) **4.** _____.

Durante el invierno, muchos de ellos tienen **5.** _____ y sus

6. _____ son fiebre, escalofríos y dolores del cuerpo. En estos casos el

doctor Dardo Chávez les da una **7.** _____ para antibióticos, y los

pacientes tienen que ir a la **8.** _____. Pero en otros casos los pacientes

simplemente tienen **9.** _____, pues tosen y estornudan mucho.

En estos casos el doctor Dardo Chávez les da **10.** _____ y

11. _____. Ahora, Uds. pueden venir conmigo para ver la

12. _____. Allí es donde esperan los pacientes que vienen en la

13. _____.

WB 5-11 | ¿Qué pasa? Describe a los siguientes pacientes. Empareja *(Match)* todas las descripciones de la columna de la derecha con los dibujos de la izquierda.

1.

2.

3.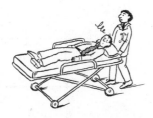

a. Le duele el estómago.

b. Está mareado.

c. Tiene escalofríos.

d. Tiene alergias.

e. Le duele la cabeza.

f. Tiene fiebre.

g. Está con el enfermero.

h. Estornuda.

WB 5-12 | ¿Loco por las medicinas? ¿Para qué son las medicinas que tiene David? Empareja las medicinas de la columna de la izquierda con sus usos de la columna de la derecha.

La usas cuando...

1. Alka Seltzer   **a.** te duele la piel.

2. Solarcane   **b.** te duele el cuerpo.

3. Halls   **c.** te duele la garganta.

4. Epsom salts   **d.** te duele el estómago.

WB 5-13 | ¿Qué les duele? Tú y tus amigos acaban de subir a El Capitán en el parque Yosemite. Forma oraciones completas para indicar qué partes del cuerpo les duelen. Sigue el modelo.

Modelo   Alberto / los pies: *A Alberto le duelen los pies.*

1. Alicia / los brazos: _____.

2. Tomás / el tobillo: _____.

3. Cara y Nidia / las rodillas: _____.

4. Yo / la espalda: _____.

ESTRUCTURA II   Describing people, things, and conditions: *Ser* versus *estar*

 To learn more about **Ser** and **Estar**, go to Heinle iRadio at www.thomsonedu.com/spanish.

WB 5-14 | El nuevo médico Ángela y Roberto están hablando del nuevo doctor de la clínica. Escoge la forma apropiada del verbo para completar sus oraciones.

1. El nombre del nuevo doctor es / eres / está / somos Juan José Valerio.

2. Están / Son / Es / Está de Copacabana, Bolivia.

3. Copacabana están / son / es / está cerca del Lago Titicaca.

4. Creo que el doctor Valerio y la doctora Vargas son / estás / están / somos / eres en la sala de espera ahora.

5. Ahora es / está / están / son las dos de la tarde, el doctor Vargas es / somos / está / estámos almorzando *(eating lunch)*.

WB 5-15 | ¿Cuánto sabes? Las siguientes oraciones son sobre gente, lugares o eventos de Bolivia y Paraguay. Vuelve a escribir cada oración con la forma apropiada del verbo **ser** o **estar.**

Modelo   El boliviano Jaime Escalante ser / estar muy inteligente.
                  El boliviano Jaime Escalante es muy inteligente.

1. Santa Cruz de la Sierra ser / estar en el este de Bolivia.

_____

2. El parque Carlos Antonio López ser / estar en Asunción.

_____

3. La Paz y Sucre ser / estar las capitales de Bolivia.

_____

4. El guaraní ser / estar la moneda oficial de Paraguay.

_____

5. La celebración de Achocalla ser / estar en La Paz.

_____

WB 5-16 | **La doctora Reyes** La doctora Reyes está revisando *(reviewing)* sus apuntes *(notes)* sobre una de sus pacientes. Completa sus apuntes con la forma apropiada de los verbos *ser* o *estar*.

Hoy **1.** _____ viernes, el 22 de febrero y **2.** _____ las dos de la tarde.

La paciente **3.** _____ Aracelia Itzapú. Ella **4.** _____ casada y

5. _____ madre de tres hijos. Ella **6.** _____ de Asunción y

7. _____ paraguaya, pero su esposo **8.** _____ boliviano. Aracelia

9. _____ baja y delgada.

Hoy día Aracelia **10.** _____ muy enferma. **11.** _____ congestionada,

12. _____ tosiendo y estornudando mucho. Dice que **13.** _____ muy

cansada también. Además, dice que **14.** _____ un poco deprimida *(depressed)*

por varias razones: acaba de morir su padre y su esposo no **15.** _____ aquí. Él

16. _____ en La Paz y **17.** _____ buscando trabajo. Creo que

18. _____ necesario para Aracelia dormir más y tomar vitaminas. La próxima cita

para Aracelia va a **19.** _____ el primero de marzo.

ESTRUCTURA III | Pointing out people and things: Demonstrative adjectives and pronouns

WB 5-17 | **¿Cómo funciona?** Hoy es el primer día de trabajo en la clínica para Leticia y tiene muchas preguntas. Completa sus preguntas con la forma correcta del adjetivo demostrativo: *este, esta, estos, estas*. Sigue el modelo.

    Modelo   ¿Ayudo a *este* señor?

1. ¿Hablo con _____ mujer?

2. ¿Trabajo en _____ sala?

3. ¿Escribo sobre _____ síntomas?

4. ¿Todos los pacientes son de _____ pueblo?

5. ¿Tratamos aquí todas _____ enfermedades?

WB 5-18 | **¡Pobre Leticia!** No está haciendo bien su trabajo. Para saber cómo la corrige su jefe *(how her boss corrects her)* completa sus comentarios con el adjetivo demostrativo correcto: ***ese, esa, esos, esas.*** Sigue el modelo.

> **Modelo**   No, ayuda a ***ese*** señor.

1. No, habla con _____ mujer.

2. No, trabaja en _____ sala.

3. No, escribe sobre _____ problemas.

4. No, los pacientes son de _____ dos pueblos.

5. No, aquí tratamos a _____ pacientes.

WB 5-19 | **Más preguntas de Leticia** Leticia todavía tiene más preguntas. Ayuda a completarlas. Sigue el modelo.

> **Modelo**   ¿Es ***esa*** *(that one there)* mujer la que tiene catarro, o es
> ***aquélla*** *(that one way over there)?*

1. ¿Es ___este___ hombre *(this man right here)* el que tiene náuseas o es ___aquél___ *(that one way over there)?*

2. ¿Son ___~~estos~~___ niños *(these boys right here)* los que necesitan jarabe o son ___aquellos___ *(those way over there)?*

3. A quién le duele el estómago, ¿a ___aquélla___ muchacha *(that one way over there)* le duele el estómago, o a ___~~este~~___ *(this one right here)?*

4. Doctor, ¿necesita ___~~esos~~ estos___ pastillas *(these pills right here)* o ___~~aquellos~~ esas___ *(those over there)?*

BIENVENIDOS A BOLIVIA

En este segmento del video, vas a aprender un poco sobre el país de Bolivia y la vida de sus ciudadanos. Los temas incluyen:

- la geografía
- la populación
- cultura

WB 5-20 | Identifica los países de Bolivia y Paraguay en el mapa.

1. _____ Escribe la letra del mapa que corresponde a Bolivia.

2. _____ Escribe la letra del mapa que corresponde a Paraguay.

WB 5-21 | En el segmento del video vas a escuchar muchos cognados que pueden facilitar *(facilitate)* tu comprensión. Algunos de estos cognados aparecen aquí. Trata de pronunciar cada palabra o frase y luego empareja *(match)* los cognados con su definición en inglés.

1. _____ altitud   **a.** descendants

2. _____ elevada   **b.** impact

3. _____ navegable   **c.** altitude

4. _____ indígena   **d.** ceramic

5. _____ descendientes   **e.** navigable

6. _____ impacto   **f.** indigenous

7. _____ artesanías   **g.** elevated

8. _____ cerámica   **h.** artisan crafts

WB 5-22 | Después de ver el segmento del video, rellena los espacios en blanco con el cognado apropiado de la actividad **WB 5-21.**

1. También se encuentra allí el Altiplano, una región de llanuras de _____ muy

   _____.

2. Casi el 70% de la población de Bolivia es de origen _____. Gran parte de

   ellos son _____ de los incas que incluyen a los aymara y a los quechua.

3. En los mercados se pueden ver sus productos agrícolas, sus _____ y su ropa

   distintiva.

4. Varios grupos indígenas son famosos por su alfarería o _____ elaboradas al

   estilo tradicional.

WB 5-23 | Después de ver el segmento del video otra vez, indica si las siguientes oraciones son **ciertas** (C) o **falsas** (F).

1. _____ Titicaca es la capital de Bolivia.

2. _____ Los Andes son unas de las montañas más altas del mundo.

3. _____ Dos grupos indígenas en Bolivia son los mayas y los incas.

4. _____ Los sombreros que llevan muchos Bolivianos son de origen inglés.

¡A ESCRIBIR!

Escribir por el Internet | You have just made a new Paraguayan friend through the Internet. Her name is Alicia Veraní, and she wants to know all about you. Write her an email and tell her all about yourself.

Strategy: Using a bilingual dictionary

A bilingual dictionary is a useful tool that, when used properly, can enhance the quality, complexity, and accuracy of your writing in Spanish. You must, however, learn to use it correctly. Here are some suggestions to help you use your bilingual dictionary properly.

1. When you look up the Spanish equivalent of an English word, you will often find several meanings for the same word, often appearing like this:
   cold: *n.* frío, catarro, resfriado
       adj. frío

2. In larger dictionaries, additional information may be given that clarifies meanings and uses.
   cold: *n.* frío *(low temperature)*; catarro *(illness)*; resfriado *(illness)*
       adj. frío

3. Pay attention to certain abbreviations in your dictionary that tell you what type of word you have found. Note the abbreviations *n.* and *adj.* in the examples above, indicating that the word is a noun or an adjective. Some of the common abbreviations you will find are listed below. Their Spanish equivalents are in parentheses.
   n. noun *(sustantivo)*
   adj. adjective *(adjetivo)*
   adv. adverb *(adverbio)*
   conj. conjunction *(conjunción)*
   prep. preposition *(preposición)*
   v. verb *(verbo)*

4. Looking up a lot of different words in a bilingual dictionary when you are writing is inefficient. If you look up too many words as you write, you may become frustrated or feel like you want to give up altogether. It is wiser and faster to use the phrases you already know in Spanish as much as possible, rather than trying to translate too many new words you don't know from English to Spanish. You will learn more and more new words as you continue reading and listening to the language.

Paso 1 Add to the following list at least five important aspects of describing yourself.

- where you and your family are from
- your nationality
- your marital status
- where your house is located
- your personality traits and your family members' personality traits

_____

_____

_____

_____

_____

Paso 2 Choose four aspects from the list on page 78, on a separate piece of paper, write several sentences to describe each aspect chosen. If you need to use the dictionary, remember the strategy you have learned for looking up words.

Paso 3 Now, on the same piece of paper, write a first draft of your email letter. Review this draft to make sure your ideas are clearly stated and that your vocabulary usage is correct.

Paso 4 Write the final draft below.

_____

_____

_____

_____

_____

_____

_____

_____

_____

_____

_____

_____

_____

_____

_____

_____

_____

ATAJO 4.0

Functions: Describing people; Talking about the present;
Vocabulary: Countries; Studies; Leisure; Family members; University;
Grammar: Verbs: **ser** & **estar**

Autoprueba

WB 5-24 | **El cuerpo humano** Escribe los nombres de las partes del cuerpo indicadas *(indicated)* en el dibujo.

1. _____
2. _____
3. _____
4. _____
5. _____

6. _____
7. _____
8. _____
9. _____
10. _____

WB 5-25 | **Los problemas médicos** Completa las oraciones con las palabras de la lista. **¡OJO!** Usa cada palabra solamente una vez. Tienes que conjugar *(conjugate)* algunos verbos.

alergia	estornudar	síntoma	enfermo(a)
escalofríos	sano(a)	enfermedad	guardar cama
náuseas	congestionado(a)	fiebre	toser
catarro	examinar	tomarle la temperatura	

1. En la primavera las flores me dan una _____ y yo _____ mucho.

2. Cuando alguien tiene _____, tose mucho.

3. El SIDA *(AIDS)* puede ser una _____ fatal.

4. A veces, cuando alguien tiene alergia, está _____.

5. El dolor del cuerpo y los _____ son _____ de la gripe.

6. Alguien que no está _____ está _____ mucho.

7. El médico _____ a sus pacientes antes de darles una receta.

8. Para saber si alguien tiene _____, el médico le _____.

9. Si alguien está mareado, puede tener _____ y por eso debe _____ para sentirse mejor.

WB 5-26 | **La rutina diaria** Mira los dibujos de la rutina diaria de Beti Villalobos y describe lo que hace todos los días. **¡OJO!** Vas a usar verbos reflexivos y no reflexivos.

1. _____
2. _____
3. _____
4. _____
5. _____
6. _____
7. _____
8. _____

WB 5-27 | **¡Cómo vuela el tiempo!** Son las ocho de la mañana en la vida de Beti Villalobos. Mira los dibujos anteriores y escribe todo lo que Beti acaba de hacer.

1. _____
2. _____
3. _____
4. _____
5. _____
6. _____
7. _____

WB 5-28 | Lorena Bobada Completa el párrafo con la forma apropiada de los verbos *ser* y *estar*.

Lorena Bobada **1.** _____ de Sucre, Bolivia. **2.** _____ estudiante de medicina y por eso **3.** _____ ahora en La Paz donde **4.** _____ la universidad. Lorena ya no **5.** _____ casada; **6.** _____ divorciada y no tiene novio. **7.** _____ soltera. Lorena **8.** _____ una mujer inteligente y **9.** _____ bastante ocupada con sus estudios. Un día ella quiere **10.** _____ cirujana *(surgeon)*. Para ella una carrera **11.** _____ muy importante y por eso ahora la vida académica **12.** _____ la única para ella.

WB 5-29 | Gemelos distintos Roberto y Gustavo son gemelos, pero tienen opiniones muy diferentes. Si Roberto quiere una cosa, Gustavo quiere la otra. Para saber más de ellos, forma oraciones usando los pronombres demostrativos. Sigue el modelo.

Modelo   Quiero ir a esta clínica
            No quiero ésta, prefiero esa clínica.

1. Prefiero esta medicina.

_____

2. Quiero ver este médico.

_____

3. Prefiero comprar esta pastilla.

_____

4. Voy a pedir estos jarabes.

_____

5. Prefiero esto.

_____

¿Quieres comer conmigo esta noche?: Venezuela

VOCABULARIO La comida

WB 6-1 | Sopa de letras Las siguientes palabras forman parte de una cena completa. Identifica las letras que faltan *(are missing)* y después, pon las letras señaladas con * *(signaled by *)* en orden en los espacios debajo del dibujo *(drawing)* para revelar la expresión idiomática *(idiom)* que el dibujo representa.

1. _*_ N _*_ A L __ D A
2. C H __ L __ _*_ __ _*_
3. __ C E __ _*_ E
4. A __ _*_ P A S
5. __ _*_ A N
6. C _*_ __ É
7. __ E R D U __ A _*_
8. V __ N _*_
9. __ A P _*_ S

Frase idiomática: ¿Qué piensa esta mujer de su admirador?

¡__ __ __ Á   HA__ __ A   __N   __ __   __ __ P __!

WB 6-2 | En la cafetería Luís habla de la cafetería de su trabajo donde siempre come. Para saber qué come, y que bebe, rellena cada espacio en blanco con una palabra apropiada de la lista. **¡OJO!** No tienes que usar todas las palabras, pero sólo puedes usar una palabra una vez.

vino	almuerzo	queso
azúcar	pavo	verduras
sal	lechuga	sándwich
jamón	pan	cerveza
vinagre	pimienta	desayuno
agua mineral	camarones	

La cafetería de la compañía es muy conveniente. A la una siempre como el

1. _____ allí con mis compañeros. Muchos días como un 2. _____ de

3. _____ y 4. _____. Me gusta mucho, sobre todo *(especially)* cuando le pongo

(I put on it) 5. _____ y 6. _____. Mi amigo Jorge no come carne, así que él

siempre come 7. _____. Pero los miércoles la cafetería no sirve mariscos y Jorge

tiene que comer 8. _____ con 9. _____.

A mí me gusta comer papas fritas con mucha **10.** _____ y a veces les pongo

11. _____. Jorge no come papas fritas porque es un poco gordo. Después de comer

siempre tomamos algo. Por lo general, yo tomo una **12.** _____, pero Jorge toma

13. _____ porque no puede tomar bebidas alcohólicas.

WB 6-3 | **¿Cómo come la gente?** ¿Qué tipo de comida sirven en el restaurante *Como* en Maracaibo? Para saber qué sirven, lee el menú y contesta las preguntas.

1. Si quieres comida de mar *(seafood)* ¿qué puedes pedir?

_____

2. ¿Tienen bebidas de fruta?

_____

3. ¿Qué bebidas alcohólicas sirven?

_____

4. ¿Qué platos de carne roja ofrecen?

_____

5. ¿Qué bebidas no alcohólicas sirven?

_____

6. ¿Qué platos ofrecen para los que no comen carne roja?

_____

7. ¿Qué sirven de postre?

_____

ESTRUCTURA I Making comparisons: Comparatives and superlatives

WB 6-4 | **Opiniones** Lupe y Lalo tratan de decidir dónde van a comer esta noche. Lee su conversación y rellena los espacios en blanco con la forma comparativa apropiada de **tan, tanto, más** o **menos. ¡OJO!** Recuerda que **tan** y **tanto** usan la palabra **como** para hacer la comparación, mientras que **más** y **menos** usan **que.**

LUPE: ¡Vamos al *Caracol*! Me encantan los mariscos allí. Son los mejores.

LALO: Sí, pero no sirven **1.** _____ carne como *El asador*. Y los platos no son

   2. _____ grandes como los platos de *Mar abierto*.

LUPE: Tienes razón, pero *El asador* no tiene **3.** _____ meseros como *El Caracol*, así

   que *(so)* su servicio no es **4.** _____ bueno como el servicio en *El Caracol*.

LALO: Bueno, ¿por qué no vamos a *Salicome?* Tienen **5.** _____ meseros que

   todos los otros restaurantes, sirven **6.** _____ carne como mariscos y los

   precios no son **7.** _____ altos como los de otros restaurantes.

LUPE: Pero no me gusta su comida. Sus mariscos tienen **8.** _____ sabor

   (taste) que los mariscos de *El Caracol*.

LALO: ¿Sabes qué? ¡Creo que debemos comer en casa!

WB 6-5 | **Lo más...** Una compañía de marketing publicó *(published)* los siguientes datos *(data)* sobre las opiniones de los estadounidenses hoy en día. Escribe los resultados en forma de comparaciones usando **más, menos, mejor, peor** y el adjetivo. **¡OJO!** Recuerda que los adjetivos tienen que concordar *(agree)* con el sustantivo *(noun)*. Sigue el modelo.

   Modelo   más nutritivo: la hamburguesa / la ensalada *
   La ensalada es más nutritiva que la hamburguesa.

   peor: los Leones de Detroit* / los Raiders de Oakland
   Los Leones de Detroit son peor que los Raiders de Oakland.

1. más cómico: Carlos Mencía* / Steve Carell

   _____

2. mejor: Round Table / Pizza Hut*

   _____

3. menos guapo: Paris Hilton* / Jessica Simpson

   _____

4. más rico: el chocolate puro* / el caramelo

   _____

5. menos dulce: la manzana* / la naranja

   _____

WB 6-6 | ¿Cómo se comparan? Tu amigo quiere llevarte *(bring you)* al nuevo restaurante *El Toro Loco,* pero tú quieres ir a tu restaurante favorito, *El Pollo Loco.* Le preguntas a tu amigo si el nuevo restaurante es tan bueno como tu favorito. Escribe sus respuestas usando comparaciones de igualdad *(comparisons of equality).* Sigue los modelos.

> Modelo   ¿Es bonito el *El Toro Loco*?
> Sí. El Toro Loco *es tan bonito como* El Pollo Loco.

> Modelo   ¿Hay mucha gente en *El Toro Loco*?
> No. *No hay tanta gente en* El Toro Loco *como en* El Pollo Loco.

1. ¿Es barato *El Toro Loco*?

   Sí. _____

2. ¿Sirven mariscos en *El Toro Loco*?

   Sí. _____

3. ¿Sirven muchas ensaladas en *El Toro Loco*?

   Sí. _____

4. ¿Es grande *El Toro Loco*?

   No _____

WB 6-7 | La nueva novia Roberto describe la familia de su nueva novia Alicia. Su familia tiene un restaurante en Venezuela. Para saber lo que dice, forma oraciones con el superlativo. Sigue el modelo.

> Modelo   Alicia / simpática / todas mis novias
> *Alicia es la más simpática de todas mis novias.*

1. Alicia / menor / hijas

   _____

2. José / mayor / hijos

   _____

3. Tomás / alto / familia

   _____

4. la familia / conocida / Maracaibo

   _____

5. su restaurante / mejor / Maracaibo

   _____

WB 6-8 | Preferencias Rafa actualiza *(is updating)* su página de Facebook. Ayúdale *(Help him)* a escribir oraciones completas con la forma superlativa correcta de los adjetivos. ¡**OJO!** Los adjetivos tienen que concordar con los sustantivos. Sigue el modelo.

> Modelo   U2 y Los Red Hot Chili Peppers / grupo musical / chévere *(cool)* / de todos
> *U2 y Los Red Hot Chili Peppers son los grupos musicales más chéveres de todos.*

1. ciclismo / deporte / divertido / de todos

   _____

2. jamón serrano / comida / deliciosa / de todos

   _____

3. *Star Wars y Lord of the Rings* / película / mejor / de todos

_____

4. Justin Timberlake / cantante / peor / de todos

_____

5. Ferrari y Porsche / coche / interesante / de todos

_____

VOCABULARIO El restaurante

WB 6-9 | ¿Cómo lo dicen? Tu amiga sale con unos amigos latinos a un restaurante venezolano, pero no sabe hablar español. Ayúdala *(Help her)* a entender qué está pasando con la selección de la mejor opción.

_____ **1.** Camarero, el menú por favor.

    a. Te invito.   **b.** Sí, ¡cómo no!   **c.** Gracias.

_____ **2.** ¿Cuál es la especialidad de la casa?

    a. Está muy fresca esta noche.   **b.** El menú.   **c.** Arepas, ¡por supuesto!

_____ **3.** ¿Qué les apetece?

    a. No, gracias.   **b.** Para mí las arepas.   **c.** Estoy a dieta.

_____ **4.** ¿Desean ver la lista de postres?

    a. ¡Ay, no, no puedo comer más!   **b.** Te invito.   **c.** ¡Buen provecho!

_____ **5.** Yo invito.

    a. ¡Salud!   **b.** Está muy rica.   **c.** Gracias, voy a dejar una propina.

WB 6-10 | Ah, *El Venezolano* Otro amigo conoce el restaurante adonde va tu amiga y le cuenta sobre una tradición latina. Para saber lo que es, completa el párrafo con una palabra apropiada de la lista. **¡OJO!** Usa la forma correcta del verbo en el presente.

    a dieta   desear   menú   propina   camarero   ligero   pedir
        recomendar   cuenta   lista de postres   picar   rico

¡Me encanta ese restaurante! Tienen de todo y el servicio es excelente. Cuando voy, nunca

tengo que ver el **1.** _____ porque sé bien lo que voy a **2.** _____. Si no tienes

mucha hambre, es decir *(that is to say)*, que sólo quieres algo para **3.** _____, puedes

pedir algo **4.** _____. Yo **5.** _____ la sopa de chipichipi. No está para

nada pesada. Pero si realmente tienes mucha hambre y **6.** _____ algo muy

7. _____, tienes que pedir el pabellón. ¡Está para chuparse los dedos! Siempre

pido el pabellón. Después de comer, el **8.** _____ te pregunta que si deseas ver la

9. _____. ¡Tienen helados y tortas muy, pero muy, ricos! Siempre estoy

10. _____, pero no me importa *(it doesn't matter to me)*; en ese restaurante siempre pido un helado. Un consejo: los restaurantes latinos son un poco diferentes de los restaurantes norteamericanos. Uds. tienen que pedir la **11.** _____ cuando todos estén listos *(are ready)* para salir. Los meseros no la llevan *(bring it)* a la mesa automáticamente. Sé que te va a gustar mucho este restaurante. A propósito, el servicio es tan bueno que tienes que dejar una buena **12.** _____, ¿sabes?

13. ¿Qué consejo le da a tu amiga?

    a. No debe ir al restaurante porque la comida es malísima.

    b. No debe pagar la cuenta. Los hombres latinos siempre la pagan.

    c. Tiene que decirle al mesero que ésta lista para ver la cuenta.

    d. Sólo van los ricos a ese restaurante, así que los precios son muy altos.

WB 6-11 | ¿Qué se dice? Indica qué se debe *(one should)* decir en las siguientes situaciones. Selecciona la mejor opción.

1. Estás en un restaurante con un amigo y van a tomar vino. Levantan sus copas y antes de tomar dicen: _____

    a. ¡Bueno provecho!

    b. ¡Dios mío!

    c. ¡Salud!

2. Le dices al mesero que quieres ver el menú. El mesero contesta:

    a. ¡Cómo no! En seguida.

    b. ¿Está fresca la langosta?

    c. Te invito.

3. Acabas tu cena y el mesero te pregunta si quieres algo más. Tú contestas:

    a. ¿Desean ver el menú de postres?

    b. ¿Está fresca la langosta?

    c. Estoy satisfecho(a), gracias.

4. Cenas con una amiga y ella dice que va a pagar la cuenta, pero tú quieres pagar la cuenta. Dices:

    a. La especialidad de la casa es el flan casero.

    b. Te invito.

    c. Estoy a dieta.

ESTRUCTURA II Describing past events: Regular verbs and verbs with spelling changes in the preterite

To learn more about the **Preterite,** go to Heinle iRadio at www.thomsonedu.com/spanish.

WB 6-12 | Palabra escondida Conjuga los verbos indicados en el pretérito para revelar las letras de la palabra escondida. Después de conjugar todos los verbos, ordena las letras en las cajas *(boxes)* para descubrir esta palabra misteriosa. **¡OJO!** La palabra escondida es a la vez *(at the same time)* algo que hicimos *(we did)* ayer y que hacemos todas las mañanas.

Verbos

1. buscar (ellos)
2. comprender (nosotros)
3. creer (usted)
4. salir (tú)
5. deber (ella)

6. comenzar (yo)
7. tocar (yo)
8. ayudar (ellas)
9. comer (ellos)
10. recibir (ustedes)
11. escribir (ella)

1. _ _ _ _ ☐ _ _ _
2. _ _ _ _ _ _ _ _ ☐ _ _
3. _ _ _ ☐ _
4. ☐ _ _ _ _ _ _
5. ☐ _ _ _ _
6. _ ☐ _ _ _
7. _ _ _ ☐ _
8. _ _ _ _ ☐ _ _ _
9. _ _ _ ☐ _ _ _
10. _ _ _ _ _ _ _ _ ☐
11. _ ☐ _ _ _ _ _

La palabra escondida es _____.

WB 6-13 | Una fiesta de sorpresa Doña Carmen le cuenta a un amigo sobre la fiesta de sorpresa que le dio *(gave to her)* su familia. Para saber lo que dice, rellena los espacios en blanco con la forma apropiada del pretérito de los verbos indicados.

1. Amalia _____ (comprar) toda la comida.
2. Carlos y Lupe _____ (preparar) las arepas.
3. Enrique _____ (invitar) a todos mis amigos.
4. Los invitados _____ (llegar) a las ocho y media.
5. Yo _____ (llegar) a las 9:00 y _____ (empezar) a bailar inmediatamente.
6. Nosotros _____ (comer) las arepas y otras cosas.

WB 6-14 | Una pachanga *(wild party)* MariCarmen y Verónica hablan de la fiesta de cumpleaños de Paco anoche. Rellena los espacios en blanco con la forma apropiada del verbo en el pretérito para saber lo que dicen. **¡OJO!** Tienes que prestar atención para saber cuál es el sujeto del verbo.

MARICARMEN: Pues, ¡qué buena fiesta anoche!, ¿no?

VERÓNICA: Sí, sí, y yo **1.** _____ (comer) un montón en la fiesta. Pero tú no

2. _____ (comer) nada. ¿Por qué?

MARICARMEN: Bueno, ayer a la una yo **3.** _____ (almorzar) con mi novio, Jorge.

Él me **4.** _____ (invitar) a ese restaurante italiano que tanto

me gusta. Yo **5.** _____ (decidir) pedir el pescado frito y él

6. _____ (decidir) pedir los camarones al ajillo. Después, nosotros

7. _____ (decidir) pedir un postre. No **8.** _____ (salir)

del restaurante hasta las tres y treinta de la tarde.

VERÓNICA: Ah, entiendo ahora. Bueno, no solamente comí mucho, sino que *(but)* también

(yo) **9.** _____ (beber) tres cervezas.

MARICARMEN: ¡Ay, mujer, eso no es nada! Tú no **10.** _____ (beber) nada en

comparación con el pobre Paco. Yo **11.** _____ (oír) que él

12. _____ (tomar) muchas cervezas y estaba *(he was)* muy

borracho *(drunk)* anoche.

VERÓNICA: Ya lo sé. Mi novio y yo **13.** _____ (llevar) a Paco a su casa. ¡Qué

suerte que tuvimos!

MARICARMEN: ¿Ustedes **14.** _____ (llevar) a Paco a casa? Ahhh, ¡por eso! A las

2:00 de la mañana yo **15.** _____ (decidir) salir para mi casa y

yo **16.** _____ (buscar) a Paco para llevarlo a su casa, pero no

lo **17.** _____ (encontrar) en ningún lado. ¿A qué hora

18. _____ (volver) a casa?

VERÓNICA: Pues, Paco **19.** _____ (llegar) a su casa a la una y media pero yo

no **20.** _____ (llegar) a mi casa hasta las cuatro de la mañana.

MARICARMEN: ¡Vero! ¿Hasta las 4:00? ¿Por qué?

VERÓNICA: Pues, porque a la una y media cuando todos **21.** _____ (llegar) a la

casa de Pablo, él **22.** _____ (comenzar) a hacer tonterías *(silly*

things). **23.** _____ (leer) y **24.** _____ (cantar) poesía

medieval en voz alta *(loudly)*. Claro, yo **25.** _____ (comenzar)

a gritarle *(yell at him)*, pero él no me **26.** _____ (oír) y

27. _____ (salir) de la casa.

MARICARMEN: Vero, pobrecita. ¿Cuándo **28.** _____ (regresar) Paco a la casa?

VERÓNICA: Una hora más tarde.

MARICARMEN: ¡Qué increíble!

WB 6-15 | Sobre la pachanga ¿Cuánto comprendiste de la conversación entre MariCarmen y Verónica en la actividad **WB 6-14?** Selecciona la mejor respuesta a cada pregunta.

1. MariCarmen didn't eat a lot at the party because . . .

    a. she didn't like the fried fish.

    b. she ate a big lunch.

    c. she drank too much and forgot to eat.

2. Last night . . .

    a. MariCarmen lost her boyfriend at the party.

    b. Paco stayed home and never went to the party.

    c. Verónica drank a few beers.

3. Vero got home late because . . .

    a. her boyfriend yelled at her and wouldn't drive her home.

    b. she had to take care of Paco.

    c. MariCarmen drove her home late.

ESTRUCTURA III — Giving detailed description about past events: Verbs with stem changes in the preterite

WB 6-16 | Formas verbales Escribe la forma indicada de cada verbo en el pretérito. **¡OJO!** No te olvides (*Don't forget*) de poner los acentos donde sea necesario (*wherever necessary*).

1. servir / yo: _____
2. servir / tú: _____
3. preferir / él: _____
4. reirse / nosotros: _____
5. sentirse / ustedes: _____
6. divertirse / yo: _____
7. divertirse / ella: _____
8. vestirse / usted: _____
9. vestirse / yo: _____
10. morir / tú: _____
11. pedir / nosotros: _____
12. dormir / él: _____
13. dormir / yo: _____

WB 6-17 | ¿Qué pasó? Lee lo que los Sepúlveda hacen a veces y después escribe lo que hicieron en el pasado. Sigue el modelo.

Modelo   A veces, Susana María duerme más de diez horas.
Anoche Susana María durmió más de diez horas.

1. A veces, yo me visto, luego visto a mi hija Susana María.

    Esta mañana _____ y luego _____ a mi hija Susana María.

2. A veces, Juan Carlos pide una Coca-Cola, pero su papá le sirve jugo.

    El otro día Juan Carlos _____ una Coca-Cola, pero su papá le

    _____ jugo.

3. A veces, Gloria se divierte mucho con su hijo.

    El jueves pasado Gloria _____ mucho con su hijo.

4. A veces, el bebé se duerme rápidamente cuando se acuesta.

Anoche el bebé _____ rápidamente cuando se acostó.

5. A veces, Julio y Tomás prefieren ver "Los Ángeles de Charlie" en la televisión.

Anoche Julio y Tomás _____ ver "Los Ángeles de Charlie" en la televisión.

6. A veces, nosotros casi nos morimos de risa *(we die of laughter)* al contar chistes.

Ayer casi _____ de risa al contar chistes.

WB 6-18 | ¿Una cita divertida? Patricio habla con Silvia sobre su cita de anoche con Laura. Completa su conversación con la forma apropiada de los vebos indicados en el pretérito.

SILVIA: ...pues, dime Patricio, ¿ **1.** _____ (divertirse) anoche con Laura?

PATRICIO: Bueno, sí y no. Ella sí **2.** _____ (divertirse) conmigo, pero no sé si yo

realmente **3.** _____ (divertirse) con ella, ¿sabes?

SILVIA: Pues, cuéntame, ¿qué pasó?

PATRICIO: Mira, yo **4.** _____ (conseguir) mi primera tarjeta de crédito y para

impresionar bien a Laura yo **5.** _____ (sugerir) que fuéramos *(that*

we go) a ese restaurante muy caro del centro. Ella dijo que sí. Esa noche yo

6. _____ (vestirme) muy elegantemente y...

SILVIA: ¿También **7.** _____ (vestirse) Laura elegantemente?

PATRICIO: Sí, Laura estaba *(was looking)* muy linda. Bueno, llegamos al restaurante y el

mesero nos **8.** _____ (servir) unas copas de vino tinto. Pero entonces

Laura **9.** _____ (pedir) una botella de champán muy caro.

SILVIA: ¿Qué hiciste?

PATRICIO: Pues, en ese momento **10.** _____ (preferir) no decir nada así que

simplemente **11.** _____ (sonreír) y no dije nada.

SILVIA: ¿Qué **12.** _____ (pedir) tú para comer?

PATRICIO: Yo **13.** _____ (pedir) el pollo asado, pero ella **14.** _____

(preferir) comer la langosta y el bistec.

SILVIA: ¿La langosta y el bistec? Esa chica sí tiene gustos muy caros ¿no? Pues, ¿hablaron

mucho durante la cena?

PATRICIO: Sí, hablamos mucho y ella **15.** _____ (reírse) mucho. Yo diría *(would*

say) que durante la cena nosotros sí **16.** _____ (divertirse) mucho.

Pero cuando el mesero me trajo la cuenta, yo casi **17.** _____ (morirse)

de miedo.

SILVIA: ¿Cuánto costó la cena?

PATRICIO: ¡260.000 bolívares!

SILVIA: ¡Caray!

PATRICIO: Sí, y después de pagar la cena, Laura **18.** _____ (sugerir) otro lugar

para tomar copas y escuchar música. Pero cuando yo le dije que mi tarjeta de

crédito ya no podiá más, ella dijo que se sentía *(she felt)* enferma y que

19. _____ (tener) que volver a casa.

SILVIA: ¡No me digas!

PATRICIO: Sí. Es la pura verdad. Entonces, nosotros **20.** _____ (despedirse) y yo

fui a casa y **21.** _____ (dormirse) en seguida.

SILVIA: ¿Y la pobre tarjeta de crédito?

PATRICIO: ¡Yo creo que la pobre tarjeta ya **22.** _____ (dormirse) para siempre!

WB 6-19 | ¿Se divirtieron? Indica si las siguientes oraciones son **ciertas** (C) o **falsas** (F)
sobre la cita de Patrcio de la actividad **WB 6-18.**

1. _____ Patricio invited Laura to an elegant restaurant.

2. _____ Patricio got dressed up, but Laura didn't dress very nicely.

3. _____ Patricio ordered a cheap bottle of wine.

4. _____ Patricio and Laura had fun during dinner.

5. _____ Patricio was surprised at how inexpensive the dinner was.

6. _____ Laura got sick at the end of the evening.

7. _____ Patricio wants to have more dates like this with Laura.

BIENVENIDOS A VENEZUELA

En este segmento del video, vas a aprender un poco sobre el país de Venezuela y la vida de
sus ciudadanos. Los temas incluyen:

- la geografía
- la población
- la capital
- el tiempo libre
- la educación

WB 6-20 | ¿Dónde está ubicada Venezuela?
Identifica el país de Venezuela en el mapa.

_____ Escribe la letra del mapa que

corresponde con Venezuela.

WB 6-21 | En el segmento del video vas a escuchar muchos cognados que pueden facilitar *(facilitate)* tu comprensión. Algunos de estos cognados aparecen aquí. Trata de pronunciar cada palabra o frase y luego empareja los cognados con su definición en inglés.

1. _____ arquitectura colonial
2. _____ obligatoria
3. _____ variedad geográfica
4. _____ eficiencia
5. _____ centro político y comercial
6. _____ héroes nacionales
7. _____ gratuita

   a. colonial architecture
   b. geographic variety
   c. efficiency
   d. gratis/free
   e. national heroes
   f. political and commercial center
   g. obligatory

WB 6-22 | Después de ver el segmento del video, rellena los espacios en blanco con el cognado apropiado de la actividad **WB 6-21.**

1. Venezuela es un país sudamericano que se caracteriza por su gran _____.

2. Caracas es una ciudad grande y moderna, un _____ del país.

3. Caracas tiene un buen sistema de metro, que la gente usa con frecuencia por su gran

   _____.

4. Se pueden ver varios ejemplos de la _____, como la hermosa Catedral.

5. Hay también varios monumentos a los _____ como Antonio José de Sucre.

6. La educación es _____ y _____ hasta la edad de catorce años.

WB 6-23 | Después de ver el segmento del video, indica si las siguientes oraciones son **ciertas** (C) o **falsas** (F).

1. _____ Caracas es la capital de Venezuela.

2. _____ Caracas está entre el mar y las montañas.

3. _____ Caracas es una ciudad pequeña y colonial.

4. _____ El metro es eficiente, pero no va a todas partes de la ciudad.

5. _____ Los jóvenes compran discos compactos en los centros comerciales.

6. _____ Antonio José de Sucre es el padre de la independencia venezolana.

¡A ESCRIBIR!

Strategy: Adding details to a paragraph

In **Capítulo 4**, you learned how to write a topic sentence for a paragraph. The other sentences in the paragraph should contain details that develop the main idea stated in the topic sentence. The following procedure will help you develop a well-written paragraph in Spanish:

1. Write a topic sentence about a specific subject.
2. List some details that develop your topic sentence.
3. Cross out any details that are unrelated to the topic.
4. Number the remaining details in a clear, logical order.
5. Write the first draft of a paragraph based on your work.
6. Cross out any ideas that do not contribute to the topic.
7. Write the second draft of your paragraph as clearly as possible.

Task: Writing about a typical student diet

One of your favorite Spanish websites is soliciting short essays about the typical diet of American college students. Write a short paragraph on this topic to submit to this site.

Paso 1: List a series of questions that people in Spanish-speaking countries might ask about the diet of an American college student. Some possibilities are ¿Es una dieta equilibrada? ¿Es una dieta variada? ¿Es una dieta de comida rápida?

Paso 2: Now, choose the most interesting of the questions you listed and answer it. Your answer will serve as the topic sentence for your paragraph.

Paso 3: Write a list of details that support the opinion (the answer to your question) you present in your topic sentence. For example, if your topic sentence is **La dieta del estudiante estadounidense no es muy equilibrada,** some examples of supporting details include, **Los estudiantes comen mucha comida rápida. La comida de las residencias universitarias es muy mala.**

Paso 4: Now write the first draft of your paragraph, incorporating your topic sentence and the sentences you wrote with supporting details. Include only details that truly demonstrate the point you make in your topic sentence.

Paso 5: Read over your first draft and correct any errors; then write a second draft below.

_____
_____
_____
_____
_____
_____
_____
_____

ATAJO 4.0

Functions: Appreciating food; Describing objects; Stating a preference
Vocabulary: Food; Food: restaurant
Grammar: Verbs: **gustar, ser, tener**; Present tense of verbs

Autoprueba

WB 6-24 | **La comida** Pon *(Put)* los nombres de las comidas en las categorías más apropiadas.

aceite	queso	naranja	calamares
cerveza	banana	sal	jugo
lechuga	flan	café	pavo
pollo	manzana	jamón	vinagre
agua mineral	res	papas	leche
chuletas de cerdo	bistec	té helado	pimiento
mantequilla	helado	camarones	vino

Carnes:

_____

Pescado/Mariscos:

_____

Bebidas:

_____

Postres:

_____

Frutas:

_____

Verduras:

_____

Condimentos:

_____

WB 6-25 | **En el restaurante** Indica la letra de la palabra o frase que mejor completa cada oración.

_____ 1. Antes de pedir la comida, el mesero nos trae...

    a. la cuenta.   **b.** la propina.   **c.** el menú.

_____ 2. Antes de comer con otros amigos, les decimos...

    a. ¡Cómo no!   **b.** ¡Estoy a dieta!   **c.** ¡Buen provecho!

_____ 3. Antes de tomar una bebida con nuestros amigos, les decimos...

    a. ¡Salud!   **b.** ¡Estoy satisfecho!   **c.** ¡Está para chuparse los dedos!

_____ 4. Si no tienes mucha hambre, pides algo...

    a. para picar.   **b.** para chuparse los dedos.   **c.** pesado.

_____ 5. Si alguien te ofrece más comida y ya no quieres comer más, puedes decir...

    a. no gracias, deseo ver la lista de postres.   **b.** no gracias, estoy satisfecho(a).   **c.** ¡Buen provecho!

_____ 6. Si quieres pagar la cuenta para tu amigo, puedes decir...

    a. te invito.   **b.** voy a dejar una propina.   **c.** la cuenta, por favor.

WB 6-26 | **¡Viva la igualdad!** Beti y su primo Martín tienen mucho en común. Usa la siguiente información para comparar a los dos primos usando **tan, tanto, tanta, tantos** y **tantas**. Sigue los modelos.

> Modelo   tener años / *Beti tiene tantos años como Martín.*
> ser inteligente / *Beti es tan inteligente como Martín.*

1. comer verduras

_____

2. almorzar en restaurantes

_____

3. pedir arepas

_____

4. ser amable

_____

5. tomar café

_____

WB 6-27 | **El más...** Escribe oraciones usando el superlativo. Sigue el modelo.

> Modelo   dos hermanas: Beti (22 años) / Lorena (19 años) / menor
> *Lorena es la menor.*

1. dos hijos: Tomás (8 años) / Guillermo (10 años) / mayor

_____

2. los primos: Alejandro (súper paciente) / Alberto (paciente) / paciente

_____

3. dos bebidas: la leche (no es dulce) / el jugo (muy dulce) / dulce

_____

4. dos jugadores: Michael Jordan (súper bueno) / Dennis Rodman (bueno) / mejor

_____

WB 6-28 | Un sábado por la tarde Completa la siguiente conversación usando el pretérito de los verbos indicados.

JULIO: Gloria, ¿ya **1.** _____ (almorzar) Juan Carlos?

GLORIA: Sí, yo **2.** _____ (almorzar) con él a las dos. Nosotros

3. _____ (comer) un sándwich y una ensalada. Yo

4. _____ (tomar) un cafecito y él **5.** _____ (beber) té

caliente. ¿Ya **6.** _____ (terminar) tu novela?

JULIO: Sí, **7.** _____ (terminar) ésa y **8.** _____ (comenzar) otra.

En una hora **9.** _____ (leer) cuarenta páginas.

GLORIA: Ah, ésa es la novela que **10.** _____ (leer) Gonzalo el mes pasado.

Yo **11.** _____ (buscar) ese libro la semana pasada para ti.

JULIO: Pues, yo lo **12.** _____ (comprar) esta mañana.

WB 6-29 | Padre e hijo Completa el párrafo con la forma correcta del pretérito de los siguientes verbos.

pedir   servir   dormirse   divertirse

Anoche Julio y Juan Carlos **1.** _____ mucho viendo un video de

Disney. Mientras lo veían, el niño **2.** _____ un refresco y su padre le

3. _____ una Coca-Cola. Más tarde el niño **4.** _____ en el sofá.

De compras: Argentina

VOCABULARIO La ropa

WB 7-1 | ¿Qué se necesita? Lee las descripciones y selecciona la palabra apropiada de la lista. **¡OJO!** No vas a usar todas las palabras, pero no puedes usar una palabra más de una vez.

bufanda	guantes	paraguas	calcetines
abrigo	chaleco	cartera	corbata
suéter	impermeable	sombrero	cinturón
traje de baño	gafas de sol	cuero	
vaqueros	zapatos	bolsa	

1. Para nadar en una piscina te pones un _____.

2. Usas un _____ con los pantalones.

3. Cuando llueve te pones un _____ y usas un _____.

4. Te pones _____ en las manos.

5. Muchos llevan _____ de la marca Levis.

6. Guardas dinero en una _____.

7. Muchas mujeres guardan sus cosas en una _____.

8. Para proteger los ojos del sol te pones _____.

9. Te llevas un _____ en la cabeza.

WB 7-2 | La ropa apropiada Choose the clothing item that would be most appropriate to wear to the following events.

_____ 1. ir a clase

_____ 2. ir a un concierto de música ranchera (country)

_____ 3. ir a una boda (wedding)

_____ 4. esquiar

_____ 5. pasar el día en la playa

a. un traje de baño

b. unas botas de cuero

c. un vestido de seda

d. un suéter de lana

e. una camisa de algodón

WB 7-3 | ¡Emergencia de moda! María Inés y Francisco Javier tienen problemas en coordinar bien su ropa. Describe su estilo único seleccionando las mejores opciones de la lista.

1. María Inés lleva (selecciona todas las opciones posibles):

   a. un abrigo

   b. una falda de rayas

   c. una chaqueta de lunares

   d. zapatos de tacón alto

   e. medias

   f. un reloj

María Inés

2. Francisco Javier lleva *(selecciona todas las opciones posibles)*:

   a. una gorra de béisbol

   b. una corbata de rayas

   c. un traje de cuadros

   d. un suéter de lunares

   e. una pulsera

   f. sandalias con calcetines

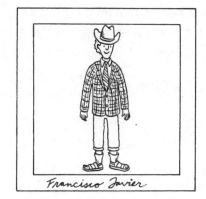

Francisco Javier

ASÍ SE DICE	Making emphatic statements: Stressed possessive adjectives and pronouns

WB 7-4 | ¡Fuera, compañero nuestro! Alejandro, un estudiante de intercambio de España, se muda *(is moving)* de su casa porque ya no se lleva bien *(get along well)* con sus compañeros. Rellena los espacios en blanco con el adjetivo posesivo apropiado para saber cómo dividen las cosas entre ellos.

TERE: ¿De quién es esta bufanda de lana? Alejandro, ¿es **1.** _____?

ALEJANDRO: No, no es **2.** _____. No llevo bufandas. Pero estos guantes sí

son **3.** _____. Los compré el año pasado.

CARLOS: Oye, Alejandro, ¿por qué tienes ese televisor en tu caja *(box)*? Es de Tere y de

mí. No es **4.** _____ y tú lo sabes.

ALEJANDRO: ¡No es de vosotros! ¡No es **5.** _____! El televisor de vosotros

está en vuestra habitación.

TERE: Esta vez Alejandro tiene razón, Carlos. Pero, Alejandro, ¿qué haces con esas

gafas de sol? Son de Carlos.

ALEJANDRO: ¡No son **6.** _____! ¡No son de Carlos! Perdió sus gafas de sol

la semana pasada.

CARLOS: No recuerdo. Pero Alejandro, ¿por qué tienes esas medias en tu maleta

(suitcase)? ¿No son de Tere?

ALEJANDRO: Ah… ah… pues, este, pues, sí. Son de Tere. Son **7.** _____ las

medias. Yo no sé cómo se metieron *(they got in)* en mi maleta. ¡Qué extraño!

TERE: ¡Sí! ¡Qué curioso!

Nombre _____   Fecha _____

WB 7-5 | ¿Cuál es mejor? Tomás y sus amigos hablan de quiénes tienen las mejores cosas. Usa el pronombre posesivo apropiado. Sigue el modelo.

> **Modelo**   La bicicleta de Ana es mejor que mi bicicleta.
> *La suya es mejor.*

1. El carro de Adolfo y Rafa es mejor que el carro de Ana.

   _____

2. Mi traje de baño es mejor que el traje de baño de Rafa.

   _____

3. Las gafas de sol de Patricio son mejores que mis gafas de sol.

   _____

4. Nuestros zapatos son mejores que los zapatos de Ana y Alicia.

   _____

ESTRUCTURA I — Talking about singular and/or completed events in the past: Verbs irregular in the preterite

WB 7-6 | Formas verbales Conjuga los verbos indicados en el pretérito.

1. dar / yo: _____
2. dar / ella: _____
3. hacer / nosotros: _____
4. hacer / ustedes: _____
5. poder / tú: _____
6. poder / yo: _____
7. tener / yo: _____
8. tener / tú: _____
9. tener / él: _____
10. estar / usted: _____
11. estar / yo: _____
12. estar / nosotros: _____
13. ser / yo: _____
14. ser / ella: _____
15. ir / ellos: _____

WB 7-7 | Una fiesta Gloria te cuenta todos los chismes de la fiesta que te perdiste anoche. Para saber lo que dice, completa las oraciones con la forma apropiada del verbo en el pretérito.

1. Muchas personas _____ (venir) a la fiesta.

2. _____ (haber) casi setenta personas en mi casa.

3. Marcos y su novia _____ (traer) mucho vino.

4. Yo _____ (ponerse) borracha y _____ (ser) la reina de la fiesta.

5. Antonio le _____ (dar) un beso a la novia de Óscar.

WB 7-8 | El viaje a Argentina Bea hizo un viaje a Argentina con su novio. Le escribió esta carta a su amiga Eva para contarle sobre un pequeño problema que tuvieron durante su viaje. Para saber lo que fue y cómo lo solucionaron, rellena los espacios en blanco con la forma apropiada del verbo indicado en el pretérito.

Querida Eva, Pues, ¿qué te puedo decir? **1.** ¡ _____ (Ser) un viaje maravilloso! Yo

2. _____ (ir) primero a Buenos Aires y **3.** _____ (estar) allí cuatro

días sola. Mi novio, Rafael, **4.** _____ (venir) el quinto (fifth) día y nosotros

5. _____ (hacer) varias cosas juntos, pues **6.** _____ (haber/hay)

muchísimas actividades para hacer en Buenos Aires. Después nosotros **7.** _____

(ir) a Mendoza. Tú **8.** _____ (decir) una vez que tu madre nació allí, ¿verdad?

Bueno, nosotros **9.** _____ (estar) en Mendoza tres días y el último día yo le

10. _____ (dar) a Rafa una sorpresa. Yo **11.** _____ (hacer) reserva-

ciones para ir a Bariloche para esquiar. Rafa no **12.** _____ (saber) de mis planes

hasta la última noche en Mendoza. Yo le **13.** _____ (traer) los boletos (tickets)

de avión esa noche en el hotel. Pero, Eva, ¿sabes qué? Rafa no **14.** _____ (querer)

ir. Él **15.** _____ (decir) que los boletos costaron demasiado. Yo le

16. _____ (decir) que no costaron mucho, pero él **17.** _____

(ponerse) enojado (angry). Yo no **18.** _____ (poder) creerlo. Yo **19.** _____

(hacer) todo lo posible para convencerlo, pero nada. Pero después de dos horas de discusión, yo

20. _____ (saber) por qué. Él también me **21.** _____ (dar) una

sorpresa: él había comprado (had bought) boletos para visitar las cataratas (falls) del Iguazú.

¡Qué romántico! Pues, tú sabes, ¡al final nosotros **22.** _____ (tener) que ir a los

dos sitios!

Bueno, ya te cuento más en otro momento.

Un beso,

Bea

WB 7-9 | **Sobre el viaje a Argentina** Contesta las preguntas sobre el viaje de la actividad WB 7-8.

1. ¿Qué problema tuvieron Bea y Rafa en este viaje?

    a. Rafa left Bea alone in Mendoza, Argentina.

    b. Rafa was upset because Bea spent too much money on this vacation.

    c. Rafa and Bea secretly planned to visit two different parts of Argentina.

    d. Bea broke her leg skiing.

2. ¿Cómo solucionaron este problema?

    a. They took both side trips.

    b. They visited Eva's mother in Mendoza.

    c. Eva decided to cancel part of the trip to save some money.

    d. Bea flew home early.

VOCABULARIO De compras

WB 7-10 | **¡De compras!** Belén es una profesional en las compras. Ahora describe sus estrategias. Completa las siguientes oraciones con una palabra apropiada de la lista.

    ofertas   barato   descuento   tarjeta de crédito   efectivo   número   por ciento

1. Nunca pago el precio de la etiqueta *(tag)*. Siempre busco las _____.

2. No compro una prenda si el _____ es menos del veinte

    _____.

3. Nunca pago en _____ cuando puedo usar mi

    _____. Así tengo más tiempo para pagar la factura *(bill)*.

WB 7-11 | **En la tienda** Escribe, en los espacios en blanco en la página 104, la letra de la palabra o frase que mejor describe cada dibujo indicado.

_____ 1. a. la talla

b. un descuento del 20 por ciento

c. el cheque

_____ 2. a. una rebaja

b. la talla de Michael Jordan

c. el número que usa Michael Jordan

_____ 3. a. Es una ganga.

b. Es muy cara.

c. Está de última moda.

_____ 4. a. No le quedan bien.

b. Cuestan mucho.

c. Hacen buen juego.

_____ 5. a. una tarjeta de crédito

b. un cheque

c. dinero en efectivo

WB 7-12 | **¡Qué buena ganga!** Ángela está de compras y quiere comprarle algo para su novio. Para saber lo que es, ordena las oraciones.

1. _____ Bueno, este traje es del estilo «retro», de los años sesenta. En su momento estuvo de última moda.

2. _____ ¡Me parece bárbaro! ¡Qué buena ganga!

3. _____ Quisiera comprar un traje nuevo para mi novio.

4. _____ No, gracias. Aquí está mi tarjeta de crédito.

5. _____ ¡Qué bueno! ¿Cuánto cuesta ese traje?

6. _____ No sé su talla, pero creo que esa talla que Ud. tiene por allí le va a quedar muy bien.

7. _____ Bien, ¿necesita algo más, señorita?

8. _____ Sí, señorita, es una ganga. ¿Sabe Ud. qué talla necesita su novio?

9. _____ Pues, normalmente ese traje cuesta unos 1.000 pesos, pero le puedo hacer un pequeño descuento. ¿Qué le parece un descuento del 30 por ciento?

10. _____ Buenas tardes, señorita, ¿en qué puedo servirle?

Nombre _____ Fecha _____

ESTRUCTURA II Simplifying expressions: Direct object pronouns

WB 7-13 | La vida de una super-modelo Mientras lees el periódico argentino *El clarín*, encuentras la siguiente entrevista con la super modelo argentina Carolina Peleritti. El reportero le hizo varias preguntas sobre cómo es ser super modelo. Completa la entrevista seleccionando la respuesta más apropiada a cada una de las preguntas. Presta atención al uso de los pronombres de objeto directo. Sigue el modelo.

Modelo ¿Levantas pesas con frecuencia?

_____ Sí, los levanta con frecuencia.

___X___ Sí, las levanto con frecuencia.

_____ Sí, me levanto con frecuencia.

1. ¿Tienes que hacer ejercicio todos los días?

_____ No, no las tengo que hacer.

_____ Sí, tengo que hacerla todos los días.

_____ Sí, lo tengo que hacer todos los días.

2. ¿Te llama todos los días tu entrenador personal?

_____ Sí, me llama todos los días.

_____ Sí, te llama todos los días.

_____ Sí, te llamo todos los días.

3. ¿Compras la ropa de última moda?

_____ No, no las compro.

_____ Sí, me compran siempre.

_____ Sí, la compro cada mes.

4. ¿Conoces a Donna Karan?

_____ Sí, me conocen.

_____ Sí, lo conozco.

_____ Sí, la conozco.

5. ¿Puedes tomar muchas vacaciones?

_____ Sí, las puedo tomar cada año.

_____ Sí, lo puedo tomar cada verano.

_____ No, la podemos tomar mucho.

6. ¿Te invitan a muchas fiestas los diseñadores famosos?

_____ Sí, los invito a muchas fiestas.

_____ Sí, me invitan a muchas fiestas.

_____ Sí, nos invitan a muchas fiestas.

WB 7-14 | Planes Amalia and Elvia hablan de las cosas que quieren comprar. Completa su conversación con el pronombre de objeto directo apropiado.

1. AMALIA: Elvia, ¿vas a comprar esa blusa?

   ELVIA: Sí, _____ voy a comprar.

2. ELVIA: Amalia, ¿tienes ahí tu tarjeta de crédito?

   AMALIA: No. No _____ tengo.

3. AMALIA: Elvia, ¿quieres comprar esas bufandas?

   ELVIA: Sí, _____ quiero comprar.

4. ELVIA: Amalia, ¿conoces estos diseñadores?

   AMALIA: No. No _____ conozco.

5. AMALIA: Elvia, ¿vas a gastar tanto dinero?

   ELVIA: Sí, _____ voy a gastar.

WB 7-15 | Un año en el extranjero Antonio regresó de un año en Argentina y ahora Carmen le hace varias preguntas sobre su viaje. Completas sus respuestas con el pronombre de objeto directo.

1. CARMEN: ¿Visitaste la Patagonia?

   ANTONIO: Sí, _____ visité tres veces.

2. CARMEN: ¿Aprendiste a jugar al fútbol?

   ANTONIO: Sí, aprendí a jugar _____.

3. CARMEN: ¿Probaste los famosos asados argentinos?

   ANTONIO: Sí, _____ probé mucho.

4. CARMEN: ¿Pudiste ver muchas películas argentinas?

   ANTONIO: Sí. Pude ver _____ todas.

WB 7-16 | Cambio de opinión Antonia fue de compras pero no le gusta lo que compró. Completa su conversación con su esposo con la forma apropiada del pronombre de objeto directo.

CARLOS: **1.** ¿_____ llamaste, Antonia?

ANTONIA: Sí, Carlos. Necesito ver **2.** _____. ¿Puedes venir aquí un rato?

CARLOS: Aquí estoy. ¿Qué pasa?

ANTONIA: No puedo encontrar mi tarjeta de crédito. **3.** ¿_____ tienes tú?

CARLOS: No mi amor. No **4.** _____ tengo. ¿Por qué **5.** _____ necesitas?

ANTONIA: Porque no me gustan los pantalones que compré ayer y **6.** _____ quiero devolver a la tienda.

CARLOS: Pero, Antonia, ayer me dijiste que tuviste que comprar **7.** _____ porque te quedaron muy bien y eran súper bonitos.

ANTONIA: Sí. Es cierto. Pero cambié de opinión.

CARLOS: ¡Antonia, tú **8.** _____ vas a matar con tus cambios de opinión!

ESTRUCTURA III	Describing ongoing and habitual actions in the past: The imperfect tense

To learn more about the **Imperfect**, go to Heinle iRadio at www.thomsonedu.com/spanish.

WB 7-17 | Investigación A las seis de la tarde ayer, hubo un robo *(robbery)* en «De moda», una tienda de ropa de Rosario. Ahora un policía está investigando el crimen y quiere saber qué hacía cada empleado a las seis de la tarde cuando ocurrió el robo. Rellena los espacios en blanco con la forma correcta del verbo en el imperfecto. Sigue el modelo.

> Modelo   María ___ (limpiar) el patio.
> María *limpiaba* el patio.

¿Qué hacía… a las seis de la tarde?

1. Luís Miguel _____ (estar) en el baño.

2. Teresa _____ (probarse) un vestido nuevo.

3. Amalia y yo _____ (pagar) las facturas en la oficina.

4. Guillermo y Santi _____ (conversar) con un cliente.

5. Francisco _____ (dormir) una siesta.

WB 7-18 | Cómo cambiaron los tiempos Ana María está hablando con su nieto y recordando el pasado y cómo eran las cosas. Para completar sus recuerdos, escribe la forma correcta de los verbos en el **imperfecto**.

1. En el pasado los jóvenes _____ (comer) más en casa.

2. En el pasado tú nunca _____ (llevar) la ropa de última moda.

3. En el pasado la ropa no _____ (costar) mucho dinero.

4. En el pasado nosotros _____ (ir) al cine para ver buenas películas.

5. En el pasado tus padres _____ (trabajar) sólo ocho horas al día.

6. En el pasado la gente joven _____ (leer) más.

WB 7-19 | Cuando yo era niña Cómo era Ana María de niña. Rellena los espacios en blanco con la forma apropiada del imperfecto para saberlo.

CARMEN: Los sábados **1.** _____ (levantarse) a las ocho y luego

2. _____ (ir) al baño. A veces, **3.** _____ (tener) mucho

sueño. Después, **4.** _____ (desayunar) mientras **5.** _____

(mirar) la televisión por media hora. Entonces **6.** _____ (bañarse) y

7. _____ (vestirse). Luego **8.** _____ (jugar) un

poco en casa o, si **9.** _____ (ver) a mis amigos en la calle,

10. _____ (jugar) juntos. **11.** _____ (tener) muchos

amigos y (nosotros) **12.** _____ (ser) un grupo muy unido. A veces

13. _____ (ir) todos a la plaza para hablar con otros amigos y otras

veces **14.** _____ (ir) al cine. (Nosotros) Nunca **15.** _____

(gastar) mucho dinero, pero siempre **16.** _____ (divertirse) mucho.

WB 7-20 | Una experiencia emocionante Elena le explicó al Sr. Romero lo que pasó la semana pasada cuando ella fue a la plaza central para hacer las compras. Para saber lo que le dijo al Sr. Romero, rellena los espacios en blanco con la forma apropiada de los verbos. Tienes que escoger entre el pretérito y el imperfecto. **¡OJO!** Repasa las reglas del texto sobre el uso de estos tiempos antes de hacer esta actividad.

1. _____ (Llover) mucho ese día y, por eso, **2.** _____ (decidir) buscar un taxi. Claro, **3.** _____ (haber) muchas otras personas que también **4.** _____ (buscar) taxis por el mal tiempo que

5. _____ (hacer). Por fin, (yo) **6.** _____ (encontrar) un taxi y me subí.

Le dije al taxista adónde **7.** _____ (querer) ir cuando de repente

8. _____ (acordarme) que mi bolsa **9.** _____ (estar) en una de las tiendas de la plaza. Me bajé del taxi y **10.** _____ (ir) corriendo hacia la tienda. Cuando **11.** _____ (llegar) a la tienda,

12. _____ (ver) mi bolsa. Yo **13.** _____ (estar) muy contenta.

BIENVENIDOS A ARGENTINA

En este segmento del video, vas a aprender un poco sobre el país de Argentina y la vida de sus ciudadanos. Los temas incluyen:

- la geografía
- Buenos Aires y los bonaerenses (la gente que vive en Buenos Aires)
- los países que han influenciado *(have influenced)* Argentina
- el tango
- los pasatiempos
- el gaucho

WB 7-21 | ¿Dónde está ubicada Argentina?
Identifica Argentina en el mapa.

_____ Escribe la letra del mapa que

corresponde al país.

WB 7-22 | En el segmento del video vas a escuchar muchos cognados que pueden facilitar tu comprensión. Algunos de estos cognados aparecen aquí. Trata de pronunciar cada palabra o frase y luego empareja los cognados con su definición en inglés.

1. _____ cono sur   **a.** Great Britain

2. _____ arquitectura neoclásica   **b.** diversion / fun

3. _____ influencias   **c.** Presidential Palace

4. _____ diversión   **d.** glacier

5. _____ Gran Bretaña   **e.** southern cone

6. _____ Palacio presidencial **f.** influences

7. _____ Congreso Nacional   **g.** National Congress

8. _____ costa Atlántica   **h.** Neoclassical architecture

9. _____ glaciar   **i.** Atlantic coast

WB 7-23 | Después de ver el segmento del video, rellena los espacios en blanco con el cognado apropiado de la actividad **WB 7-22.**

1. La Argentina, situada en el _____, es un país grande con diferentes zonas geográficas que incluyen la _____, las llanuras y los Andes.

2. Con muchas influencias de España, Italia, _____ y Alemania, Buenos Aires es una de las ciudades más cosmopolitas de las Américas.

3. Aquí tienen la Casa Rosada, que es el _____.

4. En estos dos edificios vemos ejemplos de _____.

5. El _____ provee un paisaje de enorme belleza e interés científico.

WB 7-24 | Después de ver el segmento del video otra vez, indica si las siguientes oraciones son **ciertas** (C) o **falsas** (F).

1. _____ Argentina tiene mucha diversidad geográfica.

2. _____ En el sur del país es el centro cultural de Argentina.

3. _____ Muchos dicen que Buenos Aires es la España de Sudamérica.

4. _____ El fútbol es un deporte muy popular en Argentina.

5. _____ El gaucho es como el «cowboy» de los Estados Unidos.

¡A ESCRIBIR!

Strategy: Editing your writing

Editing your written work is an important skill to master when learning a foreign language. You should plan on editing what you write several times. When checking your compositions, consider the following areas:

1. **Content**
   a. Is the title of your composition captivating? Would it cause readers to want to read further?
   b. Is the information you wrote pertinent to the established topic?
   c. Is your composition interesting? Does it capture reader interest?

2. **Organization**
   a. Does each paragraph in the composition have a clearly identifiable main idea?
   b. Do the details in each paragraph relate to a single idea?
   c. Are the sentences in the paragraph ordered in a logical sequence?
   d. Is the order of the paragraphs correct in your composition?

3. **Cohesion and style**
   a. Does your composition as a whole communicate what you are trying to convey?
   b. Does your composition "flow" easily and smoothly from beginning to end?
   c. Are there transitions between the different paragraphs you included in your composition?

4. **Style and accuracy**
   a. Have you chosen the precise vocabulary words you need to express your ideas?
   b. Are there grammatical errors in your composition (That is, subject-verb agreement; adjective-noun agreement; errors with verb forms or irregular verbs, and so on)?
   c. Are there spelling errors in your composition (including capitalization, accentuation and punctuation)?

If you consider these points as you edit your written work, the overall quality of your compositions will improve drastically!

Task: Reporting on changing fashion habits

You will write a short report to describe what fashion was like when you were younger and how it has changed over time in your opinion.

Paso 1: Before you begin to write, answer the following questions in Spanish. How has fashion changed since you were in high school? Or since your parents were in high school? What clothes did people wear that they don't wear now? What shops and designers were popular then that are not now?

_____

_____

_____

_____

Paso 2: Now write a first draft on a separate piece of paper; then revise it using the strategy you have just learned.

Paso 3: Write your revised draft below.

_____

_____

_____

_____

_____

_____

_____

_____

_____

_____

_____

_____

_____

_____

_____

_____

_____

_____

_____

_____

_____

_____

_____

ATAJO 4.0

Functions: Talking about past events; Talking about recent events

Vocabulary: Clothing; Fabrics; Colors; Stores and products

Grammar: Verbs: irregular preterite, regular preterite; Personal pronouns: direct, indirect

Autoprueba

WB 7-25 | **La ropa** Para cada categoría escribe el nombre de la prenda apropiada.

Modelo   Para las manos: *los guantes*

la blusa	el impermeable	el traje	las botas
las medias	el traje de baño	los calcetines	los pantalones
el vestido	la corbata	las sandalias	los zapatos
la falda	el sombrero		

1. Para nadar:

_____

2. Para la cabeza:

_____

3. Para los pies:

_____

4. Para las mujeres:

_____

5. Para los hombres:

_____

6. Para la lluvia:

_____

WB 7-26 | **En la tienda** Completa la conversación con la palabra o frase apropiada de la lista. **¡OJO!** No tienes que usar todas las palabras y frases.

en qué puedo servirle	moda	rebaja	ganga	número
talla	hace juego	probarme	le debo	
tarjeta de crédito	queda bien			

DEPENDIENTE: Buenas tardes, señor. **1.** ¿_____?

CLIENTE: Buenas tardes. Busco un traje nuevo. ¿Puedo **2.** _____

este traje?

DEPENDIENTE: Sí, por aquí.

CLIENTE: Ay, este traje no es de mi **3.** _____. No me

4. _____.

DEPENDIENTE: Lo siento, señor. Aquí está otro.

CLIENTE: Sí, éste es mejor. Y esta camisa, ¿qué opina? **5.** ¿_____ con

el traje?

DEPENDIENTE: Sí, es un juego perfecto. Además, está de última **6.** _____.

CLIENTE: Muy bien, ¿cuanto **7.** _____?

DEPENDIENTE: En total son 300 pesos.

CLIENTE: ¡Qué **8.** _____! ¿Puedo pagar con

                9. _____?

DEPENDIENTE: ¡Claro que sí!

WB 7-27 | ¿Son tuyos? Tu amigo insiste en preguntarte de quiénes son las cosas. Tú le contestas de forma muy enfática. Sigue el modelo.

   Modelo   ¿De quién es esta mochila? / yo
               ¡La mochila es mía!

1. ¿De quién es este sombrero? / tú

   _____

2. ¿De quiénes son estos cinturones? / Tomás y Ricardo

   _____

3. ¿De quiénes son estos zapatos? / Uds.

   _____

4. ¿De quién son estas gafas de sol? / yo

   _____

5. ¿De quién es este paraguas? / Teresa

   _____

WB 7-28 | Entre amigas Completa la conversación con el pretérito de los verbos indicados.

DELIA: ¿Adónde **1.** _____ (ir) este fin de semana?

NORA: (Yo) **2.** _____ (Ir) con mi familia a Santa Fé.

DELIA: ¿Qué **3.** _____ (hacer) Uds. allí?

NORA: **4.** _____ (Tener) que ir a una fiesta con nuestros amigos.

DELIA: Ah, **5.** ¿_____ (venir) muchas personas a la fiesta?

NORA: Sí, y todos **6.** _____ (traer) algo distinto para comer. ¡La comida

         7. _____ (estar) riquísima! ¿Y tú? ¿Qué

         8. _____ (hacer) este fin de semana?

DELIA: Bueno, para mí el fin de semana no **9.** _____ (ser) muy bueno.

         No **10.** _____ (hacer) nada. El viernes quería ir a una fiesta,

         pero a mi novio no le gusta la persona que hacía la fiesta y él no

         11. _____ (querer) ir. El sábado había una exposición de arte en

         el museo, pero yo no **12.** _____ (saber) que el museo estaba

         abierto hasta demasiado tarde.

NORA: ¡Qué pena!

WB 7-29 | A la hora de la cena Completa la conversación con el pronombre de objeto directo apropiado.

1. Preparaste una cena muy buena, Julio. ¡Eres tan simpático!

   Gracias, Gloria. —————— preparé porque sé que estás ocupada hoy.

2. Juan Carlos, ¿ya comiste tu pescado?

   Pues... no, papá. El gato —————— está comiendo.

3. ¿—————— quieres, mamá?

   Sí, tu papá y yo —————— queremos mucho, Juan Carlos.

4. De postre quiero una de esas naranjas, papá.

   Bien, Juan Carlos. Acabo de comprar —————— en el mercado.

WB 7-30 | La pequeña Elena Completa la narración sobre la niñez de Elena usando el imperfecto de los verbos apropiados de la lista.

comer   comprar   gustar   ir   limpiar   sacar   tener   vivir

De niña yo **1.** —————— cerca de Buenos Aires. (Yo)

2. —————— algunos quehaceres en casa. Por ejemplo,

3. —————— la basura y **4.** —————— mi dormitorio.

Todas los sábados mi mamá y yo **5.** —————— de compras al centro. A veces

ella no **6.** —————— nada, pero nos **7.** —————— mirar las

cosas de las tiendas. Por la tarde nosotras **8.** —————— en un café pequeño.

WB 7-31 | ¡Y ahora baila! Completa la conversación con la forma apropiada del pretérito o del imperfecto de los verbos entre paréntesis.

PACA: Anoche mientras nosotras **1.** —————— (trabajar) en la cocina,

Marcos me **2.** —————— (llamar) por teléfono.

PECA: ¿Marcos? Sabes que él y yo no nos llevamos bien. Cuando nosotros

3. —————— (ser) jóvenes, él siempre **4.** ——————

(burlarse) *(made fun)* de mí.

PACA: ¿Sí? Bueno, ahora es una persona muy simpática. De hecho *(in fact)*, él me

5. —————— (invitar) a salir a bailar el próximo sábado.

PECA: ¡Qué curioso! De joven él nunca **6.** —————— (bailar) con nadie.

Bueno, **7.** ¿—————— (aceptar) (tú) su invitación?

PACA: Sí **8.** —————— (aceptar). ¡Y vamos a salir el sábado!

Fiestas y vacaciones: Guatemala y El Salvador

VOCABULARIO Fiestas y celebraciones

WB 8-1 | Las celebraciones Completa cada oración con la palabra apropiada.

disfraz   anfitrión   velas   máscara   cohetes   pastel   brindis

1. Se oyen muchos _____ durante las celebraciones para el Día de la Independencia de los Estados Unidos.

2. El _____ es la persona que da la fiesta.

3. Para celebrar Mardi Gras en Nueva Orleans, mucha gente se lleva una _____.

4. Se ponen las _____ en el _____ de cumpleaños.

5. En los Estados Unidos la gente se pone un _____ para celebrar el día 31 de octubre.

6. Al hacer un _____ la gente dice: «¡Salud!».

WB 8-2 | ¿Qué pasó en la fiesta? Paulino no fue a la fiesta de sorpresa de Luci anoche, pero escuchó los chismes *(gossip)* sobre lo que pasó. Pon los dibujos y los detalles en orden.

1. _____ Juan Carlos le gritó a Javi y Javi se asustó.

2. _____ Todos lo pasaban bien, menos su novio, Juan Carlos.

3. _____ Anoche se reunió toda la familia de Luci.

4. _____ Juan Carlos reaccionó mal cuando vio que Javi, el ex-novio de Luci, estaba en la fiesta.

5. _____ Luci cumplió 20 años y su familia le dio una fiesta de sorpresa.

6. _____ Luci lloró y le dijo a Juan Carlos que se portaba muy mal.

7. _____ Todos los invitados le trajeron regalos.

WB 8-3 | ¡Qué dramáticos! Carlos habla de cómo reaccionan los miembros de su familia en los días festivos. Para saberlo, forma oraciones con una forma apropiada de **ponerse** + el adjetivo dado. Recuerda que los adjetivos tienen que concordar en número y género con la persona que describen. Sigue el modelo.

> Modelo   El cumpleaños: Teresa y Gabriel / triste
> *Teresa y Gabriel se ponen tristes.*

1. El Día de los Reyes Magos: Carolina / enojado

   _____

2. El Día de los Muertos: Javier y Silvia / asustado

   _____

3. El Día de la Raza: yo (Carlos) / emocionado

   _____

4. La Noche Vieja: nosotros / cansado

   _____

WB 8-4 | Nuestras costumbres Para saber lo que hacen Irene y su familia en los días festivos, rellena los espacios en blanco con la palabra apropiada de la lista. No vas a usar todas las palabras, pero ninguna palabra se usa más de una vez. **¡OJO!** Tienes que conjugar los verbos según el sujeto.

> cumpleaños   recordar   reunirse   pasarlo   olvidar
> reaccionar   hacer una fiesta   cumplir años

Cuando alguien en mi familia **1.** _____, nosotros siempre

2. _____. Nosotros **3.** _____ con todos los miembros

de la familia y siempre **4.** _____ bien. Cuando celebramos el

5. _____ de mi madre, ella siempre se pone molesta porque mi padre

nunca **6.** _____ la fecha no le compra un regalo.

ASÍ SE DICE	Inquiring and providing information about people and events: Interrogative words

🎧 To learn more about **Question Words**, go to Heinle iRadio at www.thomsonedu.com/spanish.

WB 8-5 | Una llamada a mamá Mónica le hace su llamada normal a su mamá en El Salvador, y como siempre, su mamá tiene muchas preguntas. Completa su conversación con las palabras interrogativas apropiadas. **¡OJO!** Recuerda que estas palabras siempre llevan un acento escrito.

SEÑORA LÓPEZ: ¡Bueno!

MÓNICA: ¡Hola, mamá! Soy yo, Mónica.

SEÑORA LÓPEZ: ¡Mónica! **1.** ¿_____ estás, hija?

MÓNICA: Bien, mami, bien.

SEÑORA LÓPEZ: Me alegro. Oye, **2.** ¿_____ estás ahora? ¿Estás en la

                 residencia?

MÓNICA: Sí, mami. ¿Y papi, **3.** ¿_____ está? ¿Está en casa?

SEÑORA LÓPEZ: Sí, pero ya se durmió. **4.** ¿_____ hora es allí?

MÓNICA: Son las once. Dentro de poco voy a una fiesta.

SEÑORA LÓPEZ: Mónica, **5.** ¿_____ quieres ir a una fiesta tan tarde? ¿No tienes clases mañana?

MÓNICA: Ay, mami. Sí, tengo clases, pero está bien. No pasa nada.

SEÑORA LÓPEZ: **6.** ¿_____ vas? ¿Con **7.** _____ vas?

MÓNICA: Mami, no te preocupes. No vamos a salir de la residencia. Voy con mi amiga Carola.

SEÑORA LÓPEZ: **8.** ¿_____ es Carola? **9.** ¿_____ es ella? ¿Es de Nueva York? **10.** ¿_____ tiempo hace que la conoces?

MÓNICA: ¡Mami! Tranquila. Es mi amiga y es de Manhattan, pero habla español muy bien. Es muy buena gente *(good person)*. Dime, mami, **11.** ¿_____ pasa allí? ¿Alguna novedad?

SEÑORA LÓPEZ: Pues, sí. ¡Nació *(was born)* tu primera sobrina!

MÓNICA: ¿De verdad? **12.** ¿_____ nació? **13.** ¿_____ se llama?

SEÑORA LÓPEZ: Se llama Verónica y nació anoche.

MÓNICA: **14.** ¿_____ pesa?

SEÑORA LÓPEZ: Unas ocho libras. Es grande.

MÓNICA: ¡Qué alegría, mami! Mira, voy a tener que ir, pero quería preguntarte, ¿te acuerdas *(do you remember)* del libro que me recomendaste la semana pasada?

SEÑORA LÓPEZ: **15.** ¿_____ libro?

MÓNICA: El libro de cuentos. **16.** ¿_____ era el título?

SEÑORA LÓPEZ: Ay, mi amor, ya soy tan vieja que no puedo recordar.

MÓNICA: Bueno, mami. Tal vez la próxima vez. Mira, ya me tengo que ir. Un beso para papi, y dos para mi nueva sobrina. Chao.

SEÑORA LÓPEZ: Te quiero mucho. Chao, Mónica.

To learn more about **Preterite** and **Imperfect**, go to Heinle iRadio at www.thomsonedu.com/spanish.

WB 8-6 | Una pachanga Anoche Lupe asistió a una fiesta con sus colegas *(coworkers)* de trabajo y ella dice que pasaron algunas cosas muy extrañas *(strange)*. Ahora le cuenta a Eva sobre la fiesta. Selecciona la forma correcta de los verbos indicados.

Eva, anoche (yo) **1.** (vi / veía) algo muy raro en la fiesta del trabajo. Cuando **2.** (llegué / llegaba) a la fiesta ya **3.** (hubo / había) un ambiente *(atmosphere)* muy extraño. Por ejemplo, Ofelia **4.** (bailó / bailaba) en la mesa mientras que Ledia **5.** (recitó / recitaba) poesía en un rincón *(corner)* y Kati le **6.** (habló / hablaba) a Miguel sobre su esposo famoso. De repente *(all of a sudden)*, Samuel, **7.** (corrió / corría) medio desnudo por la sala recitando palabra por palabra episodios del *Quijote*.

Eva, yo creo que tus colegas se han vuelto locos *(they've gone crazy)*. ¿Recuerdas que el año pasado ellos **8.** (fueron / iban) a la fiesta y no **9.** (se divirtieron / se divertían) para nada?

WB 8-7 | Traducciones Traduce *(Translate)* las siguientes oraciones al español. **¡OJO!** Cada oración requiere un verbo en el pretérito y otro en el imperfecto.

1. My grandmother was preparing food when the guests arrived.

_____

2. My little brother was behaving poorly and he had to go to his bedroom.

_____

3. My girlfriend called while I was watching television.

_____

4. Teri and Juan remembered the party while they were at the office.

_____

5. It began to rain as Santi was leaving the house.

_____

WB 8-8 | Un cuento de hadas *(fairy tale)* Rellena los espacios en blanco con la forma apropiada del verbo en el pretérito o el imperfecto. Lee la historia una vez antes de rellenar los espacios para comprender el contexto y luego escoge *(choose)* la forma apropiada del verbo. Al final, adivina *(guess)* qué cuento de hadas es.

1. _____ (Haber) una vez un rey que **2.** _____

(tener) cinco hijas. De todas ellas, la más joven **3.** _____ (ser) la más

bonita. La princesa **4.** _____ (tener) una pelota y siempre

5. _____ (ir) a jugar a solas con esta pelota al lado de un estanque *(pond)*

cerca del castillo. Un día la princesa **6.** _____ (perder) su pelota en el

agua del estanque. La pobre princesa no **7.** _____ (saber) nadar y por eso

no **8.** _____ (poder) recoger su pelota favorita. La princesa

9. _____ (estar) muy triste y **10.** _____ (empezar) a

llorar. De repente la princesa **11.** _____ (oír) una voz. La voz le decía,

«Princesa, ¿qué **12.** _____ (pasar) aquí? ¿Por qué lloras?» La princesa no

13. _____ (saber) de dónde **14.** _____ (venir) la voz,

pero pronto ella **15.** _____ (ver) un sapito *(little frog)*. En este momento

el sapo **16.** _____ (volver) a hablar y **17.** _____

(decir), «Yo te puedo devolver *(return)* tu querida pelota si me haces un favor». La princesa

18. _____ (preguntar) cuál **19.** _____ (ser) el favor y

el sapo le **20.** _____ (contestar) que él **21.** _____

(querer) un beso. La princesa **22.** _____ (tener) que pensar un minuto:

ella **23.** _____ (querer) su pelota, pero no **24.** _____

(saber) si **25.** _____ (poder) darle un beso al sapo. Al final

26. _____ (decidir) que sí. Ella **27.** _____ (ir) a darle

un beso al sapo.

En ese momento el sapo se zambulló *(dove)* en el agua y le **28.** _____

(devolver) la pelota a la princesa. Ahora la princesa **29.** _____ (tener) que

besarlo. Ella **30.** _____ (cerrar) los ojos y lo **31.** _____

(besar). Un segundo después la princesa **32.** _____ (saber) por qué el

sapo quería el beso.

¿Cómo se llama el cuento? **33.** _____

  a. Caperucita roja *(Little Red Riding Hood)*

  b. La princesa y el sapo *(The Frog Prince)*

  c. Los tres cerditos *(The Three Little Pigs)*

VOCABULARIO La playa y el campo

WB 8-9 | **Activos** Javi y sus amigos son muy deportistas y activos. Escribe una oración
completa para describir las actividades que hacen en cada dibujo. Sigue el modelo.

    Modelo   *Javi pasea en canoa.*

1. Nadia _____

2. Carlos _____

3. Alicia _____

4. Javi y Ángela _____

5. Rafa _____

WB 8-10 | De vacaciones Luis y Jorge fueron de vacaciones con sus amigos. Para saber cómo lo pasaron, completa el párrafo con las palabras apropiadas de la siguiente lista.

mar	lago	olas
caminar por las montañas	crema bronceadora	camping
canoa	parrillada	playa
tomar el sol	balneario	broncearse

La semana pasada Luis, Jorge y algunos amigos decidieron tomar las vacaciones. A Jorge le

gusta mucho estar en las montañas así que él quería hacer **1.** _____.

Jorge dijo que conocía un lugar precioso donde podían **2.** _____ y nadar

en un **3.** _____. Pero a los otros les gusta más estar cerca del mar y

decidieron ir a un **4.** _____.

Encontraron un hotel que estaba justo al lado *(right along side)* del **5.** _____.

El primer día de sus vacaciones salieron del hotel temprano y fueron a la

6. _____ para **7.** _____. Para protegerse contra el

sol, se aplicaron la **8.** _____. Después de **9.** _____ lo

suficiente *(sufficiently)*, decidieron hacer algunas actividades acuáticas. Primero corrieron las

10. _____ y después decidieron pasear en **11.** _____.

Esa noche para comer todos hicieron una **12.** _____. Se divirtieron mucho

y hasta *(even)* Jorge estaba muy contento.

ESTRUCTURA II — Stating indefinite ideas and quantities: Affirmative and negative expressions

WB 8-11 | Conversaciones en el café Estás en un café en San Salvador y escuchas partes de diferentes conversaciones. Lee las preguntas y respuestas y luego selecciona la palabra afirmativa o negativa apropiada para rellenar el espacio en blanco.

nunca   siempre   algo   nada   o... o   ni... ni   alguien   nadie

1. ¿Quieres tomar algo más?

No, no quiero tomar _____.

2. ¿Tomas café con leche?

   No, _____ tomo café con leche.

3. ¿Conoces a _____ de esa compañía?

   Sí, conozco a varias personas.

4. ¿Quieres hacer camping este fin de semana o prefieres correr las olas?

   Este fin de semana _____ quiero hacer camping

   _____ quiero correr las olas. Prefiero quedarme en casa.

5. ¿Viste _____ interesante en la tele anoche?

   No. No vi _____ interesante anoche.

WB 8-12 | Bienvenida, abuelita La abuela de Rafa acaba de llegar y Rafa piensa que ella le trae un regalo. Para saber si lo hizo, rellena los espacios en blanco con la palabra afirmativa o negativa apropiada.

algo   algún   algunas   algunos   ningún   ninguna   siempre   tampoco

RAFA: ¿Me trajiste 1. _____ regalo, abuelita?

ABUELA: ¡Claro! 2. _____ te traigo regalos, ¿verdad?

RAFA: Sí. ¿Me trajiste 3. _____ libros de Disney?

ABUELA: No, Rafa. No te traje 4. _____ libro.

RAFA: ¿Me trajiste 5. _____ para comer?

ABUELA: 6. _____, niño.

RAFA: Pues, ¿qué me trajiste, abuelita?

ABUELA: Te traje 7. _____ camisas...

RAFA: ¡Ay, no quiero 8. _____ camisa!

ABUELA: ...y un juego electrónico.

RAFA: ¡Gracias, abuelita!

WB 8-13 | Opuestos Forma una oración con el significado opuesto sustituyendo las palabras afirmativas con palabras negativas.

1. Hay algunas canoas para alquilar en el balneario.

   _____

2. Todos de nuestro grupo saben pescar.

   _____

3. Mónica también sabe bucear.

   _____

4. Teresa o quiere nadar o quiere broncearse.

   _____

WB 8-14 | **¿Cuánto tiempo hace?** Empareja la frase de la primera columna con su traducción de la segunda columna. **¡OJO!** No vas a usar todas las traducciones, pero ninguna se usa más de una vez.

1. _____ Hace diez años que vivo en Guatemala.

2. _____ Fui a El Salvador hace tres meses.

3. _____ ¿Cuánto tiempo hace que estudias la cultura maya?

4. _____ Hace dos años que visité las pirámides.

5. _____ ¿Hace cuánto tiempo que estuviste en Antigua?

6. _____ Hace mucho tiempo que no voy de vacaciones.

a. I went to El Salvador three months ago.

b. How long have you been studying Mayan culture?

c. I have lived in Guatemala for ten years.

d. I lived in Guatemala ten years ago.

e. It's been a long time since I've gone on vacation.

f. I visited the pyramids two years ago.

g. I've been on vacation for a long time.

h. How long ago were you in Antigua?

i. I've been in El Salvador for three months.

j. For how long have you been going to Antigua?

WB 8-15 | **¡Tanto tiempo!** La famlia de Juan es muy monótona *(monotonous)*, nunca cambian de rutina. ¿Cuánto tiempo hace que los miembros de su familia hacen las siguientes cosas? Escribe una oración usando la fórmula **hacer +** *time*. Sigue el modelo.

Modelo   Teresa / estudiar alemán / cuatro años
Hace cuatro años que Teresa estudia alemán.

1. doña María / trabajar de dependiente en una tienda / veinte años

_____

2. don José / tomar copas con sus amigos después del trabajo / treinta años

_____

3. Olivia y su hermana / jugar con las muñecas Barbie / dos años

_____

4. toda la familia / acostarse a las 11:00 de la noche / mucho tiempo

_____

5. la abuela / no salir de la casa los domingos / diez años

_____

Nombre _____ Fecha _____

BIENVENIDOS A GUATEMALA

En este segmento del video, vas a aprender un poco sobre Guatemala y sobre la vida de sus ciudadanos. Los temas incluyen:

- la geografía
- la cultura maya
- las fiestas y costumbres

WB 8-16 | **¿Dónde están ubicados Guatemala y El Salvador?** Identifica los países de Guatemala y El Salvador en el mapa.

1. _____ Escribe la letra del mapa que corresponde a Guatemala.

2. _____ Escribe la letra del mapa que corresponde a El Salvador.

WB 8-17 | En el segmento del video vas a escuchar muchos cognados que pueden facilitar tu comprensión. Algunos de estos cognados aparecen aquí. Trata de pronunciar cada palabra o frase y luego empareja los cognados con su definición en inglés.

1. _____ majestuosa   **a.** pyramids

2. _____ erupciones volcánicas   **b.** astronomers

3. _____ templos   **c.** majestic

4. _____ pirámides   **d.** temples

5. _____ astrónomos   **e.** volcanic eruptions

WB 8-18 | Después de ver el segmento del video, rellena los espacios en blanco con el cognado apropiado de la actividad **WB 8-17.**

1. Su naturaleza es _____.

2. _____ y terremotos sacuden las regiones montañosas.

3. Los _____, las esculturas y las _____ de Tikal, una antigua ciudad maya cuentan la trágica historia de esta poderosa y misteriosa civilización.

4. Los mayas fueron excelentes arquitectos, _____ y matemáticos.

WB 8-19 | Después de ver el segmento del video, indica si las siguientes oraciones son **ciertas** (C) o **falsas** (F).

1. _____ Guatemala está en Centroamérica, pero El Salvador está en Sudamérica.

2. _____ Hay más de treinta volcanes en Guatemala.

3. _____ La cultura maya existió hace más de cuatro mil años, pero ya no viven personas mayas.

4. _____ Todavía conservan tradiciones españolas en Guatemala.

¡A ESCRIBIR!

Task: Writing a summary of a favorite holiday or celebration

Paso 1: When you were young, what was your favorite holiday or celebration? How long has it been since you last celebrated? How did you celebrate? Did something special / funny / interesting happen? Answer these questions below in Spanish.

_____

_____

_____

Paso 2: Based on your responses above, write a descriptive paragraph to summarize these details. Since your description will be in the past, you will need to pay attention to your use of the preterite and the imperfect. Refer to your text to review the use of these verb forms.

Paso 3: Revise your first draft, making sure your ideas are organized and that your verb forms are accurate; then write your final draft below.

_____

_____

_____

_____

_____

_____

_____

_____

_____

_____

ATAJO 4.0

Functions: Writing about past events; Writing about theme, plot, or scene

Vocabulary: Family members; Religious holidays; Time expressions

Grammar: Verbs: Preterite & Imperfect

Autoprueba

VOCABULARIO

WB 8-20 | **Una celebración especial** Para saber cómo lo pasaron en la fiesta de Ana anoche, completa la siguiente descripción con una palabra apropiada de la lista. **¡OJO!** Vas a tener que conjugar algunos de los verbos.

anfitriona	pastel	felicidades
llorar	disfraz	reunirse
brindis	procesión	gritar
máscara	disfrazarse	velas
celebrar	recordar	invitados
pasarlo	entremeses	
cumplir	regalos	

Ayer Silvia **1.** _____ treinta años y Ana le hizo una fiesta divertida.

Había mucha cerveza, vino y sodas. También Ana preparó varios **2.** _____

y todos comieron un montón. Todos los **3.** _____ tuvieron que

4. _____ de su personaje histórico favorito. Ana se puso una

5. _____ de Marie Antoinette y su esposo, Jorge, se llevó un

6. _____ de Simón Bolívar. Después de que llegó Silvia, todos hicieron

una **7.** _____ para seleccionar quién se vestía mejor.

A las once de la noche, a la misma hora en que nació Silvia, todos **8.** _____

para **9.** _____ el momento. Hicieron un **10.** _____ y

todos **11.** _____, **12.** «¡_____!». Luego, empezaron

a comer el **13.** _____ de cumpleaños. Esta vez no tenía

14. _____ porque Silvia no quería **15.** _____ cuántos

años cumplía. A la medianoche Silvia abrió sus **16.** _____. Su novio, Raul,

le dio un anillo de diamantes y Silvia empezó a **17.** _____.

La fiesta acabó a las tres de la mañana. Todos **18.** _____ muy bien y

antes de salir todos le dieron las gracias a la **19.** _____ que había

preparado (had prepared) una fiesta tan buena.

¡La celebración fue un éxito total!

WB 8-21 | En la playa y en el campo Escribe la letra de cada actividad descrita *(described)*.

_____ 1. nadar debajo del agua con un tubo   **a.** bucear

_____ 2. nadar debajo del agua con un tanque   **b.** hacer camping

_____ 3. jugar en el agua con una tabla   **c.** tomar el sol

_____ 4. navegar en bote de vela en el mar   **d.** correr las olas

_____ 5. descansar tranquilamente en la playa   **e.** pasear en canoa

_____ 6. cocinar carne al aire libre   **f.** hacer esnórquel

_____ 7. dormir debajo de las estrellas   **g.** hacer una parrillada

_____ 8. navegar por los ríos en un bote   **h.** pasear en velero

WB 8-22 | Más preguntas Un amigo nuevo te hace preguntas por correo electrónico *(e-mail)*. Completa sus preguntas con la palabra interrogativa apropiada.

1. Soy de la Ciudad de Guatemala. ¿_____ eres tú?

2. Ahora estoy en la universidad. ¿_____ estás tú ahora mismo?

3. A mí me encanta la música de Pink Floyd. ¿_____ es tu música favorita?

4. Paso mucho tiempo en la selva con mis amigos. ¿_____ vas tú para divertirte?

5. Salimos mucho a bailar. ¿_____ haces tú para divertirte?

6. Tomo tres clases este semestre. ¿_____ clases tomas tú?

7. Estudio relaciones internacionales. ¿_____ estudias tú?

WB 8-23 | Un viaje inolvidable Lee la siguiente narración sobre un viaje memorable de Guillermo. Después, escribe la forma apropiada del pretérito o del imperfecto de cada verbo entre paréntesis.

Cuando yo **1.** _____ (ser) más joven, **2.** _____ (hacer) una vez un viaje a Belice. **3.** _____ (Ir) con toda mi familia. Mi hermanito **4.** _____ (tener) tres años y yo **5.** _____ (tener) catorce. Después de pensarlo mucho, mis padres **6.** _____ (decidir) hacer el viaje a Belice porque quedaba tan cerca de donde nosotros **7.** _____ (vivir) en Guatemala en esos años.

Recuerdo todo de ese viaje. El lugar **8.** _____ (ser) tan limpio y bonito y en las playas **9.** _____ (haber) muchos pájaros y otros animales bonitos. Yo sí **10.** _____ (poder) nadar, pero mi hermanito todavía no **11.** _____ (saber) nadar. Un día yo **12.** _____ (ir) a nadar sin él y él **13.** _____ (empezar) a llorar. ¡Pobre Juan! En realidad, pobre de mí, porque ese día mientras yo **14.** _____ (nadar) en el mar un pez grande me **15.** _____ (morder) *(to bite)*. En un instante yo

16. _____ (sentir) un dolor tremendo y **17.** _____

(gritar), «¡Mamá, ayúdame!». Mi mamá **18.** _____ (meterse) al agua y

me **19.** _____ (salvar) la vida. Después de salir del agua yo

20. _____ (tener) que ir al hospital. Al final no

21. _____ (ser) nada serio, pero de todas formas toda la situación me

22. _____ (asustar) mucho.

WB 8-24 | Significados especiales Recuerda que ciertos verbos tienen un significado especial en el pretérito o el imperfecto. Completa las siguientes oraciones con el pretérito o el imperfecto según *(according to)* el significado de la oración.

1. Anoche nosotros _____ (tener) que asistir a una reunión muy

    aburrida. No salimos hasta las diez de la noche.

2. El año pasado Elisa _____ (saber) que Esteban tenía una hermana.

    No lo _____ (saber) antes.

3. Anita quería llevarme a una celebración familiar pero yo no _____

    (querer) ir. Me quedé en casa.

4. La semana pasada Dolores trató de sacar dinero del banco pero no

    _____ (poder). La máquina «ATM» estaba descompuesta *(broken)* y el

    banco estaba cerrado.

5. Cuando yo era más joven _____ (tener) que estudiar mucho.

WB 8-25 | En el mercado Completa las oraciones con una palabra apropiada de la lista. Vas a usar ciertas palabras más de una vez.

algo   ni . . . ni   algún   ninguna   algunas   nunca

algunos   también   nada   tampoco

VENDEDOR: ¿Quiere **1.** _____, señor?

CLIENTE: Sí, quiero **2.** _____ tomates, por favor.

VENDEDOR: Bien. ¿Quiere **3.** _____ naranjas

    4. _____? Están muy frescas.

CLIENTE: No, no quiero **5.** _____ porque no como fruta.

VENDEDOR: ¿Necesita **6.** _____ huevos frescos, señor?

CLIENTE: No, **7.** _____ como huevos.

VENDEDOR: ¿Verdad? Mi esposa no come **8.** _____ frutas

    9. _____ huevos. ¡Qué coincidencia! ¿Necesita pan hoy?

CLIENTE: No gracias, no necesito **10.** _____ más.

VENDEDOR: Muy bien... catorce quetzales, por favor.

WB 8-26 | ¿Cuánto tiempo hace? ¿Cuánto tiempo hace que las siguientes personas hacen estas cosas? Escribe la respuesta con la fórmula **hacer** + *time*. Sigue el modelo.

Modelo   Juan / no comprar un traje nuevo / dos años
          Hace dos años que Juan no compra un traje nuevo.

1. Lucía / no trabajar / tres meses

_____

2. Santi y Silvina / no estar casados / un año

_____

3. nosotros / no ir al centro comercial / una semana

_____

4. yo / no tener novio(a) / demasiado tiempo

_____

5. tú / no estar en la secundaria / ¿?

_____

De viaje por el Caribe: La República Dominicana, Cuba y Puerto Rico

VOCABULARIO Viajar en avión

WB 9-1 | **Rompecabezas** (*Puzzles*) Usa las pistas (*clues*) para solucionar los rompecabezas sobre los viajes. Escribe la palabra más apropiada según la pista.

1. Una colección de maletas: __ __ __ __ p __ __ __

2. Donde guardas la ropa para un viaje: __ __ __ __ __ a

3. Un viaje directo de Miami a Puerto Rico es un vuelo sin: e __ c __ __ __

4. El momento en que el avión sale del aeropuerto: s __ __ __ __ a

5. Para saber cuándo sale un vuelo tienes que consultar un: __ __ r __ __ __ o

6. Para comprar un boleto de avión, vas a una: __ __ __ n __ __ __ de viajes.

7. Un boleto de San Francisco a Puerto Rico a San Francisco es un boleto de: __ d __ y

    __ __ __ l __ __

8. Donde esperas el avión justo antes del vuelo: __ __ e __ __ __

9. La persona que te trae bebidas y comida durante el vuelo: __ s __ __ __ __ __ t __

    de vuelo

10. El documento necesario para pasar por la aduana: __ __ __ __ p __ __ __ __

11. Las personas que viajan en un avión: __ __ __ __ __ __ __ s

WB 9-2 | **Un viaje gratis** Ganaste un viaje gratuito y ahora consultas con el agente de viajes. ¿Qué preguntas te hace? Para saberlo, rellena los espacios en blanco con la palabra apropiada de la lista. **¡OJO!** En algunos casos tienes que conjugar el verbo.

perdón   control de seguridad   viajar   avión
ventanilla   pasaporte   boleto   facturar

1. ¿Adónde quieres _____?

2. ¿Deseas un _____ de ida y vuelta o solamente de ida?

3. ¿Prefieres ir en _____ o en tren?

4. Por lo general, ¿_____ las maletas cuando viajas por avión?

5. ¿Tienes un _____ para pasar la aduana sin problemas?

WB 9-3 | Un viaje a Puerto Rico Quieres ir a Puerto Rico este verano y decides pedirle ayuda a tu amigo Ricardo. Es de San Juan y te dice todo lo que hace para planear sus viajes a Puerto Rico. Para saber lo que dice, rellena los espacios en blanco con la palabra apropiada de la lista. **¡OJO!** En algunos casos tienes que conjugar el verbo.

aeropuerto	pasaporte	asiento	facturar las maletas
inmigración	boletos	ventanilla	pasillo
escala	viaje	equipaje de mano	agente
bajarse	horario	agencia de viajes	
hacer las maletas	recoger	abordar	

Cuando hago mis planes para viajar a Puerto Rico, siempre voy a la

1. _____ donde compro los **2.** _____ . Lola, mi

3. _____ , es excelente. Siempre sabe encontrar los mejores precios.

Yo le digo las fechas de mi **4.** _____ y después ella consulta el

5. _____ de los vuelos. Aunque vivimos más cerca de San Diego, siempre

salgo del **6.** _____ de Los Ángeles porque los precios son mucho más

baratos. El único problema es que de ningún sitio tienen vuelos directos. Todos hacen una

7. _____ o en Chicago o en Miami.

Lola siempre me consigue un **8.** _____ específico en el avión. A mi me gusta

ver el paisaje desde el avión y por eso siempre me siento en la **9.** _____ .

Pero a mi novia le gusta caminar por el avión muchas veces durante el vuelo. Por eso ella

siempre se sienta en el **10.** _____ . Ahora, tú sabes que yo fumo como una

chimenea, pero ya no podemos fumar en los aviones. Está bien. Yo, lo que hago, es fumar tres o

cuatro cigarrillos antes de **11.** _____ el avión.

Antes del viaje siempre estoy muy ocupado con los preparativos. Siempre hago una lista de todo

lo que tengo que empacar *(pack)*. Entonces cuando **12.** _____ no me olvido

de nada esencial. Nunca llevo **13.** _____ porque nunca hay suficiente

espacio en el avión. Cuando llego al aeropuerto siempre tengo que **14.** _____ .

Pero no es gran cosa. Voy cómodo en el avión y al llegar a Puerto Rico,

15. _____ del avión, **16.** _____ el equipaje y ¡listo!

Bueno, creo que lo vas a pasar súper bien en Puerto Rico. Recuerda que no necesitas un

17. _____ y que no tienes que pasar por la **18.** _____

porque Puerto Rico es parte de los Estados Unidos. Y, obviamente, ¡que no olvides llevar el

traje de baño!

Nombre _____ Fecha _____

ESTRUCTURA I Simplifying expressions: Indirect object pronouns

WB 9-4 | ¿Locos de amor? Pablo e Inés están en su luna de miel y hablan de los recuerdos *(souvenirs)* que van a comprar. Para saber qué compró Pablo para Inés, completa su conversación con el pronombre de objeto indirecto apropiado.

PABLO: Inés, mi amor, ¿a mi mamá ya **1.** _____ mandamos una tarjeta postal?

INÉS: Pues, yo no **2.** _____ mandé nada, cielo. Y ahora no queda tiempo. A tus padres **3.** _____ compramos un recuerdo; no necesitan tarjeta postal.

PABLO: Tienes razón, mi amor. Pero me siento mal porque ellos ya **4.** _____ mandaron dos cartas a nosotros, ¡y ellos no están de vacaciones!

INÉS: Pero tus padres son así. ¡No te preocupes *(Don't worry)*! No van a estar enojados. Ahora, a tu hermana, ¿qué **5.** _____ compraste ayer en San Juan?

PABLO: Nada, mi amor, porque no sabía que quería algo de San Juan.

INÉS: Pues, Pablito, a ti **6.** _____ pidió una estatua de Lladró, que son muy caras donde vive ella. ¿No lo recuerdas, cielo?

PABLO: No, no recuerdo nada. Creo que estoy demasiado enamorado de ti como para pensar en otras personas.

INÉS: Ah, ¡qué mono eres! Pues, ayer cuando estabas de compras, a mí **7.** _____ compraste algo?

PABLO: Claro que sí. ¡A ti **8.** _____ compré mil años más conmigo!

INÉS: ¡Qué romántico! Pero, Pablo, entonces, ¿a quién **9.** _____ vas a regalar este equipo de buceo que tienes escondido *(hidden)* en el armario?

PABLO: Eh, eh, pues, mi amor, sabes cuánto me gusta bucear… y el año pasado yo **10.** _____ pedí un equipo de buceo y tú nunca **11.** _____ regalaste el equipo que quería… y pues el precio era muy bueno….

INÉS: ¡PABLO! Creo que tienes que volver a San Juan, «mi amor».

¿Qué recuerdo le regaló Pablo a Inés? **12.** _____

WB 9-5 | ¿Qué hiciste? Tu amiga, Teresa Enrollada, siempre tiene dificultades. Ella te cuenta un problema y tú le preguntas cómo va a solucionar su problema. Escribe tus preguntas usando un pronombre de objeto indirecto. Sigue el modelo.

> Modelo La profesora está enojada y quiere hablar conmigo. (¿hablar?)
> *¿Le vas a hablar?*
> o *¿Vas a hablarle?*

1. Mis amigos quieren copiar mi tarea. (¿enseñar / tarea?)

_____

2. Mi ex-novio necesita trescientos dólares. (¿dar / dinero?)

_____

3. Tengo que hacerte una pregunta importante. (¿hacer / pregunta?)

_____

4. Mi nuevo amigo del Internet quería una foto de mí. (¿mandar / foto?)

_____

5. Este amigo del Internet quiere mandarnos una foto a nosotros dos. (¿mandar / foto?)

_____

WB 9-6 | Planes Julio y sus compañeros de casa van de viaje a la República Dominicana y a Haití. Ahora están hablando de lo que cada persona va a hacer para planear el viaje. ¿Qué hacen? Forma oraciones completas con los elementos que siguen, incorporando pronombres de objeto indirecto.

1. Carlos / comprar / una maleta / a Anita

_____

2. Julio / prometer / hacer las reservaciones / a sus compañeros

_____

3. Alicia y Mabel / mandar / un correo electrónico / a su primo en Santo Domingo

_____

4. el señor Martínez / ir a recomendar / un hotel / a nosotros

_____

5. yo / ir a explicar / los planes / a ti

_____

ESTRUCTURA II Simplifying expressions: Double object pronouns

WB 9-7 | ¡Feliz cumpleaños! Carmen le cuenta a una amiga sobre la fiesta de cumpleaños de Olga que tuvo lugar _(took place)_ anoche. Completa su historia con un pronombre de objeto directo o un pronombre de objeto indirecto. **¡OJO!** Vas a usar sólo uno en cada caso y no los dos juntos.

Ayer fue el cumpleaños de Olga y ella **1.** _____ pasó muy bien. Todos sus

amigos **2.** _____ dieron muchos regalos. **3.** _____

compraron en diferentes tiendas especializadas del viejo San Juan. Por ejemplo, Paco

4. _____ compró una blusa de seda. A Olga le gustó mucho la blusa y ella

5. _____ dio un beso a Paco.

Mateo, el novio de Olga, también **6.** _____ dio un regalo especial.

A nosotros Mateo **7.** _____ dijo que iba a ser algo increíble, y realmente

fue increíble. Después de que Olga abrió todos sus regalos, Mateo miró a Olga y

8. _____ dijo: «Olga, **9.** _____ quiero mucho, y tú

10. _____ sabes. Y también creo que tú **11.** _____

quieres a mí, ¿verdad? Pues, **12.** _____ compré este regalo, **13.** ¡ábre

_____ ahora mismo!». Cuando Olga **14.** _____ abrió,

empezó a gritar. Era un anillo de diamantes. De repente ella **15.** _____

miró a nosotros y **16.** _____ dijo: «¡Voy a casarme con Mateo!».

WB 9-8 | Regalos para todos Ernesto le pregunta a Fernando sobre los regalos que dio y recibió en el Día de los Reyes Magos. Selecciona la mejor respuesta a las preguntas de Ernesto según los dibujos. Sigue el modelo.

Modelo ¿Quién te dio las maletas?

__X__ Tú me las diste.

_____ Uds. me las dieron.

_____ Nos las dieron Uds.

1.

2.

3.

4.

1. ¿A quién le regalaste el libro?

_____ Me lo regaló mi abuela.

_____ Me la regaló mi abuela.

_____ Se lo regalé a mi abuela.

2. ¿A quién le regalaste los discos compactos?

_____ Se las regalé a mis hermanas.

_____ Se los regalé a mis hermanas.

_____ Me las regaló mis hermanas.

3. ¿Quién les compró las bicicletas a ti y a tu hermana?

_____ Nos las compraron nuestros padres.

_____ Se las compramos a nuestros padres.

_____ Nos los compraron nuestros padres.

4. ¿A quién le mandaste dinero?

_____ Se los mandé a mis sobrinos.

_____ Nos los mandaron mis sobrinos.

_____ Se lo mandé a mis sobrinos.

WB 9-9 | **¡Qué buen servicio!** La familia Suárez está pasando una semana de vacaciones en el hotel Meliá de San Juan, Puerto Rico. Completa las siguientes conversaciones entre un empleado *(employee)* del hotel y el Señor Suárez. Forma oraciones usando los pronombres de objeto directo e indirecto. Sigue el modelo.

> **Modelo**   SR. SUÁREZ: Señor, ¿me puede cambiar el cuarto?
> EMPLEADO: *Sí, se lo cambio.*

1. SR. SUÁREZ: Señor, ¿nos puede traer una plancha?

EMPLEADO: Sí, _____.

2. SR. SUÁREZ: Señor, ¿a mis hijos les puede enseñar la piscina?

EMPLEADO: Sí, _____.

3. SR. SUÁREZ: Señor, ¿me puede explicar cómo funciona el televisor?

EMPLEADO: Sí, _____.

4. SR. SUÁREZ: Señor, ¿a mi esposa le puede servir el almuerzo?

EMPLEADO: Sí, _____.

WB 9-10 | **¡Házmelo!** Alfonso se enferma el último día de sus vacaciones y Javier le tiene que hacer varias cosas. Para saber qué le pide a Javier, usa los elementos abajo para formar mandatos y usar los pronombres de objeto directo e indirecto. **¡OJO!** Cuando usas los dos pronombres con el mandato, tienes que usar un acento escrito sobre la vocal acentuada. Sigue el modelo.

> **Modelo**   Tengo sed y necesito un vaso de agua. (traer / el vaso de agua / a mí)
> *Tráemelo, por favor.*

1. A mi novia todavía no le compré su regalo. (comprar / el regalo / a mi novia)

_____

2. Tengo que preparar mis maletas, pero no puedo. (preparar / las maletas / a mí)

_____

3. Tengo que mandarles la tarjeta postal a mis padres, pero no puedo. (mandar / la tarjeta postal / a ellos)

_____

4. Quiero comer fruta. (servir / fruta / a mí)

_____

5. Necesito aspirina. (dar / la aspirina / a mí)

_____

6. Necesitamos reconfirmar los vuelos. (reconfirmar / los vuelos / a nosotros)

_____

Nombre _____ Fecha _____

VOCABULARIO El hotel

WB 9-11 | Hoteles El Hotel Lagarto y el Hotel Sol y Luna son dos hoteles muy diferentes de San Juan, Puerto Rico. Mira los dibujos y decide si las siguientes oraciones son **ciertas** (C) o **falsas** (F).

1. _____ El Hotel El Lagarto no tiene ascensor.

2. _____ Los cuartos del Hotel El Lagarto tienen baño privado.

3. _____ El Hotel El Lagarto no tiene aire acondicionado.

4. _____ Los cuartos del Hotel El Lagarto son muy cómodos

5. _____ El Hotel Sol y Luna es un hotel de cuatro estrellas.

6. _____ Los cuartos del Hotel Sol y Luna no están muy limpios.

7. _____ Los cuartos del Hotel Sol y Luna tienen camas dobles.

WB 9-12 | ¿Un hotel de cuatro estrellas? El señor Vargas quiere quedarse en un hotel de cuatro estrellas cuando va a la República Dominicana. Para saber si encuentra uno, completa su conversación con la recepcionista del Hotel Las Brisas con una palabra apropiada de la lista.

aire acondicionado	ascensor	baño privado	cama doble
camas sencillas	cómodos	cuarto	cuatro estrellas
limpio	llave	quedarse	quejarse

SEÑOR VARGAS: Buenos días. Quiero un **1.** _____ para dos personas, por favor.

RECEPCIONISTA: ¿Con una **2.** _____ o con dos

3. _____ , señor?

SEÑOR VARGAS: Una doble, por favor, con un **4.** _____.

RECEPCIONISTA: Bien. Tengo un cuarto en el sexto piso: número 606. ¿Está bien, señor?

SEÑOR VARGAS: Pues, el hotel tiene **5.** _____, ¿verdad?

RECEPCIONISTA: No, señor. Lo siento. Ése es el encanto del hotel. A nuestros clientes les

ofrecemos un descanso de la edad moderna.

SEÑOR VARGAS: Pues, hace mucho calor allí. ¿Tiene **6.** _____ el cuarto?

RECEPCIONISTA: No, señor, pero cada cuarto sí tiene abanico *(handheld fan)*. ¡No se preocupe,

señor! Nuestros cuartos son muy **7.** _____.

¿Cuántas noches quiere **8.** _____?

SEÑOR VARGAS: Tres noches, pero no sé si puedo aguantar *(put up with)* el calor y las

escaleras.

RECEPCIONISTA: No va a haber ningún problema, señor. A Ud. nuestro pequeño paraíso le va

a gustar mucho. Éste no es un hotel de **9.** _____, pero

todo está muy **10.** _____ y Ud. no va a

11. _____ de nada.

SEÑOR VARGAS: Pues, no sé. ¿Puedo ver el cuarto antes de decidir?

RECEPCIONISTA: Sí, señor. Aquí tiene la **12.** _____.

¿Es el hotel Las Brisas un hotel de cuatro estrellas?

13. _____

ASÍ SE DICE Giving directions: Prepositions of location, adverbs, and relevant expressions

WB 9-13 | Medios de transporte ¿Cuáles son los siguientes modos de transporte? Ordena las letras para revelar las palabras.

1. icaicletb: _____

2. rbaoc: _____

3. xita: _____

4. cheoc: _____

5. tremo: _____

6. úbotasu: _____

WB 9-14 | En la ciudad Lee la siguiente descripción de la ciudad y selecciona la preposición más apropiada según el mapa.

La plaza está en el centro de la cuidad. Hay un parque que está **1.** (lejos de / detrás de / cerca de) la biblioteca. Hay un museo **2.** (entre el / a lado del / a la derecha del) banco y la oficina de correos. **3.** (Lejos del / Entre / Al lado del) parque está la gasolinera. La gasolinera está **4.** (a la derecha de / delante de / lejos de) la terminal de autobuses. **5.** (Enfrente de / Lejos de / Al lado de) la terminal está la estación de trenes, que está **6.** (a la izquierda del / a la derecha del / lejos del) mercado central. **7.** (A la derecha del / En frente del / Detrás del) hotel hay una iglesia. La iglesia está **8.** (lejos de / entre / cerca de) la oficina de correos. El aeropuerto está **9.** (cerca de / lejos de / enfrente de) la cuidad.

WB 9-15 | ¿Cómo llego? La señora López está en el hotel de la ciudad que aparece en el mapa de la actividad anterior. Quiere saber cómo llegar a varias partes de la ciudad y pide direcciones en la recepción. ¿Cómo le contestan en la recepción? Mira otra vez el plano de la ciudad y completa las siguientes conversaciones con las palabras apropiadas de la lista. **¡OJO!** Puedes usar la misma palabra más de una vez y no tienes que usar todas las palabras.

a.

a la izquierda	cuadras
hacia	cruce
a la derecha	perdón
doble	en avión
a pie	siga

SEÑORA LÓPEZ: **1.** _____ , señora, ¿cómo llego a la estación de trenes?

RECEPCIONISTA: Es muy fácil, señora. Usted puede ir **2.** _____ . Salga

(Leave) del hotel y **3.** _____ a la derecha.

4. _____ la calle y **5.** _____ derecho

6. _____ el sur dos **7.** _____ . La

estación está **8.** _____ .

b.

cuadras	derecha
hacia	a pie
pararse	doble
lejos	izquierda
perdón	en autobús
un taxi	siga

SEÑORA LÓPEZ: Y dígame, por favor, ¿cómo llego al aeropuerto?

RECEPCIONISTA: Pues, el aeropuerto queda un poco **1.** _____ de la ciudad,

pero usted tiene varias opciones. Puede ir **2.** _____ , pero

es más fácil llamar **3.** _____ . Salga del hotel y

4. _____ a la **5.** _____ .

6. _____ derecho tres **7.** _____ y

8. _____ a la **9.** _____ . De allí el

aeropuerto queda unos 25 kilómetros **10.** _____ el oeste.

ESTRUCTURA III — Giving directions and expressing desires: Formal and negative *tú* commands

WB 9-16 | Mandatos Escribe la forma apropiada del mandato según las indicaciones. Sigue los modelos.

Modelos   tú, negativo / hablar: *no hables*
                 usted, positivo / comer: *coma*

1. usted, positivo / viajar: _____
2. ustedes, negativo / fumar: _____
3. tú, negativo / llegar: _____
4. usted, positivo / bañarse: _____
5. ustedes, negativo / abrir: _____
6. tú, negativo / ir: _____
7. usted, positivo / bajarse: _____
8. tú, negativo / pedir: _____
9. ustedes, positivo / salir: _____
10. tú, negativo / dormirse: _____

WB 9-17 | De compras Es la primera semana que Gloria está en San Juan y no conoce la ciudad. Les pide indicaciones a muchas personas. Completa las siguientes conversaciones usando los mandatos formales de los verbos indicados.

En la calle

GLORIA: Perdón, señor. ¿Sabe Ud. si hay un supermercado por aquí?

SEÑOR ORTEGA: Sí, señora. **1.** _____ (Seguir) Ud. derecho hasta la

esquina.

Luego, **2.** _____ (doblar) a la derecha en la calle

Unamuno y **3.** _____ (pasar) dos cuadras más hasta la

Sexta Avenida. Allí está el supermercado.

GLORIA: Gracias, señor.

SEÑOR ORTEGA: De nada, señora.

En el supermercado

EMPLEADO: Señora, **4.** _____ (decirme) qué quiere Ud.

GLORIA: **5.** _____ (Darme) medio kilo de esas naranjas, por favor.

Y, ¿están frescos los melones?

EMPLEADO: Sí, **6.** _____ (mirar) Ud. Están súper frescos.

GLORIA: Muy bien. Y, ¿dónde puedo encontrar la sección de carnes?

EMPLEADO: Lo siento, señora. Aquí no vendemos carnes. **7.** _____

(Ir) a la carnicería. Queda muy cerca de aquí.

GLORIA: Bien. Entonces, eso es todo. Gracias.

EMPLEADO: De nada. **8.** _____ (Tener) Ud. un buen día. ¡Y

9. _____ (volver) pronto!

GLORIA: Gracias. ¡Adiós!

WB 9-18 | ¡Despiértense! Ernesto y sus amigos querían pasar las vacaciones de primavera en un club deportivo en Puerto Rico, pero su agente de viajes se equivocó y los alojó *(lodged them)* en un balneario para gente que quiere bajar de peso *(lose weight)*. A las seis de la mañana del primer día el director del club viene a despertarlos. ¿Qué les manda? Forma mandatos con los siguiente elementos. **¡OJO!** Los pronombres van conectados al final de los mandatos afirmativos y van delante de los mandatos negativos. Sigue los modelos.

Modelos   A todos: levantarse
¡Levántense todos!

A Ernesto: no dormirse otra vez
¡No te duermas otra vez!

1. A todos: vestirse rápidamente

_____

2. A Ernesto: no ducharse

_____

3. A todos: ponerse los zapatos de tenis

_____

4. A todos: echarse a correr diez millas

_____

5. A Ernesto: no pararse para descansar

_____

6. A todos: subirse la escalera

_____

7. A todos: quitarse los zapatos y meterse a la piscina

_____

BIENVENIDOS A CUBA

En este segmento del video, vas a aprender un poco sobre Cuba y sobre la vida de sus ciudadanos. Los temas incluyen:

- la geografía
- el clima
- la agricultura
- el gobierno
- La Habana y sus habitantes
- el arte local
- el vestido típico
- el turismo

WB 9-19 | En el segmento del video vas a escuchar muchos cognados que pueden facilitar tu comprensión. Algunos de estos cognados aparecen aquí. Trata de pronunciar cada palabra o frase y luego empareja los cognados con su definición en inglés.

1. _____ exuberante
2. _____ vegetación
3. _____ plantaciones
4. _____ tabaco
5. _____ comunista
6. _____ revolucionario
7. _____ organizaciones políticas
8. _____ contaminación atmosférica

a. political organizations
b. plantations
c. exuberant
d. revolutionary
e. tobacco
f. communist
g. atmospheric contamination
h. vegetation

WB 9-20 | Después de ver el segmento del video, rellena los espacios en blanco con el cognado apropiado de la actividad **WB 5-20.**

1. Por su clima tropical, Cuba es un país rico en _____ _____ .

2. Abundan las plantaciones de _____ y azúcar.

3. El Partido _____ de Cuba, el PCC, es la fuerza superior que gobierna la sociedad.

4. La mayoría de las _____ y sociales están situadas en la Plaza de la Revolución.

5. Las bicicletas cuestan poco, son fáciles de estacionar y reducen la _____ .

WB 9-21 | Después de ver el segmento del video otra vez, selecciona la mejor respuesta a las siguientes preguntas.

1. ¿Cuáles de estos pares *(pairs)* de países están más cerca de Cuba?

   a. México y Venezuela

   b. Estados Unidos y España

   c. México y Estados Unidos

   d. Puerto Rico y España

2. ¿Cuál de las siguientes opciones es el símbolo nacional de Cuba?

   a. la guayabera

   b. la caña

   c. la palma

   d. el carro Chevy

3. ¿Cuáles son las dos actividades comerciales más importantes ahora en Cuba?

   a. el turismo y la pesca

   b. el turismo y el petróleo

   c. el petróleo y el béisbol

   d. el béisbol y el boxeo

4. ¿Cuántos habitantes hay en La Habana?

    a. 2 millones   **c.** 10 millones

    b. 5 millones   **d.** 12 millones

5. ¿Qué es el Malecón?

    a. un coche de los años 50   **c.** una tienda de helados

    b. un cine en La Habana   **d.** una larga avenida al lado del mar

6. ¿Quién es José Martí?

    a. el presidente de Cuba   **c.** el héroe nacional de Cuba

    b. la persona que descubrió Cuba   **d.** el dueño de la tienda de helados

7. ¿Cuál es el medio de transporte preferido en La Habana?

    a. la bicicleta   **c.** el barco

    b. el carro Chevy   **d.** el tren

¡A ESCRIBIR!

Strategy: Using commands to give directions

If you're traveling in a Spanish-speaking country or city, chances are you might need to ask for directions. In addition, you might even have to give directions! The most important element of explaining to someone how to get from one place to another is accuracy. If you explain your directions clearly and concisely, people will be able to follow them easily.

Here are six basic requirements for giving directions to a place:

1. Choose the easiest route.

2. Be very clear in your directions.

3. Give the directions in chronological order.

4. Use linking expressions such as **Primero..., Luego..., Después de eso..., Entonces..., Usted debe..., Después...,** and **Finalmente...** .

5. Identify clearly visible landmarks such as:

la avenida *avenue*	**el cruce de caminos** *intersection*
el bulevar *boulevard*	**el edificio** *building*
la calle *street*	**el letrero** *sign*
el camino *road*	**el puente** *bridge*
la colina *hill*	**el semáforo** *traffic light*

6. When possible, include a sketch of the route.

Modelo *Para llegar a mi casa del aeropuerto, siga estas indicaciones. Primero, siga la calle del aeropuerto hasta la salida. Doble a la derecha y siga por el bulevar Glenwood dos kilómetros hasta el primer semáforo, donde hay un cruce de caminos. Entonces, doble a la izquierda y siga por el camino Parkers Mill dos kilómetros (pasando debajo de un puente) hasta la calle Lane Allen. En esa calle, doble a la derecha y siga otros dos kilómetros hasta el segundo semáforo. Después, doble a la izquierda en el camino Beacon Hill y siga derecho medio kilómetro hasta el camino Normandy. Doble a la izquierda y vaya a la cuarta casa a la derecha. Allí vivo yo, y ¡allí tiene su casa!*

Task: Giving directions from the airport to a place in town

The Álvarez family is coming from Puerto Rico to visit your city for the first time. They want to know what they should do while there, where they should stay, and of course, where they should go for fun. Write a letter to Señor Álvarez describing your city and giving directions for how to get to your favorite place in the city from the closest airport.

Paso 1: Using the strategy above, write out the directions from the airport to your favorite part of the city.

_____

_____

_____

_____

Paso 2: Using the directions you wrote above, write out a first draft of the letter and include information about where the Alvarez family should stay and what they should do in your favorite part of the city.

Paso 3: After revising your first draft, write out your second draft below.

_____

_____

_____

_____

_____

_____

_____

_____

ATAJO 4.0

Functions: Asking for and giving directions; Linking ideas; Expressing distance; Expressing location

Vocabulary: City; Directions and distance; Means of transportation; Metric systems and measurements

Grammar: Verbs: imperative: **usted(es), ser** and **estar; tener** and **haber**

Autoprueba

VOCABULARIO

WB 9-22 | **Viajes** Empareja la descripción de la primera columna con las palabras de la segunda columna.

_____ 1. maletas y mochilas   **a.** la aduana

_____ 2. las horas de salida y llegada   **b.** el horario

_____ 3. las personas que viajan   **c.** el equipaje

_____ 4. donde hacen la inspección de las maletas   **d.** los pasajeros

_____ 5. donde los turistas presentan los pasaportes   **e.** el pasaporte

_____ 6. donde los turistas compran sus boletos de viaje   **f.** la inmigración

_____ 7. el documento oficial para entrar en otro país   **g.** la agencia de viajes

WB 9-23 | **En el hotel** El Sr. Morales tiene que pasar tres noches en un hotel en San Juan y el gerente le cuenta algunos detalles del hotel. Completa su descripción usando palabras de la lista.

> aire acondicionado   cuartos   limpios   sencillas   ascensor   cuatro estrellas
> privado   sucios   cómodo   dobles   recepción

Éste es un hotel de lujo, es decir de **1.** _____ . En este hotel todos los

2. _____ siempre están **3.** _____ y nunca están

4. _____ . Según su preferencia, tenemos habitaciones con camas

5. _____ o **6.** _____ . Todas tienen baño

7. _____ . Como esta zona es tropical y normalmente hace mucho calor,

todas las habitaciones también tienen **8.** _____ . La mejor habitación está

en el octavo piso, pero no se preocupe, tenemos **9.** _____ . Si durante su

visita necesita cualquier cosa, por favor, llame a la **10.** _____ . Le pueden

traer todo lo que Ud. necesite. Creo que Ud. va a estar muy **11.** _____ en

este hotel.

WB 9-24 | ¿Dónde está todo? Mira el mapa. Estás en la avenida Constitución. Completa las oraciones con las preposiciones apropiadas de la lista. No repitas ninguna palabra.

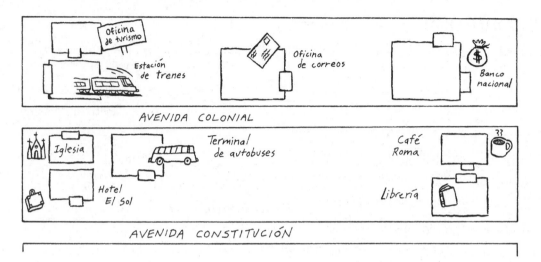

a la derecha   a la izquierda   al lado   detrás   enfrente   entre

1. La terminal de autobuses está _____ de la iglesia.

2. El Hotel El Sol está _____ de la iglesia.

3. La estación de trenes está _____ de la oficina de correos.

4. La oficina de correos está _____ la estación de trenes y el Banco nacional.

5. El Banco nacional está _____ de la oficina de correos.

6. Café Roma está _____ de la librería.

WB 9-25 | Indicaciones Ana Marie está perdida en una calle de Santo Domingo y le pide indicaciones a alguien en la calle. Completa las indicaciones con las palabras apropiadas. Vas a usar una de las siguientes palabras dos veces.

cruce   doble   hacia   siga   suba

Para llegar a su hotel de aquí, **1.** _____ esta calle y

2. _____ derecho por dos cuadras más. **3.** _____ a la

izquierda y luego **4.** _____ una cuadra en la calle Palacios.

5. _____ derecho **6.** _____ el sur y el hotel estará a

la derecha.

WB 9-26 | Una carta Completa la siguiente conversación con pronombre de objeto indirecto.

JUAN CARLOS: Celina, **1.** _____ escribí una carta a mis padres hoy.

GLORIA: ¿Qué **2.** _____ dijiste?

JUAN CARLOS: A mi mamá **3.** _____ dije que estoy muy contento aquí y a

mi papá **4.** _____ dije que necesito más dinero. Pero es

interesante porque cuando fui a enviar **5.** _____ la carta,

encontré que ellos **6.** _____ habían escrito (had written)

una carta a mí.

GLORIA: ¡Qué coincidencia! ¿Qué **7.** _____ decían a ti?

JUAN CARLOS: Pues, **8.** _____ decían que estaban bien y que no

9. _____ iban a enviar más dinero. Al final, decidí no

mandar **10.** _____ la carta.

WB 9-27 | Elena, la buena Elena siempre les hace favores a sus amigos. Escribe sus respuestas a las preguntas de sus amigos usando los pronombres de objeto directo e indirecto.

1. Elena, ¿me puedes prestar (loan) tu chaqueta azul?

   _____

2. Elena, ¿nos preparas una cena especial?

   _____

3. Elena, ¿nos puedes escribir el ensayo?

   _____

4. Elena, ¿te podemos pasar nuestra tarea?

   _____

5. Elena, ¿le puedes comprar un regalo a Rosa?

   _____

WB 9-28 | Antes de salir del mercado Completa la siguiente conversación con un mandato formal de los verbos entre paréntesis. **¡OJO!** En algunos casos tienes que usar un pronombre.

CLIENTE: **1.** _____ (Perdonar), señor. Por favor,

2. _____ (darme) una bolsa plástica para estos tomates.

VENDEDOR: Cómo no, señora. **3.** _____ (Tomar) Ud. esta bolsa limpia.

CLIENTE: Gracias. **4.** _____ (Decirme) una cosa, señor. ¿Sabe Ud. si

hay un banco cerca de aquí?

VENDEDOR: Pues, sí. **5.** _____ (Salir) del mercado y

6. _____ (ir) dos cuadras todo derecho. El banco está a la

izquierda.

CLIENTE: ¡Muchas gracias! **7.** _____ (Tener) Ud. un buen día.

VENDEDOR: Y Ud., también señora. **8.** _____ (Volver) pronto. Hasta

luego.

●10 Las relaciones sentimentales: Honduras y Nicaragua

VOCABULARIO Las relaciones sentimentales

WB 10-1 | Palabras revueltas Pon en orden las letras de las siguientes palabras relacionadas con las relaciones sentimentales.

1. samitda: _____ _____ _____ _____ _____ _____ _____

2. tica: _____ _____ _____ _____

3. cirasepaón: _____ _____ _____ _____ _____ _____ _____ _____ _____

4. sader la noma: _____ _____ _____ _____ _____ _____ _____
   _____ _____ _____ _____

5. roma: _____ _____ _____ _____

6. promimcoso: _____ _____ _____ _____ _____ _____ _____ _____ _____ _____

WB 10-2 | ¿Qué palabra es? Lee las pistas y escribe las palabras de relaciones sentimentales que describen.

1. Otro nombre para el amor que demuestran los novios
   _____ _____ _____ _____ _____ _____ _____

2. El viaje que hacen los novios después de casarse
   _____ _____ _____ _____ _____ _____ _____ _____ _____ _____ _____ _____ _____

3. Lo opuesto al matrimonio
   _____ _____ _____ _____ _____ _____ _____ _____ _____ _____

4. Lo que hacen los novios que no se llevan bien y deciden vivir aparte
   _____ _____ _____ _____ _____ _____ _____ _____ _____ _____

5. Decoración utilizada en la ceremonia
   _____ _____ _____ _____

6. Lo que lleva la novia durante la ceremonia y lo que tira después

7. El período de la relación amorosa justo antes del matrimonio
   _____ _____ _____ _____ _____ _____ _____ _____ _____

8. Nombre para la ceremonia que inicia el matrimonio
   _____ _____ _____ _____

WB 10-3 | La boda de Juan Antonio y María Teresa Carmen está explicándole a su amiga Nuria algo sobre la boda de su hermano Juan Antonio. Para saber cómo fue, completa su descripción con una palabra o frase apropiada de la siguiente lista.

casarse	quería	rompió	ramo de flores	novios	recién casados
amor	boda	salió	novia	se besaron	

Juan Antonio 1. _____ con su 2. _____, María Teresa, por tres

años. Ellos están muy contentos ahora, pero no siempre ha sido así. Hace un año María

Teresa 3. _____ con Juan Antonio porque encontró a otro hombre. Pero después de varios meses María Teresa se dio cuenta de que **4.** _____ mucho a mi

hermano y ellos se reunieron y decidieron **5.** _____.

Ellos hicieron muchos planes para el día de la **6.** _____ y ese día fue fantástico.

María Teresa se vistió de blanco y llevó un **7.** _____, que consistía de rosas rojas,

símbolo del **8.** _____. Mi hermano llevaba un traje elegante y estaba muy guapo.

Cuando el ministro les dijo a los **9.** _____, «ustedes son hombre y mujer», ellos

10. _____ y salieron de la iglesia. Después, todas fuimos a una recepción en

honor de los **11.** _____. Estoy muy contenta de que todo salió bien con ellos a

pesar de sus dificultades.

ESTRUCTURA I — Describing recent actions, events, and conditions: The present perfect

WB 10-4 | ¡Lo he perdido! Marta ha perdido algo en la universidad. Para saber lo que es,
completa la siguiente conversación con formas apropiadas del verbo **haber.**

MARTA: Hola, soy Marta.

CATALINA: Hola, soy Catalina. ¿Qué te **1.** _____ pasado?

MARTA: **2.** _____ perdido mi bolsa con mi pasaporte. ¿La

           3. _____ visto tú por aquí?

CATALINA: Pues, no. Lo siento. No **4.** _____ visto ninguna bolsa.

           ¿De dónde eres?

MARTA: Soy de Managua. Mi hermana y yo **5.** _____ venido a la

           universidad para estudiar la informática.

CATALINA: ¡Qué bueno! Uds. son nicaragüenses. ¿**6.** _____ llamado Uds.

           a la policía?

MARTA: No, nosotras no lo **7.** _____ hecho todavía. Lo vamos a hacer

           ahora mismo.

CATALINA: Bien. ¡Buena suerte!

WB 10-5 | Formas verbales Indica la forma correcta del presente perfecto de los siguientes
verbos. **¡OJO!** El presente perfecto requiere una forma del verbo **haber** y el participio
pasado. Sigue el modelo.

    Modelo   yo, cantar: *he cantado*

1. yo, hablar: _____

2. tú, comer: _____

3. él, dormir: _____

4. ella, ir: _____

5. nosotros, abrir: _____

6. vosotros, decir: _____

7. ellos, hacer: _____

8. ustedes, volver: _____

9. yo, escribir: _____

10. tú, ver: _____

WB 10-6 | Los últimos detalles Linda y su mamá están hablando de las preparaciones para la boda de Linda. Completa su conversación con la forma correcta del verbo indicado en el presente perfecto. **¡OJO!** Recuerda que varios de los verbos tienen participios irregulares.

LINDA: Bueno, mamá, ¿qué más tenemos que hacer?

MAMÁ: **1.** ¿_____ (comprar) las invitaciones?

LINDA: Sí, y ya les **2.** _____ (mandar) invitaciones a todos los invitados.

MAMÁ: **3.** ¿_____ (pagar) el vestido de boda?

LINDA: Ahhh... Se me olvidó. Y tampoco **4.** _____ (hablar) con el sastre *(tailor)* sobre las alteraciones. Y mamá, ¿sabes si papá ya **5.** _____ (reservar) su smoking *(tuxedo)*?

MAMÁ: Sí, Linda. ¡No te preocupes! Tu papá ya lo **6.** _____ (hacer). ¿No **7.** _____ (ver) el recibo?

LINDA: No, mamá. Papá todavía no me lo **8.** _____ (traer). Se lo voy a pedir. Bueno, mamá, ¿algo más?

MAMÁ: No, Linda, creo que nosotras **9.** _____ (recordar) todo. Ay, a lo mejor queda un detalle. Tu novio, ¿ **10.** _____ (decir) que quiere casarse contigo?

LINDA: ¡Mamá!

WB 10-7 | Queridos abuelos Hace dos meses que Miguel y Ana están casados y ahora Ana les escribe una carta a sus abuelos para decirles cómo les va con todo. ¿Qué les ha pasado hasta ahora? Forma oraciones con los siguientes elementos usando el presente perfecto.

Modelo   nosotros / pasarlo bien
Nosotros lo hemos pasado bien.

Queridos abuelos,

1. nosotros / volver / de la luna de miel

_____

2. la vida de casados / ser / perfecto

_____

3. cada día / Miguel / decir / que me quiere mucho

_____

4. nuestros amigos / escribirnos / muchas cartas

_____

5. nosotros / abrir / una cuenta bancaria

_____

6. Y, ¿saben qué?, ¡el conejo / morir!

_____

Con mucho cariño,

Ana y Miguel

Describing reciprocal actions: Reciprocal constructions with _se, nos,_ and _os_

WB 10-8 | **La pareja famosa** Julio y Ana María están enamorados. Todos sus amigos están hartos _(fed up)_ porque Julio y Ana María demuestran su cariño por todas partes. Míralos en los siguientes dibujos y describe todo lo que ellos hacen y qué les molesta a sus amigos. Escribe oraciones completas usando las formas recíprocas. Puedes seleccionar entre las siguientes acciones.

abrazarse y mirarse profundamente

besarse en público

contarse secretos en público

escribirse cartas durante la clase

hablarse por teléfono

> **Modelo** _Se hablan por teléfono hasta muy tarde._

1. _____

_____

2. _____

_____

3. _____

_____

4. _____

_____

WB 10-9 | **¡La guerra de los Rosas!** Claudia y Juan José Rosas están a punto de *(about to)* divorciarse y están hablando ahora con su consejero *(counselor)* matrimonial. Se están quejando de su relación. ¿Qué dicen? Completa sus oraciones con la forma recíproca correcta del verbo entre paréntesis.

1. Claudia y yo no _____ (verse) mucho.

2. Juan José y yo no _____ (hablarse) por teléfono durante el día.

3. Claudia y yo no _____ (mirarse) cariñosamente.

4. Juan José y yo _____ (conocerse) demasiado.

5. Claudia y yo no _____ (comunicarse) bien.

VOCABULARIO La recepción

WB 10-10 | **La recepción** ¿Cuáles de las siguientes actividades son parte de una recepción de boda tradicional de los Estados Unidos? Indica estas actividades con una X.

1. _____ Los novios van de pesca inmediatamente después de la ceremonia.

2. _____ Los invitados felicitan a los novios.

3. _____ La celebración tiene lugar en un lugar especial.

4. _____ Los novios se ponen patines y pasean por el salón.

5. _____ La novia les tira su vestido a las chicas solteras.

6. _____ Todos los invitados se visten de gala.

7. _____ El novio pasa la aspiradora.

8. _____ La pareja baila con la música de la orquesta.

9. _____ La pareja entra en el salón y todos los invitados aplauden.

10. _____ Los padres de la novia planchan la ropa.

WB 10-11 | Así se hace Maríbel le está contando a su amiga Ángela cómo son las recepciones en su país. Para saber cómo son, completa la descripción con la palabra apropiada de la siguiente lista. ¡OJO! Tienes que conjugar los verbos en el presente del indicativo.

agarrar   aplaudir   asistir   banquete   felicitar   orquesta   terminar

Después de la ceremonia todos los invitados **1.** _____ a una fiesta elegante para celebrar el matrimonio. Todo empieza con un brindis para los novios. Después los invitados toman su champán *(champagne)* y **2.** _____ a los recién casados.

Generalmente el **3.** _____ comienza a las nueve de la noche. Hay todo tipo de comida rica, y mientras comen los invitados, la **4.** _____ toca música moderna y tradicional.

Después de la cena, todos se divierten mucho bailando y charlando hasta muy tarde. Al final, la novia tira su ramo de flores y una chica lo **5.** _____. Eso significa que ella va a casarse pronto. La fiesta **6.** _____ cuando los novios se van. Todos

7. _____ y los recién casados salen para su luna de miel.

ASÍ SE DICE   Qualifying actions: Adverbs and adverbial expressions of time and sequencing of events

WB 10-12 | Adverbios Forma adverbios de los siguientes adjetivos. Sigue el modelo.

> **Modelo**   frecuente: *frecuentemente*

1. inmediato _____

2. nervioso _____

3. regular _____

4. tranquilo _____

5. constante _____

6. rápido _____

WB 10-13 | Don Juan Berta acaba de conocer a Esteban, el "don Juan" de su residencia universitaria. Ahora le está haciendo preguntas a Cristina sobre cómo es este don Juan. ¿Cómo contesta Cristina? Escribe la respuesta de Cristina, convirtiendo el adjetivo en adverbio para describir el verbo.

> **Modelo**   ¿Cómo les habla Esteban a las chicas? / paciente
> *Les habla a las chicas pacientemente.*

1. ¿Cómo conquista a las chicas Esteban? / fácil

_____

2. ¿Cuándo llama a las chicas? / frecuente

_____

3. ¿Cómo besa a las chicas? / apasionado

_____

4. ¿Cómo corta con las chicas? / rápido

_____

WB 10-14 | Las vacaciones de Pedro Pedro le escribió un correo electrónico a su keypal sobre sus vacaciones. Termina el email, rellenando los espacios en blanco con los adverbios apropiados de la siguiente lista.

a veces   cada   nunca   siempre   solamente   todos los días

1. _____ año voy de vacaciones a las lindas playas de Nicaragua. Cuando era joven **2.** _____ iba con mi familia, pero ahora que soy mayor, voy solo. De hecho, prefiero viajar solo; **3.** _____ invito a nadie. Normalmente paso tres semanas, pero este año, **4.** _____ voy a poder pasar una semana. Pero, ¡voy a aprovechar el tiempo! **5.** _____ voy a bañarme en el mar y después voy a explorar la selva.

6. _____ me gusta pasar tiempo en Managua con algunos de mis amigos, pero este año con tan poco tiempo, creo que voy a quedarme cerca de la playa y la selva. Sé que lo voy a pasar súper bien!

ESTRUCTURA II Using the Spanish equivalents of *who, whom, that,* and *which*: Relative pronouns

WB 10-15 | Chismes *(Gossip)* Antonio le está contando los últimos chismes a sus amigos de la residencia. Para saber qué dice, rellena los espacios en blanco con la forma apropiada del pronombre relativo: **que, quien** o **lo que.**

1. Marta, la chica _____ vive en el tercer piso está saliendo con Roberto.

2. La chica con _____ salía Roberto el mes pasado está saliendo ahora con el hermano de Roberto.

3. _____ le sorprende a Roberto es que esa chica está saliendo también con el chico con _____ cortó hace dos meses.

4. Carlos rompió la computadora _____ está en la habitación de Tomás.

5. Tomás cree que su compañero, a _____ le prestó *(loaned)* la computadora la rompió.

6. Carlos no le dijo a Tomás _____ pasó.

WB 10-16 | **Más chismes** Antonio y sus amigos siguen con sus chismes. Escribe las respuestas a las preguntas usando el pronombre relativo apropiado. Sigue los modelos.

Modelos   Teresa, ¿quién es la persona a quien más quieres?
Juan Carlos es *la persona a quien más quiero.*

Antonio, ¿qué es lo que más te molesta?
La falta de cortesía es *lo que más me molesta.*

1. Carlos, ¿quién es la chica que habla con tu hermano?

   Ángela es _____.

2. Toni, ¿cuál es la comida que más te gusta?

   El burrito loco es _____.

3. José, ¿quién es la persona con quien sales ahora?

   Alicia es _____.

4. Elvia, ¿qué es lo que más te molesta?

   La tarea es _____.

WB 10-17 | **Planes de boda** Ana habla con una amiga sobre sus planes de boda. Completa sus oraciones con el pronombre relativo apropiado.

1. Mi padre es la persona _____ me va a ofrecer a mi novio.

2. Mi hermana es la persona a _____ voy a tirar mi ramo.

3. El vestido es la cosa _____ todavía necesito comprar.

4. El dinero es _____ necesitamos para pagar por todo esto.

BIENVENIDOS A NICARAGUA

En este segmento del video, vas a aprender un poco sobre Nicaragua y sobre la vida de sus ciudadanos. Los temas incluyen:

- la geografía
- las ciudades principales
- el clima
- la vida nocturna

WB 10-18 | En el segmento del video vas a escuchar muchos cognados que pueden facilitar tu comprensión. Algunos de estos cognados aparecen aquí. Trata de pronunciar cada palabra o frase y luego empareja los cognados con su definición en inglés.

1. _____ compiten
2. _____ colonial
3. _____ volcanes
4. _____ tranquilidad
5. _____ ritmos contagiosos

   a. tranquility
   b. infectious rhythms
   c. compete
   d. volcanoes
   e. colonial

WB 10-19 | Después de ver el segmento del video, rellena los espacios en blanco con el cognado apropiado de la actividad **WB 10-18**.

1. En Nicaragua, el país más grande de Centroamérica, los caballos y las bicicletas todavía _____ con los carros.

2. Las calles de León recuerdan un pasado _____.

3. Con sus playas blancas, sus montañas y sus _____, éste es un país tropical de bellos paisajes.

4. Durante el mediodía, las plazas mantienen un aire de _____.

5. Los muchos clubes de Managua prenden sus luces y su música de _____ llama al pueblo para disfrutar.

WB 10-20 | Después de ver el segmento del video otra vez, selecciona la mejor respuesta a las siguientes preguntas.

1. _____ ¿Quién es Rubén Dario?
   a. el padre de la independencia de Nicaragua
   b. un conquistador español
   c. el presidente de Nicaragua
   d. un famoso poeta nicaragüense

2. _____ ¿Cuáles de los siguientes datos describen la ciudad de León? Selecciona todas las respuestas correctas.
   a. Tiene la catedral más grande de Latinoamérica.
   b. Es la capital de Nicaragua.
   c. Tiene más de cien mil habitantes.
   d. La construcción de su catedral tomó más de cien años.

3. _____ ¿Cuál es uno de los platos favoritos de Nicaragua?
   a. paella
   b. rana
   c. iguana
   d. perro

4. _____ ¿Cuáles de los siguientes datos describen Nicaragua? Selecciona todas las respuestas correctas.
   a. Es un país comunista.
   b. Tiene un clima tropical.
   c. Sus países vecinos incluyen Costa Rica y Panamá.
   d. Pasó más de setenta años en una guerra *(war)* civil.

¡A ESCRIBIR!

Strategy: Writing a descriptive paragraph

Descriptive paragraphs occur in many contexts. They are often found in works of fiction such as novels and short stories, but they also appear in newspaper articles, advertising materials, educational publications, and personal letters. A descriptive paragraph contains sentences that describe people, places, things, and/or events. In this chapter we focus on describing events. To express how often events take place or how often you or others do something, you can use adverbs of frequency such as the following:

a veces	*sometimes*
cada año / todos los años	*each / every year*
dos veces a la semana	*twice a week*
muchas veces	*often*
nunca	*never*
raras veces	*rarely, infrequently*
siempre	*always*
todos los días	*every day*
una vez al mes	*once a month*

You can also modify these expressions to express a wide variety of time frames: **dos veces al mes, tres veces a la semana, cada mes,** and so on.

Task: Writing a descriptive paragraph

Now you will apply the strategy to describe the activities you do with your "fantasy family."

Paso 1 Begin by assuming that all your dreams have come true. Make a list of all the activities you and your family do now that life is perfect.

_____

_____

Paso 2 Now think about how frequently you do these activities. Next to each one write a phrase describing the frequency. Remember to use the adverbs you learned in your text.

Paso 3 Now write a well-developed paragraph to describe these activities, with whom you do them, and with what frequency. Revise the paragraph and write the second draft below.

_____

_____

_____

_____

_____

_____

ATAJO 4.0

Functions: Expressing time relationships; Linking ideas; Talking about habitual actions

Vocabulary: Family members; Leisure; Time expressions

Grammar: Adverbs; Adverb types

Autoprueba

VOCABULARIO

WB 10-21 | El noviazgo Gregorio y María hablan de su relación. Para saber lo que dicen, completa su conversación con la palabra apropiada de la siguiente lista. **¡OJO!** Si seleccionas un verbo, tienes que conjugarlo. No repitas ninguna palabra.

amor   casados   enamorarse   matrimonio   cariño   enamorados   llevarse   noviazgo

GREGORIO: Mi amor, ¿no es cierto que nuestro **1.** _____ comenzó el día que nos

conocimos?

MARÍA: Sí, cariño, fue **2.** _____ a primera vista, ¿verdad?

GREGORIO: Claro porque **3.** _____ en un instante.

MARÍA: Tan grande era nuestro **4.** _____ desde el principio.

GREGORIO: Ay, cómo recuerdo nuestra primera cita. Me invitaste al cine y luego fuimos

a un café.

MARÍA: Sí, y **5.** _____ tan bien juntos, estábamos **6.** _____. ¡Ay!

GREGORIO: Y al poco tiempo te hice una propuesta de **7.** _____.

MARÍA: Y cinco años después, ¡todavía estamos **8.** _____!

WB 10-22 | La boda Monica le está contando a su amiga cómo son típicamente las bodas norteamericanas. Completa su descripción usando palabras y frases de la siguiente lista. **¡OJO!** Si seleccionas un verbo, es posible que tengas que conjugarlo.

agarrar	aplaudir	banquete	besarse
casarse	divorciarse	felicitar	luna de miel
novios	orquesta	ramo de flores	recepción
recién casados	separarse	tener lugar	brindis

Muchas veces los **1.** _____ deciden **2.** _____ en una iglesia. Cuando

3. _____ delante del altar, ya están casados. Después de esa ceremonia, los

4. _____ salen de la iglesia y todos **5.** _____. Luego todos salen para

la **6.** _____.

A veces estas fiestas **7.** _____ en un restaurante o en un parque bonito.

Allí es típico tener un **8.** _____ elegante, pero antes de comer alguien les hace un

9. _____ a la pareja. Todos los invitados **10.** _____ a los novios y

entonces empiezan a comer. Después de comer, la **11.** _____ empieza a tocar

y todos salen a bailar. Más tarde, la novia tira el **12.** _____ y una chica lo trata

de **13.** _____.

Finalmente, los novios salen para la **14.** _____ y los otros continúan la fiesta.

Con suerte, los novios no **15.** _____, pero típicamente, el 50 por ciento de los

novios **16.** _____ después de siete años de matrimonio.

WB 10-23 | ¿Qué han hecho? Leonel acaba de volver de un viaje de negocios y quiere saber qué han hecho los diferentes miembros de su familia durante la última semana. ¿Cómo contestan? Forma oraciones completas con los siguiente elementos, usando el presente perfecto.

1. Pablo / leer / tres libros

_____

2. Teresa y Ángela / ver / una película nueva

_____

3. mamá y yo / escribirle / cartas a la familia

_____

4. yo / divertirse / con mis amigos

_____

5. tú / volver / de un viaje largo

_____

WB 10-24 | El romance de Ken y Barbie ¿Cuál es la historia de la relación entre Ken y Barbie? Forma oraciones recíprocas con los siguientes elementos. Recuerda que tienes que conjugar los verbos en el pretérito y usar los pronombres apropiados. Sigue el modelo.

Modelo   Ken y Barbie / presentarse / un día en la playa
Ken y Barbie se presentaron un día en la playa.

1. Ken y Barbie / conocerse / en Malibú

_____

2. ellos / mirarse / intensamente

_____

3. ellos / abrazarse / fuertemente

_____

4. ellos / enamorarse / inmediatamente

_____

5. ellos / casarse / en junio de ese año

_____

WB 10-25 | Miguel lo hace así ¿Cómo hace Miguel las cosas? Cambia los adjetivos a adverbios y escribe una oración completa para describir cómo hace Miguel las siguiente cosas.

1. leer el periódico / detenido *(careful)*

_____

2. hablar con las chicas / nervioso

_____

3. comer / rápido

_____

4. sacar buenas notas / fácil

_____

5. ir a fiestas / frecuente

_____

WB 10-26 | La rutina Arcelia describe su rutina diaria. Completa su descripción con el adverbio apropiado de la siguiente lista.

a veces   muchas veces   nunca   siempre   solamente   todos los días   una vez

1. _____ me despierto a las seis de la mañana porque tengo muchísimas cosas que hacer en un día típico. **2.** _____ tengo ganas de volver a dormirme, pero no puedo, así que me levanto en seguida. **3.** _____ los sábados y domingos puedo levantarme tarde, ya que son mis días de descanso. Cuando me levanto, me visto *(get dressed)* rápidamente y en seguida me voy corriendo a la universidad.

4. _____ voy a un café para tomar un cafecito, pero normalmente no tengo tiempo porque mi primera clase empieza a las siete y media.

5. _____ pensé que tenía tiempo para el café, pero no lo tenía. Llegué tarde a la clase y el profesor me regañó enfrente de todos. ¡Qué vergüenza!

Después de la clase como el desayuno. **6.** _____ pierdo el desayuno con mis amigos porque es casi la única oportunidad que tengo para descansar durante todo el día. Después de desayunar, voy a mis otras clases, y finalmente, a trabajar. Vuelvo a la casa a las nueve y media de la noche y **7.** _____ estoy cansada.

WB 10-27 | **¿Cómo lo hago?** La novia de Jorge está fuera del país y Jorge quiere mandarle un correo electrónico, pero no sabe hacerlo. Para ayudarlo, escribe las instrucciones para mandar un email, usando los adverbios de secuencia que aprendiste en tu libro de texto: **primero, luego, después, entonces** y **finalmente.**

_____ Te compras software para el email.

_____ Te sacas una cuenta electrónica de Internet.

_____ Le pides a tu novia su dirección electrónica.

_____ Le envías el mensaje.

_____ Puedes escribir el mensaje que quieres mandar.

1. _____

2. _____

3. _____

4. _____

5. _____

WB 10-28 | **¿El nuevo novio de Valeria?** Para saber cómo es este nuevo novio, completa cada oración con el pronombre relativo apropiado.

1. Es el chico _____ vive con su hermano.

2. Tiene ese coche viejo _____ siempre hace tanto ruido.

3. Valeria está loca porque no sabe _____ dice todo el mundo de él.

4. Creo que el chico con _____ salía antes era mucho más guapo.

1 | *El mundo del trabajo: Panamá*

VOCABULARIO Las profesiones y los oficios

WB 11-1 | Letras desordenadas Pon en orden las letras de los siguientes nombres de profesiones.

1. dabaogo _____
2. rloepuequ _____
3. narquebo _____
4. ótagarfof _____
5. enioringe _____
6. urisaqita _____
7. ostepridia _____
8. dorcanot _____

WB 11-2 | ¿Qué profesión es? Lee las siguiente descripciones y escribe el nombre de la profesión que describe.

1. Traduce textos de un idioma a otro: _____
2. Protege a los ciudadanos de una ciudad: _____
3. Puede arreglar el lavabo: _____
4. Diseña casas y edificios: _____
5. Escribe programas para computadoras: _____
6. Médico que cuida los dientes: _____
7. Supervisor en el lugar de trabajo: _____
8. Prepara comida en un restaurante: _____

ESTRUCTURA I Making statements about motives, intentions, and periods of time: *Por* vs. *para*

To learn more about **Por** and **Para**, go to Heinle iRadio at www.thomsonedu.com/spanish.

WB 11-3 | ¿*Por o para*? Lee las oraciones en la página 162 con las preposiciones **por** y **para**. Luego pon la letra de la razón por la que se usa **por** o **para** al lado de la oración.

a. in order to / for the purpose of	**g.** duration of time
b. during	**h.** cost
c. through	**i.** destination
d. employment	**j.** specific time
e. opinion	**k.** member of a group
f. on behalf of	

_____ **1.** Alicia tiene que estudiar para el examen.

_____ **2.** Claudio gana $40,00 por hora.

_____ **3.** Antonio sale para el trabajo a las seis.

_____ **4.** Antonio trabaja para Telefónica.

_____ **5.** Para Carmela, ser dentista es muy agradable.

_____ **6.** Julia iba a trabajar por su amiga ayer.

_____ **7.** Juan Carlos trabajó por treinta años.

_____ **8.** Compró el CD para Julieta.

_____ **9.** Para ser extranjera, Teresita habla español muy bien.

_____ **10.** Nidia necesita el artículo para el martes que viene.

WB 11-4 | Entrevista Ernesto es el jefe de una compañía y va a entrevistar a un candidato. Ayúdale con las preguntas. Rellena los espacios en blanco con **por** o **para.**

1. ¿ _____ cuántos años ha trabajado Ud.?

2. ¿ _____ qué compañías ha trabajado?

3. _____ Ud., ¿cuál es el mejor lugar en el mundo hispano _____ trabajar y vivir?

4. ¿Cree Ud. que es difícil _____ un norteamericano vivir y trabajar en un país extranjero?

5. ¿Cuánto dinero piensa Ud. ganar _____ hora?

6. ¿ _____ cuándo piensas comenzar el nuevo trabajo?

WB 11-5 | ¿Puedes ir? Tita y Sara hacen planes para ir de compras, pero Sara tiene que trabajar. Completa su conversación con **por** o **para.**

SARA: ¿Aló?

TITA: Hola, Sara, habla Tita. Oye, ¿quieres ir de compras hoy **1.** _____ la tarde?

SARA: Sí, me encantaría, pero hoy tengo que trabajar **2.** _____ Amanda. Está enferma hoy y no puede trabajar.

TITA: ¡Otra vez! Ésta es la tercera vez este mes. **3.** _____ ser una chica tan joven, está enferma muchísimo.

SARA: Ya lo sé. **4.** _____ mí ya es demasiado, pero ¿qué puedo hacer? Es mi hermanita.

TITA: Bueno, **5.** ¿_____ cuántas horas tienes que trabajar hoy?

SARA: Sólo dos o tres. **6.** ¿_____ qué no pasas **7.** _____ mi casa a las siete de la tarde?

TITA: A las siete va a haber mucho tráfico así que voy a salir **8.** _____ tu casa a las seis. ¿Sabes qué? ¿Va a estar allí Mónica?

SARA: No lo sé. ¿Qué quieres con Mónica?

TITA: Pues, mi hermano, Carlos, le compró algo **9.** _____ su cumpleaños, pero le da mucha vergüenza dárselo. Entonces, se lo voy a llevar yo.

SARA: ¡Ay, **10.** _____ Dios! ¡Esa Mónica tiene a todos los chicos pero locos de verdad!

VOCABULARIO La oficina, el trabajo y la búsqueda de un puesto

WB 11-6 | Una de estas cosas no es como las otras. Selecciona la palabra que no va con las otras de la lista.

1. _____
- **a.** fax
- **b.** fotocopiadora
- **c.** sueldo
- **d.** computadora

2. _____
- **a.** solicitud
- **b.** impresora
- **c.** candidato
- **d.** currículum

3. _____
- **a.** jubilarse
- **b.** puesto
- **c.** entrevista
- **d.** beneficios

4. _____
- **a.** reunión
- **b.** empresa
- **c.** sala de conferencias
- **d.** llenar

5. _____
- **a.** contratar
- **b.** correo electrónico
- **c.** solicitar
- **d.** entrevista

WB 11-7 | ¡Un buen trabajo! Carolina Corral le escribe un correo electrónico a su hermana, Tita, para decirle un poco sobre lo que está haciendo su hijo, Jorge. Completa la carta en la página 164 rellenando los espacios en blanco con una palabra apropiada de la siguiente lista. ¡OJO! Tienes que conjugar algunos de los verbos en el pretérito.

beneficios	llenar	correo electrónico
currículum	solicitud	jubilarse
llamar	contratar	puesto
reunirse	entrevista	tiempo completo
candidato	pedir un aumento	
empresa	sueldo	

Hola Tita:

Espero que estés bien *(you are well)* en todo. Aquí te cuento que mi querido Jorgito acaba de graduarse

de la universidad y ahora busca trabajo con una **1.** _____ internacional. La se-

mana pasada encontró un **2.** _____ con AT&T en el campo de telecomunicaciones.

Ya que las telecomunicaciones son su especialidad, Jorge va a ser un buen **3.** _____

para el trabajo. Jorge **4.** _____ a la compañía por teléfono y pidió una

5. _____.

   Se la mandaron inmediatamente y en seguida *(right away)* él la **6.** _____ y

la mandó de vuelta. Y, ¡ahora quieren hacerle una **7.** _____!

   Es un trabajo de **8.** _____, es decir, cinco días a la semana desde las ocho

de la mañana hasta las seis de la tarde. Tal vez va a ser difícil, pero la compañía ofrece muy buenos

9. _____. Le van a pagar los seguros médicos privados y le van a dar tres

semanas de vacaciones durante el primer año. Además, el **10.** _____ es relati-

vamente alto para un principiante *(beginner)*: ¡ofrecen 20.000 balboas al año! Jorge dice que después

de su primer año, si todo va bien, él puede **11.** _____. También dice que la per-

sona que antes hacía este trabajo acaba de **12.** _____ y él, al final de su carrera

de veinte años con la compañía, ganaba 60.000 balboas al año. La única desventaja del trabajo, para

mí, es que Jorge va a tener que viajar mucho. Pero, bueno, en esta época de tecnología, siempre puedo

mandarle algún **13.** _____ para estar en contacto con él.

   Jorge quiere prepararse bien, así que hoy va a **14.** _____ con su consejero y

él le va a ayudar a pulir *(polish)* su **15.** _____. Jorge quiere saber si ha incluido

toda la información necesaria porque sabe que es una parte muy importante de la presentación.

Jorge está súper preocupado porque quiere este trabajo, pero yo sé que AT&T lo va a

16. _____. Claro, es mi hijo, así que él ¡es perfecto! Bueno, Tita, ya te aviso si

tengo alguna noticia del trabajo.

Un abrazo fuerte y un besito, Carolina

ESTRUCTURA II
Expressing subjectivity and uncertainty: The subjunctive mood

To learn more about the **Subjunctive Mood**, go to Heinle iRadio at www.thomsonedu.
com/spanish.

WB 11-8 | El diario Tomás encontró el diario de Laura, su colega, y empezó a leerlo. ¿Qué
encontró en el diario? Para saberlo, lee los siguientes pensamientos de Laura. Nota que cada
oración usa el subjuntivo. Escribe el verbo que está en el subjuntivo y escoge la letra de la
razón por la que se usa en cada caso. Sigue el modelo. Al final, indica lo que descubre Tomás.

   Modelo   Quiero que Tomás me hable más.
               hable / a. (volición)

a. volition   **b.** negation   **c.** doubt   **d.** emotion

1. Dudo que la novia de Tomás lo quiera. _____

2. Siento que la novia de Tomás tenga otro novio. _____

3. Estoy muy contenta de que Tomás trabaje conmigo. _____

4. No hay otra mujer que conozca mejor a Tomás que yo. _____

5. Estoy muy triste que Tomás no sepa cómo es su novia. _____

6. El siquiatra recomienda que yo hable con Tomás sobre mis sentimientos. _____

7. Es imposible que yo le diga a Tomás cómo me siento. Tengo demasiado miedo. _____

8. _____ ¿Qué descubre Tomás al leer el diario de Laura?

a. que Laura va a jubilarse

b. que Laura va a divorciarse de su esposo

c. que a Laura no le gusta su trabajo

d. que Laura está enamorada de Tomás

WB 11-9 | Los consejos Después de descubrir el secreto de Laura, Tomás le pide consejos a su jefe. ¿Qué consejos le da? Selecciona el consejo más lógico en cada caso. Sigue el modelo.

Modelo *a.* **a.** Recomiendo que ya no hables con Laura en el trabajo.
b. Es necesario que consultes con el médico.

1. _____ **a.** Es necesario que consultes con la jefe de Laura.
b. Estoy contento que quieras ser arquitecto.

2. _____ **a.** Dudo que la fotocopiadora no funcione.
b. La compañía no permite que sus empleados tengan relaciones amorosas.

3. _____ **a.** Es probable que Laura cambie de opinión.
b. No creo que debas comprarle flores.

4. _____ **a.** Recomiendo que dejes de leer su diario.
b. No es cierto que la nueva candidata sea más bonita que Laura.

VOCABULARIO Las finanzas personales

WB 11-10 | Finanzas Escoge la palabra financiera descrita *(described)* en cada oración.

a. los gastos   e. la cuenta
b. el cajero automático   f. rebota
c. la factura   g. pedir un préstamo
d. el recibo   h. a plazos

1. _____ Es lo que las compañías te envían cada mes para cobrar los servicios que te dan, como el teléfono, la televisión por cable, la electricidad etc.

2. _____ Si necesitas dinero para comprar un coche puedes hacer esto.

3. _____ Si compras algo en una tienda, te dan este papel después de que les pagas.

4. _____ Si escribes un cheque y no tienes el dinero en tu cuenta bancaria, esto ocurre con tu cheque.

5. _____ Es el dinero que tienes que gastar cada mes.

WB 11-11 | Gemelos distintos Juan y Juana son gemelos, pero son muy distintos con respecto a sus hábitos financieros. Para saber cómo son diferentes, mira los dibujos y rellena los espacios en blanco con una palabra o verbo apropiado de la lista. Si es verbo, vas a tener que conjugarlo para usarlo.

a plazos   facturas   cajero automático   prestar   cuenta de ahorros
presupuesto   depositar   sacar   efectivo   tarjeta de crédito

JUANA

JUAN

a. Todos los días Juana **1.** _____ dinero en su **2.** _____ .

Todos los días Juan **3.** _____ dinero del **4.** _____ .

JUANA

JUAN

b. Juana compra poco y siempre paga en **1.** _____ . Sólo gasta lo que le permite su **2.** _____ .

Juan compra mucho y lo paga todo con su **3.** _____ .

JUANA

JUAN

c. Juana siempre le **1.** _____ dinero a Juan porque él nunca lo tiene.

Juan no puede pagar sus **2.** _____ en total. Siempre tiene que pagar **3.** _____ .

ESTRUCTURA III | Expressing desires and intentions: The present subjunctive with statements of volition

To learn more about the **Subjunctive Mood**, go to Heinle iRadio at www.thomsonedu. com/spanish.

WB 11-12 | Situaciones Tus amigos te piden ayuda con varias situaciones. Lee cada situación y escoge el consejo más lógico en cada caso.

1. _____ Un amigo quiere estudiar en Costa Rica el próximo año. El problema es que no ha ahorrado suficiente dinero y necesita 1.000 dólares más. ¿Qué sugieres que haga?
   a. Recomiendo que te levantes más temprano.
   b. Insito en que pidas un préstamo.
   c. Prohíbo que pagues tus facturas en los meses próximos.

2. _____ Una amiga tuya acaba de cortar con su novio. Dice que piensa en él todo el día y no sabe qué hacer. ¿Qué le recomiendas?
   a. Prefiero que le ofrezcas dinero por ser tu novio.
   b. Deseo que solicites un nuevo puesto de trabajo.
   c. Recomiendo que busques otro novio.

3. _____ Dos amigos tuyos necesitan un lugar donde vivir porque acaban de botarlos *(kick them out)* de su propio apartamento y ahora quieren vivir contigo. ¿Qué les recomiendas?
   a. Prefiero que comiencen a buscar apartamentos baratos.
   b. Deseo que saquen dinero del cajero automático.
   c. No quiero que se diviertan.

WB 11-13 | ¡Tantos consejos! Hoy Ramón va a dejar su trabajo y todos sus amigos quieren darle consejos. ¿Qué le dicen? Para saberlo, rellena los espacios en blanco con la forma apropiada del verbo en el **presente del subjuntivo.**

1. Antonia recomienda que Ramón le _____ (escribir) una carta a su jefe.

2. Tomás quiere que Ramón _____ (hablar) directamente con su jefe.

3. María Dolores prefiere que Ramón no _____ (venir) al trabajo hoy.

4. Carmen quiere que Ramón le _____ (dar) una semana más al jefe antes de dejar el puesto.

5. José insiste en que Ramón no _____ (dejar) el puesto y que simplemente le _____ (pedir) un aumento.

WB 11-14 | Marimandona Gloria es la jefe de una compañía y siempre les dice a sus empleados que hagan algo. Luz Consuelo le está contando a un amigo qué les dice su jefe. Forma oraciones completas con los elementos dados. ¡OJO! Tienes que usar el presente del subjuntivo en la frase subordinada. Sigue el modelo.

   Modelo   Gloria / querer / Juan Carlos y Antonio / traerle café / todas las mañanas
             Gloria quiere que Juan Carlos y Antonio le traigan café todas las mañanas.

1. Gloria / insistir en / todos los empleados / trabajar / diez horas al día

_____

2. Gloria / no permitir / Magaly y yo / usar / el correo electrónico

3. Gloria / prohibir / nosotros / hacerle / preguntas

_____

4. Gloria / no querer / yo / divertirme / durante las horas de trabajo

_____

5. Gloria / mandar / Alejandro / servirle / el almuerzo / todos los días

_____

WB 11-15 | Tertulia Estás en el café donde Cecilia, Felipe y otros amigos se reúnen todos los días. Como siempre, están charlando sobre su vida y los problemas del mundo. Cada uno expresa sus deseos y tú los escuchas. ¿Qué dicen? Rellena los espacios en blanco con la forma correcta de los verbos indicados. Tienes que decidir entre el presente del indicativo y el presente del subjuntivo.

1. Ellos _____ (insistir) en que la policía _____ (ser) más justa.

2. Felipe _____ (desear) que el presidente _____ (saber) más de las necesidades de la gente.

3. Felipe _____ (desear) que _____ (haber) más trabajos para todos.

4. Cecilia _____ (recomendar) que tú no _____ (dormirse) mientras hablan.

5. Ellos _____ (esperar) que todos nosotros _____ (ir) de vacaciones más a menudo.

6. Felipe y Cecilia _____ (preferir) que todos nosotros _____ (estar) felices.

7. Ellos _____ (querer) que nosotros no _____ (tener) que trabajar demasiado.

WB 11-16 | ¡Qué horror! Tere tiene que cuidar a su primo, un niño travieso *(rascal)*. Decide mandarle un email a su mamá, quien está trabajando en su oficina, para decirle lo que está haciendo su hijo. Rellena los espacios en blanco con la forma apropiada del verbo entre paréntesis. Tienes que decidir si necesitas usar el infinitivo o el presente del subjuntivo. **¡OJO!** Es necesario usar el subjuntivo sólo cuando hay un cambio de sujeto .

Hola Lupe,

Te cuento que ahora quiero 1. _____ (matar) a tu hijo. Manuel insiste en

no 2. _____ (acostarse) y no sé qué hacer. Deseo que Manuel

3. _____ (dejar) de jugar con sus juguetes porque ya es demasiado tarde, pero

prefiere que nosotros 4. _____ (jugar) más. De hecho, insiste en que nosotros

5. _____ (seguir) jugando. No deseo 6. _____ (ser) antipática,

pero te juro que ¡este niño me tiene loca! Espero que tú 7. _____ (poder) ayudarme.

Me interesa saber qué recomiendas que yo 8. _____ (hacer) con este niño travieso.

Por favor, ¡contéstame pronto!

Tere

BIENVENIDOS A PANAMÁ

En este segmento del video, vas a aprender un poco sobre Panamá y sobre la vida de sus ciudadanos. Los temas incluyen:

- el canal de Panamá
- la naturaleza
- los indígenas
- la Ciudad de Panamá

WB 11-17 | En el segmento del video vas a escuchar muchos cognados que pueden facilitar tu comprensión. Algunos de estos cognados aparecen aquí. Trata de pronunciar cada palabra o frase y luego empareja los cognados con su definición en inglés.

1. _____ marítimas
2. _____ labores
3. _____ cascadas
4. _____ planeta
5. _____ Carnaval
6. _____ palpitante

a. palpatating
b. planet
c. maritime
d. cascades / waterfalls
e. Carnival
f. labors / work

WB 11-18 | Después de ver el segmento del video, rellena los espacios en blanco con el cognado apropiado de la actividad **WB 11-17.**

1. El país es conocido internacionalmente por su canal, una de las vías _____ más importantes del mundo.

2. Miles de embarcaciones de todas partes del _____ pasan de un océano al otro en el Canal de Panamá.

3. Aquí habitan los indígenas kuna, conocidos por sus bellas _____ bordadas, sus molas.

4. La nueva ciudad de Panamá es una ciudad cosmopolita de mucha actividad económica internacional de día y de _____ actividad musical de noche.

5. Esto es bien evidente en la fiesta que todo panameño espera con anticipación: _____.

6. Tierra de volcanes y _____, de bosques y selvas, de paz y armonía.

WB 11-19 | Después de ver el segmento del video otra vez, selecciona la mejor respuesta a las siguientes preguntas.

1. _____ ¿Cuántos barcos *(ships)* pasan por el Canal de Panamá?
   a. millones
   b. cientos
   c. miles
   d. un billón

2. _____ ¿Dónde viven los indígenas kuna de Panamá?
   a. en la ciudad de Panamá
   b. en las islas de San Blas
   c. entre norte y Sudamérica
   d. en el desierto

3. _____ ¿Cómo se llama el arte de los kuna?
   a. molas
   b. bellas
   c. bordadas
   d. cunitas

4. _____ ¿Cuánto tiempo dura el Carnaval?
   a. una semana
   b. cuatro días
   c. un mes
   d. un fin de semana

¡A ESCRIBIR!

Strategy: Writing from an idea map

An idea map is a tool for organizing your ideas before you begin developing them in a composition. In this section you are going to use an idea map to write a paragraph about the personal qualities that make you an ideal employee. Using an idea map will help you organize your thoughts about this topic before you write about it.

Writing task: Writing about what makes you an ideal employee

Paso 1 Spend 10 minutes thinking about the personal qualities that make you a good employee. Write each of these qualities down on a piece of paper. Do not worry about grammar or spelling at this point. Just get your ideas on paper.

Paso 2 Try to categorize the ideas you have just written. For example, did you mention information about your character? about your professional experience? about your academic history? These categories can help you to organize your paragraph.

Paso 3 For each of your qualities, draw a line to a space on the paper where you can write an example that demonstrates this quality. For example, if you mentioned that you have studied in one of the best universities in the country, write the name of the university in the space. These examples will help form the content of your paragraph.

Paso 4 Look at the map you have drawn and write a sentence that summarizes all the information you have included. This will be the topic sentence of your paragraph. An example: **Tanto mi experiencia profesional como mi preparación académica me hacen el (la) empleado(a) ideal.**

Paso 5 Write your paragraph following the organization of your map.

Paso 6 After writing a first draft, review the grammar and spelling and then write a second draft below.

_____

_____

_____

_____

_____

_____

_____

_____

_____

_____

_____

_____

_____

_____

_____

_____

_____

_____

ATAJO 4.0

Functions: Expressing hopes and aspirations; Expressing intention
Vocabulary: Professions, trades, working conditions
Grammar: Verbs: present; Verbs: subjunctive

Autoprueba

VOCABULARIO

WB 11-20 | **¿Qué debe hacer?** Ernesto está un poco confundido sobre su futura carrera. Quiere hacerlo todo. Ahora está describiendo lo que le gusta hacer. Para cada una de sus descripciones, escribe el nombre de la profesión que describe.

1. Me gusta dibujar y diseñar edificios.

   _____

2. Me gusta cortar pelo.

   _____

3. Me encantan los números.

   _____

4. Quiero escribir artículos interesantes.

   _____

5. Me interesa escribir programas de software.

   _____

6. Quiero enseñar en una escuela.

   _____

7. Me encantan las lenguas.

   _____

8. Quiero proteger a la gente.

   _____

9. Me interesa analizar los problemas que tiene la gente.

   _____

10. Me fascinan los dientes.

   _____

WB 11-21 | **Solicitando trabajo** Juan Antonio trabaja para un servicio de empleos. Hoy le está explicando a Ana María los pasos que tiene que seguir para conseguir un buen puesto. Para saber lo que dice, rellena los espacios en blanco con la palabra apropiada de la lista.

beneficios	solicitar	imprimir	empleados
entrevista	contratar	sueldo	llamar
proyectos	impresora	despedir	tiempo parcial
computadora	solicitud	jubilarte	
fotocopias	currículum	tiempo completo	

Si vas a **1.** _____ un puesto, lo primero que tienes que hacer es

actualizar *(to update)* tu **2.** _____. Tienes que escribirlo en la

3. _____ e **4.** _____ el documento en un papel muy

fino. Recomiendo una **5.** _____ laser. Después, tienes que hacer muchas

6. _____ porque lo vas a mandar a muchas compañías.

Si encuentras un trabajo que te interesa, tienes que pedir una **7.** _____ de

la compañía. Creo que debes **8.** _____ por teléfono para pedirla. Así vas a

tener tu primera oportunidad de impresionar a los empleados de la compañía. Si les caes

bien, pueden ofrecerte una **9.** _____ inmediatamente.

Si te invitan a la compañía, vístete bien. Lleva un traje azul o negro. Ese día te van a explicar

mejor el puesto y los **10.** _____ que vas a tener que llevar a cabo.

También te van a describir los **11.** _____ que les ofrecen a los

12. _____. Ése no es el momento de hablar del **13.** _____.

Si la compañía decide que te quiere **14.** _____, te lo van a decir y

entonces puedes hablar de dinero.

Antes de aceptar el trabajo, tienes que establecer si es un puesto de

15. _____ o de **16.** _____. También vas a querer

hablar más de los beneficios. Vas a querer saber cuál es la edad para **17.** _____

, y vas a querer saber qué seguros ofrecen si te tienen que **18.** _____.

WB 11-22 | **Consejos financieros** Vas a comprar un coche nuevo y tus padres quieren darte
algunos consejos. ¿Qué te dicen? Rellena los espacios en blanco con la palabra apropiada.
Si es un verbo, tienes que conjugarlo y tienes que decidir entre el infinitivo y el presente de
subjuntivo.

a plazos   cuenta de ahorros   prestar   ahorrar   depositar   presupuesto

cajero automático   en efectivo   sacar   cheques   facturas   tarjeta de crédito

Primero, tienes que **1.** _____ mucho dinero. Para hacerlo, recomendamos

que **2.** _____ dinero en tu **3.** _____ todas las

semanas. También, recomendamos que no **4.** _____ dinero del

5. _____ todos los días. Es mejor escribirte un **6.** _____

y sólo gastar el dinero que sabes que puedes gastar.

Claro, esperamos que no uses tu **7.** _____. Debes pagar todo con tus

8. _____ porque así al fin del mes no vas a recibir **9.** _____

que te espanten *(frighten you)*. Para comprar el coche, nosotros te queremos

10. _____ el dinero. Así puedes pagar **11.** _____ y no

vas a tener que pagar **12.** _____ y perder dinero en interés.

ESTRUCTURAS

WB 11-23 | **De vacaciones** Marta ha estado de vacaciones y ahora ha vuelto a su oficina. Completa su conversación con Elena. Rellena los espacios en blanco con las preposiciones **por** o **para.**

MARTA: ¿Sabes qué, Elena? La semana pasada estuve en un crucero y pasamos

        1. _____ el canal de Panamá. ¡Fue fantástico! Regresé anoche

        2. _____ la tarde.

ELENA: ¡Que bueno, Marta! **3.** ¿_____ cuánto tiempo estuviste en el crucero?

MARTA: Fue un crucero de catorce días. No te diste cuenta de que yo no estaba aquí.

ELENA: Ay, Marta, lo siento, pero no. Tuve que preparar un informe **4.** _____ el

        jefe y él lo quería **5.** _____ hoy. No noté nada porque estaba trabajando

        como loca.

MARTA: Ay, sí, Héctor, el jefe horrible. **6.** _____ ser padre de dos hijos tan

        simpáticos, es un hombre demasiado antipático. Pues, dime, ¿lo terminaste?

ELENA: Sí, casi. Sólo hace falta sacar una fotocopia, pero la máquina está descompuesta.

        ¿No hay otra **7.** _____ aquí?

MARTA: Sí, en la oficina de Juan. Pero antes de irte, compré este regalito **8.** _____

        ti. Si no te gusta, selecciona otro. Compré un montón de cosas en el Caribe

        9. _____ muy poco dinero.

ELENA: Bueno, gracias. Pues, ahora, ¿qué vas a hacer?

MARTA: Me siento un poco cansada todavía. Creo que voy **10.** _____ la casa

        para descansar. No le digas nada a Héctor.

ELENA: No, no le digo nada. ¡Adiós!

MARTA: Chao.

WB 11-24 | El amor y los negocios Mientras trabajas en la computadora de un colega de trabajo, encuentras el siguiente correo electrónico que alguien le escribió a un hombre que trabaja en la compañía rival. Selecciona los verbos apropiados de la lista para acabar el correo. Conjuga los verbos en el presente del subjuntivo.

divertirse   enamorarse   escribir   ir   llamar

mandar   mirar   pensar   perder   tener

Querido amor:

Gracias por tu mensaje. También he pensado mucho en ti. Quiero que me 1. _____ más

emails y que me 2. _____ por teléfono a veces. Espero que 3. _____ un

buen día hoy, y que no te 4. _____ ningún otra mujer. También prefiero que tú no

5. _____ en otras mujeres. ¡Sabes que soy muy celosa! Sabes que te quiero mucho y

espero con todo el corazón que tú 6. _____ de mí. Sé que tu jefe no quiere que sus

empleados 7. _____ mucho tiempo con los emails, pero te pido que me

8. _____ por lo menos uno al día y así voy a saber que estás pensando en mí. Quiero

invitarte a salir el viernes que viene. Quiero que nosotros 9. _____ al nuevo restaurante

caribeño y que 10. _____ mucho.

Espero verte muy pronto.

Con todo mi cariño,

Paula

WB 11-25 | Entre amigos Completa la siguiente conversación entre dos colegas de trabajo. Rellena los espacios en blanco con una forma apropiada del verbo indicado. Tienes que decidir entre el infinitivo y el presente de subjuntivo.

LUIS: Tengo ganas de descansar un poco, Jorge. Quiero 1. _____ (salir) a

tomar algo. ¿Quieres 2. _____ (venir) conmigo al Coyote Pub?

JORGE: No, prefiero que nosotros 3. _____ (seguir) trabajando un poco más.

Sólo nos queda una hora más.

LUIS: Tienes razón, pero quiero que 4. _____ (trabajar) rápidamente para

así terminar temprano.

JORGE: Bueno, pero después de terminar no quiero 5. _____ (ir) al Coyote.

Mi esposa insiste en que yo siempre 6. _____ (volver) a casa después

del trabajo. Así que prefiero que tú me 7. _____ (acompañar) a mi casa

para tomar algo. ¿Qué te parece?

LUIS: Pues, está bien. Entonces te acompaño.

El medio ambiente: Costa Rica

VOCABULARIO La geografía rural y urbana

WB 12-1 | Palabras revueltas Usa las pistas y pon las letras en orden para revelar las palabras de geografía rural y urbana.

1. Lugar donde usas tu carro: acaterrer _____

2. La subes y bajas: licona _____

3. Un ritmo rápido de la vida: dolarecea _____

4. Mucha población en una zona pequeña: andes _____

WB 12-2 | ¿Una vida tranquila? Completa los perfiles *(profiles)* de las siguientes personas, rellenando los espacios en blanco con las palabras apropiadas de la lista.

bosque   colinas   rascacielos   cultiva   basura   finca

transporte público   agricultor   tierra   metrópolis   arroyo   ruido   bellos

1. Juan Carlos es _____. Trabaja en el campo cultivando la

   _____.

2. María Teresa vive cerca de Chicago. No tiene que batallar el tráfico porque usa el sistema

   de _____, pero sí tiene que aguantar *(put up with)* el

   _____ y la _____, es decir, los problemas típicos

   de la vida en la _____.

3. Manuel Antonio y Ana Lisa viven en una _____ donde tienen muchos

   animales. Desde la ventana de la casa pueden ver toda la naturaleza del lugar. Al lado de

   la casa pasa un _____ donde se bañan en los días calurosos *(warm)*.

   Los fines de semana, ellos montan a bicicleta y andan por las _____

   altas donde se cultiva café.

4. Francisco Javier es accionista y vive en un apartamento en un _____

   de la cuidad de Nueva York. El edificio está al lado de un parque que tiene árboles muy

   _____. El apartamento tiene un balcón donde él

   _____ flores.

WB 12-3 | Geografía Lee las pistas y escribe la palabra a que se refiere.

1. La causa de mucho ruido urbano: el _____

2. Cuerpo de agua parecido a un río: el _____

3. Demasiada gente concentrada en una metrópolis: la _____

4. Lo que ya no se usa y se tira: la _____

5. Echar agua a las plantas: _____

6. La _____ del Amazonas

7. Sin problemas o complicaciones: _____

8. Autobuses, metros y trenes son formas del _____ público.

9. Lugar donde se producen varios productos: una _____

10. Lugar donde se cultivan plantas: una _____

11. Edificios altísimos: los _____

12. La persona que cultiva la tierra: el _____

13. La persona que trabaja en el campo: el _____

14. Destinación popular para una luna de miel: la _____

ESTRUCTURA I Expressing emotion and opinions: Subjunctive following verbs of emotion, impersonal expressions, and *ojalá*

To learn more about the **Subjunctive,** go to Heinle iRadio at www.thomsonedu.com/spanish.

WB 12-4 | Emociones ¿Qué opinan los estudiantes de la clase de la profesora Ramírez sobre el medio ambiente y el futuro? Selecciona la forma apropiada del verbo entre paréntesis.

1. Espero que los agricultores (cultivan / cultiven) más hierbas naturales.

_____

2. Es importante que todos (conservan / conserven) los recursos naturales.

_____

3. Me preocupa que nosotros no (tratamos / tratemos) bien la tierra.

_____

4. Es imperdonable que (hay / haya) tanta basura en las calles.

_____

WB 12-5 | Consejería Trabajas para un consejero y hoy te pide que le ayudes con los consejos que les va a dar a sus clientes. Selecciona el consejo más lógico para cada caso.

1. _____ Carlos quiere visitar un lugar bello y tranquilo.
  a. Es necesario que vaya al bosque de Monteverde.
  b. Es mejor que visite la metrópolis.

2. _____ Alicia busca una alternativa al carro porque no le gusta el tráfico.
  a. Es importante que deje de trabajar.
  b. Es lógico que tome el transporte público.

3. _____ A Adolfo y Érika les preocupa que no lleven una vida tranquila.
   a. Es posible que tengan miedo de cultivar plantas.
   b. Es necesario que no trabajen tanto.

4. _____ A Silvia le molesta que sus vecinos tiren tanta basura a la calle.
   a. Es importante que se queje del problema con sus vecinos.
   b. Es ridículo que le moleste la basura.

WB 12-6 | La primera visita a Costa Rica ¿Qué piensan Luis y Ana de Costa Rica después de su primer día en el país? Completa su conversación con la forma apropiada del presente del subjuntivo del verbo entre paréntesis.

ANA: ¡Es increíble este país! ¿No te parece, Luis?

LUIS: Sí, Ana. ¡Qué bueno que nosotros **1.** _____ (estar) aquí y no en Atlanta!

ANA: Me alegro de que el lugar **2.** _____ (ser) tan bonito y tranquilo.

LUIS: Tranquilo, sí. Es increíble que acá en San José, la capital, no **3.** _____ (haber) mucho tráfico ni mucho ruido.

ANA: Es cierto. Me sorprende a mí que en un lugar tan grande, la ciudad no **4.** _____ (tener) muchos problemas de sobrepoblación, como la contaminación, el tráfico, la basura, etcétera.

LUIS: De acuerdo. Es muy interesante eso porque vivimos en una ciudad más pequeña pero nos quejamos siempre de que la gente no **5.** _____ (respetar) el medio ambiente. Es una lástima que todo el mundo no **6.** _____ (poder) ser como Costa Rica.

ANA: Bueno, Luis, es imposible que todo el mundo **7.** _____ (ajustarse) *(to adjust itself)* al modelo de Costa Rica. Pero de todas formas, sería *(it would be)* una situación ideal.

LUIS: Pues, sí. Oye, mañana es necesario que nosotros **8.** _____ (hacer) el tour por el bosque nuboso Monteverde. ¿Está bien?

ANA: Sí, pero, ¿por qué es necesario hacerlo mañana?

LUIS: Pues, mañana es viernes, y si no lo hacemos mañana es posible que el sábado no **9.** _____ (ir) a poder hacerlo porque va a haber mucha gente.

ANA: Tienes razón, pero entonces es importante que tú **10.** _____ (llamar) ahora para hacer la reserva.

LUIS: Bueno, la voy a hacer ahora mismo.

WB 12-7 | Una reunión de Greenpeace Estás en una reunión de Greenpeace y todos los miembros están expresando sus opiniones sobre varios temas importantes. Para saber lo que dicen, forma oraciones con los elementos dados. Recuerda que solamente los verbos en la claúsula subordinada van a estar en el presente del subjuntivo.

> Modelo   Yo / sentir / algunas de nuestras actividades / ser radicales.
> *Yo siento que algunas de nuestras actividades sean radicales.*

1. Nosotros / tener miedo de / nuestros esfuerzos / no tener éxito / en este caso

   _____

2. Javier / esperar / nuestro grupo / conservar / el medio ambiente

   _____

3. Ojalá / el gobierno / nos apoyar

   _____

4. Es una lástima / las grandes compañías / no hacer / más inversiones «verdes»

   _____

5. Es ridículo / la gente / tener miedo / de nosotros

   _____

6. Nosotros / sentir / mucha gente / no entender / los objetivos de Greenpeace

   _____

VOCABULARIO La conservación y la explotación

WB 12-8 | Problemas y soluciones Identifica cuáles son problemas ambientales y cuáles son soluciones. Pon las letras con su categoría correcta.

Problemas ambientales: _____

Soluciones: _____

   a. la destrucción de la capa de ozono

   b. explotar la energía solar

   c. el desperdicio

   d. la contaminación del aire

   e. reciclar productos de plástico, metal, vidrio *(glass)* y papel

   f. la reforestación

   g. desarrollar métodos alternativos de transporte público

   h. la destrucción de los bosques

   i. la escasez de recursos naturales

   j. acabar con la contaminación de las grandes fábricas

Nombre _____ Fecha _____

WB 12-9 | Una clase de ecología Jorge acaba de tomar una clase de ecología y dice que la clase le ha cambiado la vida. ¿Cómo ha cambiado Jorge? Completa el siguiente párrafo con la palabra apropiada de la lista para saberlo.

capa de ozono   escasez   reciclar   conservar   medio ambiente   recursos naturales

contaminación   naturaleza   resolver   energía solar   proteger   transporte público

Antes de tomar la clase de ecología yo nunca pensaba en la **1.** _____. Nunca me preocupaban los problemas del **2.** _____ como la **3.** _____ de petróleo o la destrucción de la **4.** _____. Sin embargo, en la clase aprendí que cada persona tiene que **5.** _____ nuestros **6.** _____ y que tenemos que **7.** _____ el aire y la tierra. Ahora sé que tengo que hacer mi parte para **8.** _____ nuestros problemas ambientales. Voy a **9.** _____ todos los productos de plástico y de papel que uso en mi casa para evitar el desperdicio. También, voy a tratar de usar **10.** _____ para calentar mi piscina. Finalmente, siempre que sea posible, voy a tomar el autobús o cualquier otra forma de **11.** _____ para así no contribuir a la **12.** _____ del aire. Sé que yo solo no puedo cambiar el mundo, pero en la clase aprendí que puedo hacer mi parte para cambiarlo.

ESTRUCTURA II

Expressing doubts or uncertainty and hypothesizing: The subjunctive with verbs or expressions of doubt and uncertainty and adjective clauses

To learn more about the **Subjunctive,** go to Heinle iRadio at www.thomsonedu.com/spanish.

WB 12-10 | ¿Qué hacemos ahora? Luis y Ana todavía están en Costa Rica y están planeando cómo quieren pasar los próximos días de vacaciones. Para saber lo que dicen, completa su conversación con la forma apropiada de los verbos entre paréntesis. **¡OJO!** Tienes que decidir si el verbo debe estar en el presente del indicativo subjuntivo.

LUIS: Ana, mañana creo que nosotros **1.** _____ (deber) ir al parque nacional Volcán Poás. Tomás y María también van mañana. ¿Qué te parece?

ANA: Bueno, no pienso que ellos **2.** _____ (ir) mañana. Me dijeron que iban a otro lugar. Pienso que **3.** _____ (ser) mejor ir a Puntarenas mañana. Allí es donde está el parque nacional Palo Verde.

LUIS: No creo que **4.** _____ (estar) allí el Palo Verde. En Puntarenas pienso que **5.** _____ (poder) visitar las playas y tal vez el parque de Manuel Antonio.

ANA: Ay, Manuel Antonio. Sí, lo quiero ver. No creo que **6.** _____ (quedar) muy lejos del hotel La Mariposa, ¿verdad?

LUIS: Es cierto que La Mariposa **7.** _____ (estar) al lado del parque. Pero, bueno… ¿Qué hacemos, entonces?

ANA: Mañana es lunes y es dudoso que **8.** _____ (haber) mucha gente en cualquier lugar, así que todo depende de ti.

LUIS: Como no estamos seguros que Tomás y María **9.** _____ (visitar) el Volcán Poás mañana, ¿por qué no los llamamos y así averiguamos? Si van mañana, los podemos acompañar.

ANA: Pienso que **10.** _____ (ser) una buena idea.

WB 12-11 | **¡Qué preciosidad!** Luis y Ana decidieron ir al parque nacional Manuel Antonio y ahora están comentando el viaje y el lugar. Para saber lo que dicen, completa su conversación con la forma correcta de los verbos entre paréntesis. **¡OJO!** Tienes que decidir si los verbos deben estar en el presente del indicativo subjuntivo.

LUIS: No creo que el viaje a Quepos **1.** _____ (pasar) rápidamente.

ANA: Yo creo que nosotros **2.** _____ (tardar) demasiado tiempo en llegar.

LUIS: María y Tomás piensan que los titís *(squirrel monkeys)* **3.** _____ (venir) a jugar en la playa de Manuel Antonio.

ANA: Yo dudo que los titís **4.** _____ (venir) a jugar en la playa.

LUIS: Yo creo que **5.** _____ (haber) más de 600 tipos de aves en el parque de Manuel Antonio.

ANA: No es cierto que **6.** _____ (haber) tantos aves en ese lugar.

LUIS: No estoy seguro que el parque **7.** _____ (estar) abierto toda la noche.

ANA: Es imposible que el parque **8.** _____ (cerrar) temprano.

WB 12-12 | **Más planes** Ahora Ana y Luis están planeando un viaje al Volcán Poás. Para saber lo que dicen, completa su conversación con la frase más lógica. **¡OJO!** Antes de empezar, repasa el uso del subjuntivo en las frases adjetivales en tu libro de texto.

1. Tenemos que buscar el autobús _____.
   a. que va a Poás
   b. que dure por lo menos tres horas
   c. que sea muy barato

2. Queremos un autobús _____.
   a. que es muy barato
   b. que dure por lo menos tres horas
   c. que pueda hacer el viaje de San José a Poás

3. Es mejor alquilar un coche _____.
   a. que dura cuatro horas
   b. que pueda hacer el viaje de San José a Poás
   c. que es muy barato

4. Tomás tiene un coche _____.
   a. que dure por lo menos tres horas
   b. que vaya directamente a Poás
   c. que puede hacer el viaje de San José a Poás

5. Podemos tomar ese servicio de taxi _____.
   a. que es muy barato
   b. que dure por lo menos tres horas
   c. que vaya directamente a Poás

6. En el hotel no conocen ningún servicio de taxi _____.
   a. que es muy barato
   b. que sea muy barato
   c. que puede hacer el viaje de San José a Poás

7. Necesitamos buscar un tour del parque _____.
   a. que dure por lo menos tres horas
   b. que vaya directamente a Poás
   c. que dura cuatro horas

WB 12-13 | Lo que quieran ¿Cómo es la vida de Andrea y sus amigos y cómo quieren que sea? Para saberlo, forma oraciones con los elementos dados. **¡OJO!** Tienes que decidir si los verbos deben estar en el indicativo o el subjuntivo. Sigue el modelo.

   Modelo   Andrea / querer vivir / en una ciudad / no tener contaminación
            Andrea quiere vivir en una ciudad que no tenga contaminación.

1. Carmen / tener / una casa / estar en la ciudad

_____

2. Carmen y Andrea / buscar / compañeros de casa / ser simpáticos

_____

3. Alberto / tener / un coche / usar / poca gasolina

_____

4. Ramón / necesitar / un trabajo / pagar / mucho dinero

_____

BIENVENIDOS A COSTA RICA

En este segmento del video, vas a aprender un poco sobre Costa Rica y sobre la vida de sus ciudadanos. Los temas incluyen:

- la geografía
- la ecología
- la artesanía
- la flora y la fauna

WB 12-14 | En el segmento del video, vas a escuchar muchos cognados que pueden facilitar comprensión. Algunos de estos cognados aparecen aquí. Trata de pronunciar cada palabra o frase y luego empareja los cognados con su definición en inglés.

1. _____ multicolores   **a.** geometric designs

2. _____ exóticas   **b.** multicolored

3. _____ pintoresco   **c.** picturesque

4. _____ fachadas   **d.** exotic

5. _____ diseños geométricos   **e.** complex

6. _____ compleja   **f.** façades *(fronts)*

WB 12-15 | Después de ver el segmento del video, rellena los espacios en blanco con el cognado apropiado de la actividad **WB 12-14.**

1. Costa Rica, un pequeño país centroamericano, tiene una geografía _____.

2. Tiene ríos, montañas y valles y una gran variedad de flora y de fauna

   _____.

3. En la provincia de Alajuela está el _____ pueblo agrícola de Sarchí,

   famoso en todo el mundo por sus carretas _____ de madera, símbolo de la

   artesanía costarricense.

4. Según la leyenda, un campesino decidió pintar su carreta con alegres

   _____ y colores brillantes.

5. Se ve reflejado el orgullo que tienen los ciudadanos de su fama artística en los letreros,

   las murallas, en las _____ de los edificios.

WB 12-16 | Después de ver el segmento del video otra vez, selecciona la mejor respuesta a las siguientes preguntas.

1. _____ ¿Qué han hecho los costarricenses para conservar su naturaleza?
   a. Han construido muchos rascacielos.
   b. Han establecido áreas protegidas.
   c. Han promocionado más ecoturismo.
   d. Han aumentado el transporte público.

2. _____ ¿De qué pueblo son las famosas carretas?
   a. Sarchí   **c.** San José
   b. Alajuela   **d.** Guácima

3. _____ ¿Para qué se usan las carretas hoy en día?
   a. como transporte público   **c.** para hacer carreras
   b. para estudiar geometría   **d.** para representar la artesanía local

4. _____ ¿Qué se puede ver en Guácima?
  a. las mariposas
  b. las tortugas
  c. las carretas
  d. los rascacielos

¡A ESCRIBIR!

Strategy: Making your writing persuasive

Writers often try to convince readers to understand or adopt particular points of view.

Persuasive writing is used by writers of editorials, by political figures, and often by professionals such as attorneys, medical personnel, educators, and reviewers or critics. In this section, you will write an essay in which you try to convince your reader of your point of view regarding a particular environmental issue. The following words and phrases will allow you to connect your ideas in this type of composition.

To express opinions . . .		*To show contrast . . .*	
creo que	*I believe*	**pero**	*but*
pienso que	*I think*	**aunque**	*although*
en mi opinión	*in my opinion*	**por otro lado**	*on the other hand*

To support opinions . . .		*To summarize . . .*	
primero	*first*	**por eso**	*therefore*
una razón	*one reason*	**finalmente**	*finally*
por ejemplo	*for example*	**en conclusión**	*in conclusion*

Task: Writing a persuasive essay

Paso 1 Form your opinion about one of the following topics (one that you didn't select in your textbook).

- El problema global más grande
- La mejor manera de resolver los problemas del mundo
- Si es justo mantener los animales en los zoológicos
- Si el gobierno debe permitir la manipulación genética

Paso 2 On a separate sheet of paper write a sentence that demonstrates your opinion about the topic you selected. Then write two to three reasons that support your opinion. Finally, write your essay. Remember that the essay must include:

- Introductory statement of your opinion
- Reasons in favor of your opinion, along with specific examples where possible
- Conclusion—a summary of your opinion.

Paso 3 After writing the first draft, revise the content and check the grammar. Try to incorporate several of the expressions you learned in this chapter to express your opinion. If you use these phrases, decide whether they require the indicative or the subjunctive. When you are finished, write your final draft here.

_____

_____

_____

_____

_____

_____

_____

_____

_____

_____

_____

_____

_____

_____

_____

_____

_____

_____

_____

ATAJO 4.0

Functions: Persuading; Expressing an opinion; Agreeing and disagreeing; Comparing and contrasting

Vocabulary: Animals; Automobile; Geography; Means of transportation

Grammar: Verbs: present; Verbs: subjunctive

Autoprueba

VOCABULARIO

WB 12-17 | **La geografía rural y urbana** Completa los espacios en blanco con las palabras apropiadas de las listas.

acelerado   recogen   basura   ruido   bella   sobrepoblación   contaminación

tráfico   medio ambiente   transporte público   metrópolis

a. La Ciudad de Nueva York es una de las **1.** _____ más conocidas en

todo el mundo. Como en cualquier otra ciudad grande, el ritmo de la vida es muy

2. _____ en Nueva York y allí es común encontrar problemas asociados con

la **3.** _____. Estos problemas incluyen el **4.** _____, el

5. _____ y la **6.** _____ del aire. Sin embargo, la ciudad tiene

un sistema de **7.** _____ que facilita el movimiento de gente y también pro-

tege el **8.** _____. Para ser una ciudad tan grande, no está demasiado sucia.

La gente no arroja mucha **9.** _____ a las calles y hay muchas personas que

la **10.** _____ cuando alguien lo hace. A pesar de ser grande, es una ciudad

11. _____.

arroyos   regar   campesinos   tranquila   cultivar   colinas

b. A diferencia de la vida urbana, la vida rural es bastante **1.** _____, pero es

todavía bastante dura. Los **2.** _____ trabajan desde muy temprano de la

mañana. Sus trabajos incluyen **3.** _____ la tierra, **4.** _____

las plantas y atender a los animales. Sin embargo, las zonas rurales pueden ser muy pin-

torescas. Las **5.** _____ y los **6.** _____ ayudan a crear un am-

biente bastante agradable para trabajar, vivir y jugar.

capa de ozono   explotar   desarrollar   petróleo   desperdicio   reciclar   destrucción

recursos naturales   energía solar   reforestar   escasez   resolver

c. Tanto en las zonas urbanas como en las zonas rurales hay problemas ecológicos que hay que

1. _____ para proteger el medio ambiente. Si no hacemos algo rápidamente,

vamos a acabar todos los **2.** _____, como el **3.** _____. Algunas

soluciones incluyen **4.** _____ los bosques, preservar la **5.** _____

y **6.** _____ programas para limpiar el aire. También es importante

7. _____ otras formas de energía como la **8.** _____. Cada

individuo puede hacer su parte para evitar el **9.** _____ y la

10. _____ de la naturaleza. Por ejemplo, todos pueden **11.** _____

las botellas, latas (cans) y papeles que usan en la casa. Si todos hacen su parte, no vamos a

tener que hablar de la **12.** _____ de los recursos importantes.

WB 12-18 | Entre amigos Completa la siguiente conversación usando apropiadamente el infinitivo o el subjuntivo de los verbos entre paréntesis.

JORGE: Me alegro de que nosotros **1.** _____ (estar) en Costa Rica otra

vez. Me gusta **2.** _____ (poder) explorar las selvas y ver todas

las especies de animales.

LUIS: Sí, creo que es bueno **3.** _____ (venir) a Costa Rica cada año,

pero siento que Moni y Alicia no **4.** _____ (estar) aquí con

nosotros.

JORGE: ¿Cómo? ¡Es ridículo que tú **5.** _____ (decir) eso! Es mejor que

las novias no nos **6.** _____ (acompañar) en estos viajes.

LUIS: ¡Jorge! Me sorprende que **7.** _____ (pensar) así. Creo que es una

lástima que Moni y Alicia no **8.** _____ (ir) a poder disfrutar de

la belleza de Costa Rica.

JORGE: Bueno, Luis, cálmate. Quiero mucho a mi novia. Pero también creo que es

importante que los hombres **9.** _____ (tener) su tiempo libre,

¿no? Y otra cosa: ojalá que esta conversación **10.** _____ (ser)

secreto nuestro, ¿eh?

WB 12-19 | Hablando del viaje Carmen y Tere están hablando del viaje que van a tomar a Costa Rica. Para saber lo que dicen, forma oraciones usando los siguientes elementos. Tienes que determinar si los verbos deben estar conjugados en el presente de indicativo o en el presente de subjuntivo.

1. TERE: yo / creer / estas vacaciones / ser / excelentes

CARMEN: sí, pero yo / dudar / David / querer venir / este año

TERE: _____

CARMEN: _____

2. TERE: Gabriela / no estar segura / el hotel / ser / bueno

CARMEN: yo / estar segura / todos los hoteles / ir a ser / muy buenos

TERE: _____

CARMEN: _____

3. TERE: en San José nosotros / tener que buscar / un restaurante / servir / gallo pinto

(Costa Rican dish of rice, beans, and cilantro)

CARMEN: yo / conocer / un buen restaurante / servir / gallo pinto

TERE: _____

CARMEN: _____

4. TERE: yo / querer visitar / una reserva biológica / tener muchas especies exóticas

CRMEN: Manuel Antonio / ser una reserva preciosa / tener todo tipo de animal exótico

TERE: _____

CARMEN: _____

El mundo del espectáculo: Perú y Ecuador

VOCABULARIO Programas y películas

WB 13-1 | ¡Vamos a ver! Lee las pistas y escribe las palabras relacionadas con la programación y las películas.

1. El lugar donde ves una película es el _____.

2. ESPN es un _____ de televisión.

3. «The Office» es una _____.

4. Para informarte sobre lo que ha pasado durante el día, ves las _____.

5. «The Oprah Winfrey Show» es un programa de _____.

6. Los _____ son programación, cuyo objetivo es el de vender productos.

7. Samuel L. Jackson hace muchas películas de _____.

8. Una película en otro idioma es una película _____.

9. «Days of Our Lives» es una _____.

10. «Jeopardy» es un programa de _____.

WB 13-2 | Teleprogramas Estás viendo el guía de programación. Lee cada descripción y luego identifica el tipo de programa o de película que van a poner en televisión. Sigue el modelo.

> Modelo   La periodista Carmen Rico Godoy preparará en el estudio-cocina alguna de sus recetas preferidas.
> *el programa educativo*

1. En un futuro próximo, la gran astronave comercial «Nostromo» se dirige a la Tierra tras una larga ausencia, transportando un cargamento de minerales extraterrestres.

   _____

2. Desde llegar a convertirse en la estrella de un circo hasta dedicarse a gondolero en Venecia, el oso Yogui y sus amigos, Bu-Bu y Cindy, viven sus aventuras en el parque Jellystone.

   _____

3. La misma noche en que una nueva víctima de Jack el Destripador es encontrada, un hombre alquila una habitación en casa de los señores Burton.

   _____

4. Transmisión de un partido de fútbol entre la selección joven peruana, actual subcampeona del mundo, y su homóloga danesa.

   _____

5. Comprueba científicamente que el hombre alcanza la plenitud física a los veinte años, que se mantiene en buena forma durante una década y que a los treinta años comienza el declive físico.

   _____

6. El meteorólogo José Antonio Maldonado ofrece la predicción del tiempo para las próximas horas, tanto en nuestro país como en el resto de Europa.

_____

7. El coronel Thursday llega a Fort Apache para hacerse cargo del mando. Fort Apache es un puesto avanzado en la frontera de Arizona, cuyos oficiales y soldados han luchado mucho contra los indios.

_____

ESTRUCTURA I | Talking about anticipated actions: Subjunctive with purpose and time clauses

To learn more about the **Subjunctive,** go to Heinle iRadio at www.thomsonedu.com/spanish.

WB 13-3 | ¿Vamos o no vamos? Ana y Julia están conversando sobre si van a ir al cine con Antonio y Tomás o no. Completa su conversación seleccionando la conjunción más lógica en cada caso.

ANA: Julia, Antonio nos invitó al cine, pero no sé si quiero ir. ¿Quieres ir?

JULIA: Bueno, Ana, voy **1.** (con tal de que / para que / a menos que) vaya también David, el

hermano de Antonio. ¿Sabes que me gusta mucho? Si él no va, yo no voy.

ANA: Julia, ¡no seas tan difícil! **2.** (Cuando / Aunque / Después de que) no vaya David, te

vas a divertir mucho con Antonio y conmigo. También nos va a acompañar Tomás.

JULIA: ¿Tomás? Ay, no, por favor. Ese tipo me molesta demasiado. No voy entonces. **3.** (Para

que / Cuando / Hasta que) veas a Antonio y Tomás, diles que estoy muy enferma y

por eso no podía acompañarte. A propósito _(By the way),_ ¿qué película van a ver?

ANA: No te lo voy a decir **4.** (tan pronto como / cuando / a menos que) nos acompañes. Si no

vas, ¿qué te importa qué película vemos?

JULIA: Ay, chica, **5.** (antes de que / en caso de que / después de que) te enojes conmigo, te voy

a decir que sí los voy a acompañar... **6.** ¡(para que / tan pronto como / hasta que)

invites a David! ¡Por favor!

ANA: Julia, David no puede ir al cine esta tarde; tiene que trabajar. Pero, mira, **7.** (sin que /

en caso de que / después de que) salgamos del cine, vamos a visitar a David en su

lugar de trabajo. ¿Qué te parece?

JULIA: Me parece muy bien. Pero no voy a salir de la casa **8.** (sin que / para que / aunque) me

digas el título de la película que vamos a ver. ¡Espero que sea la nueva película de

Almodóvar!

ANA: Sí, Julia, es la nueva de Almodóvar.

WB 13-4 | **La telenovela del momento** Varios estudiantes están hablando de la nueva telenovela, «Decepciones». Para saber lo que dicen, forma oraciones completas usando los elementos dados. ¡**OJO**! Tienes que poner el verbo de la cláusula subordinada en el subjuntivo.

Modelo   Gerardo ir a casarse con Juanita / aunque / Juanita estar enamorada de otro hombre
Gerardo va a casarse con Juanita aunque Juanita esté enamorada de otro hombre.

1. Javier / no ir a volver a Lima / hasta que / la policía encontrar al asesino

     _____

2. Elena / tomar tratamientos médicos / para que / ella y Omar poder tener un bebé

     _____

3. Manuel / nunca firmar su nombre a las cartas que escribe a Analisa / en caso de que / su esposo las leer

     _____

4. Alberto y Claudia / ir a divorciarse / a menos que / Alberto cortar con su novia

     _____

5. Santi / ir a estar mejor / tan pronto como / los médicos le operar

     _____

WB 13-5 | **Los hábitos de Jorge** Jorge es adicto a la televisión y tiene hábitos muy peculiares. Para saber cuán *(how)* peculiar es Jorge, selecciona la frase que mejor termine cada oración. Luego, explica tu selección, indicando si la oración implica:

a. una acción habitual;

b. algo que va a ocurrir en el futuro;

c. algo que es cierto;

d. algo que es incierto.

Sigue los modelos.

Modelos   Jorge empieza a ver la tele tan pronto como [llegue a casa / llega a casa].
                                TIPO
llega a casa   *a. acción habitual*

Aunque su madre [le diga / le dice] que no vea tanta televisión, sigue haciéndolo.
                                TIPO
le dice   *c. algo cierto*

1. Jorge ve las telenovelas cuando [no pasen documentales / no pasan documentales]

                                TIPO

     _____   _____

2. Jorge piensa comprar otro televisor después de que [le paguen en el trabajo / le pagan en el trabajo].

                                TIPO

     _____   _____

3. Jorge siempre ve por los menos cinco horas de televisión al día aunque [tenga mucha tarea / tiene mucha tarea].

TIPO

_____   _____

4. Jorge nunca quita la televisión hasta que [vea la nieve en la pantalla / ve la nieve en la pantalla].

TIPO

_____   _____

5. Jorge piensa estudiar cine tan pronto como [termine sus estudios actuales / termina sus estudios actuales].

TIPO

_____   _____

WB 13-6 | **¿Qué hacemos esta noche?** Daniel quiere hacer algo divertido esta noche y le manda el siguiente correo electrónico a su amigo Carlos. Para saber lo que dice, rellena los espacios en blanco con la forma apropiada del verbo. Usa el presente del indicativo o el presente del subjuntivo según sea necesario.

Hola Carlos,

Esta noche no sé qué vamos a hacer. La verdad es que no me importa mucho exactamente qué hacemos, con tal de que nosotros **1.** _____ (hacer) algo divertido. Hoy es el cumpleaños de Amalia y su novio le va a hacer una fiesta. Aunque **2.** _____ (ser) una fiesta de cumpleaños, creo que lo van a pasar bien allí. Otra opción es ir al cine del centro para ver una película. Me gusta ese cine porque tan pronto como **3.** _____ (salir) las películas nuevas, las pasan allí, y no cobran demasiado dinero. Prefiero ver una película de intriga a menos que tú **4.** _____ (querer) ver algo diferente.

Mira, Carlos, cuando tú **5.** _____ (recibir) este mensaje, llámame y podemos decidir qué hacemos. En caso de que yo no **6.** _____ (estar) en casa, llámame en casa de Elvia —ella va a ayudarme con mi tarea de matemáticas. No te preocupes, ¡no voy a salir con Elvia esta noche! De hecho (In fact), no voy a hacer planes para esta noche hasta que tú me **7.** _____ (llamar).

VOCABULARIO Las artes

WB 13-7 | En el Museo de Arte de Lima Para promover el interés por experimentar el arte, el Museo de Arte de Lima ofrece varios talleres, o cursos, sobre varios tipos de arte. Mira su folleto sobre los temas de los talleres que ofrecen este mes y escribe el nombre de cada tipo de arte representado. Selecciona entre las siguientes opciones:

el papel	la danza
la arquitectura	el teatro
la música	el ballet
la pintura	la escultura
la fotografía	la música
el retrato	la ópera

1. _____
2. _____
3. _____
4. _____
5. _____
6. _____
7. _____
8. _____
9. _____

WB 13-8 | Trivia El programa de concursos, «Trivia» tiene una página web para los televidentes que quieren jugar desde su casa. Hoy decides jugar tú y tienes que seleccionar la respuesta correcta.

1. Quentin Tarantino es _____
   a. un cantante famoso.
   b. un director de películas.
   c. un escultor de la Edad de Oro.

2. Federico García Lorca era _____
   a. músico famoso.
   b. fotógrafo español.
   c. poeta español.

3. Antonio Banderas _____
   a. hizo el papel del amante del Tom Hanks en «Philadelphia».
   b. dirigió la película «Snakes on a Plane».
   c. escribió una ópera clásica.

4. Enrique Iglesias es _____
   a. bailarín.
   b. cantante.
   c. escultor.

5. Salma Hayek es _____
   a. cantante mexicana.
   b. poeta española.
   c. actriz mexicana.

ESTRUCTURA II | Talking about unplanned or accidental occurrences: No-fault *se* construction

WB 13-9 | ¿Qué significa? Selecciona la mejor traducción de cada oración.

1. _____ A ti se te acaba el dinero.
   a. You ran out of money.
   b. You lost all your money.
   c. Your money is running out on you.

2. _____ A Juan se le escaparon las palabras para explicar el problema.
   a. Juan had too many things to say about the problem.
   b. Juan ran out of words to explain the problem.
   c. Juan is running out of words to explain the problem.

3. _____ A Jorge se le rompió una obra de arte de su abuela.
   a. Jorge's grandmother broke his piece of art.
   b. Jorge's grandmother's piece of art broke on him.
   c. Jorge broke his art piece at his grandmother's house.

4. _____ A Alicia y Juan se les perdió la llave de su coche.
   a. Alicia's and Juan's car key got lost.
   b. Juan lost Alicia's car key.
   c. Alicia lost Juan's car key.

WB 13-10 | ¡No tenemos la culpa! Gilberto y sus dos hermanos, Jorge y César, trabajan en el Museo de Arte de Lima, pero han tenido demasiados «accidentes» costosos *(costly)*. Ahora su jefe quiere despedirlos *(fire them)* y le está diciendo a Gilberto todas las razones para su decisión. Cada vez que el jefe les acusa de hacer algo malo, Gilberto le dice que ellos no tienen la culpa. ¿Cómo le contesta Gilberto? Escribe su respuesta usando una construcción con **se.** Sigue el modelo.

   Modelo   Gilberto, has perdido tres cuadros valiosos.
             Bueno, se me perdieron los cuadros.

1. Gilberto, tus hermanos dejaron caer *(dropped)* dos floreros muy caros.

   _____

2. Gilberto, tú y tus hermanos rompieron una escultura muy valiosa anoche.

   _____

3. Gilberto, tú no recordaste limpiar la sala de arte clásico.

_____

4. Gilberto, tu hermano perdió a dos clientes en el tour del museo ayer.

_____

5. Gilberto, tú y tus hermanos dejaron escapar a tres ladrones la semana pasada.

_____

ASÍ SE DICE | Describing completed actions and resulting conditions: Use of the past participle as adjective

WB 13-11 | Una oportunidad más para Gilberto El jefe de Gilberto decidió darle una oportunidad más para hacer bien su trabajo en el museo y Gilberto está tratando de hacer todo lo posible para ser eficiente. Siempre que el jefe le dice que Gilberto haga algo nuevo, Gilberto contesta que ya está hecho. ¿Qué dice? Escribe su respuesta usando un adjetivo con el verbo **estar** para indicar que lo que pide el jefe ya está hecho. Sigue el modelo.

Modelo   Gilberto, abre la puerta principal.
La puerta ya *está abierta*.

1. Gilberto, cubre los cuadros de Picasso con la tela.

Los cuadros de Picasso ya _____ _____.

2. Gilberto, cierra las puertas de la sala de arte folclórico.

Las puertas ya _____ _____.

3. Gilberto, pon los anuncios para la nueva exhibición en las paredes.

Los anuncios ya _____ _____ en las paredes.

4. Gilberto, invita a los patrocinadores *(sponsors)* del museo a la cena especial.

Los patrocinadores ya _____ _____.

5. Gilberto, lava las esculturas de esa sala.

Las esculturas ya _____ _____.

6. Gilberto, resuelve el problema que tienen los otros trabajadores.

El problema ya _____ _____.

WB 13-12 | Cultura peruana Tomás tiene que escribir una pequeña reseña sobre la escultura y el cine en Perú. Cambia las siguientes oraciones a oraciones en la voz pasiva usando el verbo **ser** + el participio pasado. Sigue el modelo.

Modelo   Armando Robles Godoy dirigió la película peruana *La muralla verde*.
La película peruana *La muralla verde fue dirigida* por Armando Robles Godoy.

1. Los españoles introdujeron los patrones occidentales a la escultura peruana.

Los patrones occidentales _____ _____ a la escultura peruana por los

españoles.

2. En el siglo XX don José Pardo estableció la Escuela de Artes y Oficios en Perú.

En el siglo XX la Escuela de Artes y Oficios en Perú _____ _____ por don José Pardo.

3. También en el siglo XX varios escultores, profesores y estudiantes de artes plásticas formaron un grupo de escultores peruanos.

También en el siglo XX un grupo de escultores _____ _____ por varios escultores, profesores y estudiantes de artes plásticas.

4. Iniciaron el cine peruano en 1897.

El cine peruano _____ _____ en 1897.

5. En 1929 presentaron la primera película con sonido en Perú.

La primera película con sonido _____ _____ en Perú en 1929.

6. En 1934 filmaron *Resaca,* la primera película peruana con sonido.

En 1934 *Resaca,* la primera película peruana con sonido, _____ _____.

WB 13-13 | ¿Cómo está? Para saber más de Daniel, un estudiante de la Universidad de Lima, selecciona la respuesta más lógica.

1. Antes de tomar un examen difícil:
   a. estoy preocupada.
   b. soy preocupado.
   c. estoy preocupado.

2. Cuando tengo que entregar mis tareas:
   a. son preparadas.
   b. estoy preparadas.
   c. están preparadas.

3. Mi cuarto normalmente:
   a. estoy desorganizado.
   b. es desorganizado.
   c. está desorganizado.

4. Después de tomar cuatro tazas de café:
   a. soy despierto.
   b. estoy despierto.
   c. estoy despiertos.

5. Al final de cada mes todas mis facturas:
   a. están pagadas.
   b. estoy pagado.
   c. soy pagado.

WB 13-14 | ¡Imagínate tú! Imagínate que eres un/una actor/actriz famoso(a) y cada aspecto de tu vida aparece en las revistas todos los días. ¿Qué diría *(would say)* la tapa *(cover)* de la revista ¡Hola! esta semana? Lee las cosas que supuestamente te ocurrieron la semana pasada y escribe los titulares *(headlines)* con el verbo **ser** y el participio pasado. Sigue el modelo.

Modelo   Tú escribiste la novela «Circo» bajo otro nombre.
           La novela «Circo» fue escrita por (tu nombre).

Nombre _____ Fecha _____

1. Tú acompañaste a Penelope Cruz a una cena.

   _____

2. Alguien te robó el perro.

   _____

3. Tú ganaste el premio Oscar en Hollywood.

   _____

4. Tú descubriste dos ratones en tu casa.

   _____

BIENVENIDOS A PERÚ

En este segmento del video, vas a aprender un poco sobre Perú y sobre la vida de sus ciudadanos. Los temas incluyen:

- la geografía
- los indígenas
- la artesanía
- la arquitectura
- la naturaleza

WB 13-15 | En el segmento del video vas a escuchar muchos cognados que pueden facilitar tu comprensión. Algunos de estos cognados aparecen aquí. Trata de pronunciar cada palabra o frase y luego empareja los cognados con su definición en inglés.

1. _____ continente
2. _____ palacio
3. _____ bestias
4. _____ acueductos
5. _____ caimán
6. _____ descendientes

a. aqueduct
b. caiman/alligator
c. palace
d. continent
e. descendants
f. beasts/animals

WB 13-16 | Después de ver el segmento del video, rellena los espacios en blanco con el cognado apropiado de la actividad **WB 13-15.**

1. Los Andes son las montañas más altas del _____.

2. Aquí se ven las ruinas de Puca Pucara con la maravilla de su arquitectura,

   unos _____ que todavía funcionan.

3. Otros piensan que era como un _____ para el rey de los incas.

4. Los _____ de los incas siguen viviendo en los Andes.

5. Utilizan la llama y la alpaca como _____ de carga y para lana.

6. Es un vía importante de transporte, y también presenta la oportunidad de ver y estudiar

   muchos animales de los trópicos como este _____.

Nombre _____ Fecha _____

1. Tú acompañaste a Penelope Cruz a una cena.

2. Alguien te robó el perro.

3. Tú ganaste el premio Oscar en Hollywood.

4. Tú descubriste dos ratones en tu casa.

BIENVENIDOS A PERÚ

En este segmento del video, vas a aprender un poco sobre Perú y sobre la vida de sus ciudadanos. Los temas incluyen:

- la geografía
- los indígenas
- la artesanía
- la arquitectura
- la naturaleza

WB 13-15 | En el segmento del video vas a escuchar muchos cognados que pueden facilitar tu comprensión. Algunos de estos cognados aparecen aquí. Trata de pronunciar cada palabra o frase y luego empareja los cognados con su definición en inglés.

1. _____ continente
2. _____ palacio
3. _____ bestias
4. _____ acueductos
5. _____ caimán
6. _____ descendientes

a. aqueduct
b. caiman/alligator
c. palace
d. continent
e. descendants
f. beasts/animals

WB 13-16 | Después de ver el segmento del video, rellena los espacios en blanco con el cognado apropiado de la actividad **WB 13-15.**

1. Los Andes son las montañas más altas del _____.

2. Aquí se ven las ruinas de Puca Pucara con la maravilla de su arquitectura, unos _____ que todavía funcionan.

3. Otros piensan que era como un _____ para el rey de los incas.

4. Los _____ de los incas siguen viviendo en los Andes.

5. Utilizan la llama y la alpaca como _____ de carga y para lana.

6. Es un vía importante de transporte, y también presenta la oportunidad de ver y estudiar muchos animales de los trópicos como este _____.

Capítulo 13 **197**

WB 13-17 | Después de ver el segmento del video otra vez, selecciona la mejor respuesta a las siguientes preguntas.

1. _____ ¿Cuántos habitantes tiene el país de Perú?
   a. 32 millones
   b. 32.000
   c. 28 millones
   d. 28.000

2. _____ ¿Cuál es la capital de Perú?
   a. Lima
   b. Cusco
   c. Puca Pucara
   d. La Paz

3. _____ ¿Qué lengua hablan los indígenas de Perú?
   a. mapuche
   b. náhuatl
   c. quechua
   d. guaraní

4. _____ ¿Por cuántos años fue Perú colonia de España?
   a. 30
   b. 300
   c. 3000
   d. 13

5. _____ ¿En qué año se hizo independiente de España?
   a. 1492
   b. 1842
   c. 1820
   d. 1824

6. _____ ¿Cómo se llama el sitio arqueológico más famoso del país?
   a. Lima
   b. Pucu Pucara
   c. Machu Picchu
   d. Río Amazonas

¡A ESCRIBIR!

Strategy: Identifying elements of a critical essay

Every day we evaluate many conditions, situations, and people. Sometimes, for personal or professional reasons, we write down our comments and opinions about them. Critical essays often appear in newspapers, magazines, and other similar publications and frequently deal with topics discussed in this chapter, such as art, literature, film, and television. When beginning to write a critical essay, use the following guidelines to help you get started:

1. Choose a subject or topic that interests you.
2. Write a brief introduction about the subject you choose.
3. List three or four things that you like about your subject.
4. Think of one or two things that could be done realistically to improve your subject and write these ideas down.
5. Come to a conclusion about your subject.

Task: Writing a critical essay

Paso 1 Recall the steps for writing this type of essay.

1. Selecciona el tema.
2. Escribe una breve introducción.
3. Haz una lista de tres o cuatro cosas que te gustan.
4. Piensa en una o dos cosas que puedes hacer para mejorar el sujeto.
5. Escribe una conclusión.

Paso 2 Now it's time to select your topic. Write your essay about one of these topics:

- una película nueva
- un concierto
- un programa de televisión
- un disco compacto
- una novela que te gusta

Paso 3 Write a first draft on a separate piece of paper. Once you have that draft, think about whether you can include more details to better explain the point you wish to make about your topic. Decide also whether you need to delete some details that are not particularly relevant to explaining your point of view. Afterward, review the grammar and make any necessary changes. Pay special attention to your spelling, use of accents, use of the verb gustar, and use of the subjunctive.

Paso 4 Write your final draft below.

_____

_____

_____

_____

_____

_____

_____

_____

_____

_____

_____

_____

 ATAJO 4.0

Functions: Writing an essay; Writing an introduction; Writing a conclusion; Expressing an opinion

Vocabulary: Arts; Poetry; Prose; Musical instruments

Grammar: Verbs: subjunctive

Autoprueba

VOCABULARIO

WB 13-18 | Las películas y los programas Empareja los nombres de las personas con el tipo de programa o película que se asocia con ellos.

1. _____ Mia Hamm   **a.** un drama
2. _____ Dan Rather   **b.** una comedia
3. _____ Bugs Bunny   **c.** las noticias
4. _____ John Wayne   **d.** los dibujos animados
5. _____ Al Roker   **e.** un programa deportivo
6. _____ Adam Sandler   **f.** una película del oeste
7. _____ Vanna White   **g.** el pronóstico del tiempo
8. _____ Dave Letterman   **h.** un programa de concursos
9. _____ Stephen Spielberg   **i.** un programa de entrevistas
10. _____ Meryl Streep   **j.** una película de ciencia ficción

WB 13-19 | El mundo de las bellas artes Rellena los espacios en blanco con la palabra apropiada de la siguiente lista.

> actriz   concierto   arquitectura   cuadro   fotografía   bailarín
>
> danza   fotógrafo   cantante   director   compositor

1. El pianista va a dar un _____ mañana en el parque.
2. El arte de sacar fotos se llama _____ y quien lo practica es el

   _____ .
3. Una persona que dirige una película o una obra de teatro es el _____ .
4. Una mujer que interpreta un papel en una obra de teatro se llama

   _____ .
5. El arte de diseñar edificios se llama la _____ .
6. Lo que pinta el pintor se llama un _____ .
7. Un hombre que practica el baile es _____ .
8. El tango es una _____ de Argentina.
9. Una persona que escribe música es _____ .
10. Una persona que canta es _____ .

WB 13-20 | Consejos para la cita Esta noche Paulo tiene cita con la mujer de sus sueños, Silvia. Su amigo Carlos trata de darle consejos para que todo salga bien. Para saber lo que dicen, rellena los espacios en blanco con una forma apropiada del verbo. Tienes que leer la conversación y entender bien el contexto para decidir si el verbo debe ir en el presente del subjuntivo o el presente del indicativo.

CARLOS: Hola, Paulo, ¿qué me cuentas? ¿Cómo estás?

PAULO: ¡Estoy súper bien! Sabes que Silvia por fin viene a visitarme, bueno, con tal de que

1. _____ (limpiar) la casa antes de que ella

2. _____ (venir).

CARLOS: ¿Silvia? ¿Te va a visitar a ti? Pero tu casa es un desastre. ¿Qué vas a hacer para

que Silvia no **3.** _____ (asustarse) cuando

4. _____ (llegar)?

PAULO: Mira, Carlos, aunque mi casa sí **5.** _____ (estar) un poco sucia,

no es un desastre. La puedo limpiar.

CARLOS: Pues, suponiendo que sí puedes limpiar la casa, ¿qué van a hacer Uds.?

PAULO: No lo sé. Creo que voy a alquilar un video de Jackie Chan. Creo que a Silvia le va a

gustar. Pero, en caso de que no le **6.** _____ (gustar), también

voy a alquilar mi película favorita, Smokey and the Bandit. Sé que con una de ésas

no puedo perder.

CARLOS: ¡Paulo, Paulo! ¿Cuándo **7.** _____ (ir) a aprender? ¿Cuántas

veces te lo tengo que decir? Cuando **8.** _____ (invitar) a tu casa

a una chica como Silvia, tienes que enfocarte en ella. Tienes que preguntarle a ella

qué quiere ver. Esta noche, pregúntale a Silvia qué quiere ver y entonces, cuando

ella te **9.** _____ (decir) el título de la película, Uds. dos pueden

ir juntos a la tienda para alquilarla.

PAULO: Entonces, ¿no crees que una película de Jackie Chan le vaya a gustar?

CARLOS: Paulo, aunque le **10.** _____ (gustar), tienes que esperar hasta

que ella **11.** _____ (decidir) qué es lo que prefiere ver. ¡Qué

cabezota *(stubborn person)* eres!

WB 13-21 | Pero ¡no fue nuestra culpa! Tú y tu mejor amiga tuvieron un día horrible ayer. Les ocurrieron varios accidentes. ¿Qué les pasó? Forma oraciones usando no-fault **se**. Sigue el modelo.

Modelo   Tú rompiste dos vasos de cristal.
          Se me rompieron dos vasos de cristal.

1. Tú y tu amiga dejaron caer una escultura en la casa de otra amiga.

   _____

2. Tu amiga dejó escapar a los niños que cuidaba.

   _____

3. Tú no recordaste una cita con tu novio.

   _____

4. Tú y tu amiga acabaron todo el dinero que tenían para el mes.

   _____

5. Tú perdiste la llave de tu coche.

   _____

WB 13-22 | ¿Ya está hecho? Tú estás encargado del comité para planear la fiesta más grande del año de la universidad. Ahora estás anotando lo que ya está hecho y quién lo hizo. Completa esta lista, escribiendo primero una oración con el verbo **estar** + el participio pasado y después una oración con el verbo **ser** + el participio pasado para indicar quién lo hizo. Sigue el modelo.

Modelo   escribir las invitaciones / Teresa
          Las invitaciones ya están escritas.
          Fueron escritas por Teresa.

1. invitar a los estudiantes / Jaime y Juan

   _____

   _____

2. confirmar el entretenimiento / Analisa

   _____

   _____

3. organizar la lista de música / Rosa y Eva

   _____

   _____

4. preparar la comida / Marta y Esteban

   _____

   _____

5. colgar las decoraciones / Julio

   _____

   _____

La vida pública: Chile

VOCABULARIO La política y el voto

WB 14-1 | La plataforma de Valeria El periódico de la universidad publicó hoy la plataforma de Valeria Denevi, una de las candidatas para el puesto de presidente del gobierno estudiantil. Para saber lo que dice, rellena los espacios en blanco con la palabra apropiada de la lista. **¡OJO!** Es posible que tengas que conjugar algunos verbos.

poder   votar   democrático   voto   candidata   deber

apoyar   elegir   elecciones   aprobar   dictadura

Las **1.** _____ vienen pronto y yo necesito su **2.** _____. Yo soy la mejor

3. _____ para representar y **4.** _____ a los estudiantes de esta universidad.

Si ustedes me **5.** _____ presidente prometo dos cosas: no voy a **6.** _____

el aumento de la matrícula que intenta imponer la administración y voy a insistir en que la

universidad le compre una computadora a cada estudiante. Yo creo en el sistema

7. _____ y nunca voy a abusar el **8.** _____ de este puesto. De hecho,

prometo establecer un comité de estudiantes para informarme continuamente de las

necesidades de los estudiantes y para aconsejarme en las decisiones más importantes.

Recuerden por favor que el gobierno de esta universidad no es una **9.** _____.

Ustedes no solamente tienen el privilegio, sino que tienen el **10.** _____ de

11. _____. Sólo así podemos mejorar esta universidad. Por favor, ¡voten por mí!

WB 14-2 | Rompecabezas Lee cada pista y determina la palabra política que describe.

1. Fidel Castro:

___ ___ ___ ___ ___ ___ ___ ___ ___

2. Partido político de George W. Bush:

___ ___ ___ ___ ___ ___ ___ ___ ___ ___ ___

3. Acción de nombrar por elección:

___ ___ ___ ___ ___ ___

4. Regla:

___ ___ ___

5. Líder de un gobierno democrático:

___ ___ ___ ___ ___ ___ ___ ___ ___ ___

6. Opuesto de liberal:

___ ___ ___ ___ ___ ___ ___ ___ ___ ___ ___

7. Discusión pública entre candidatos:

___ ___ ___ ___ ___

8. Sinónimo de proteger:

___ ___ ___ ___ ___ ___ ___ ___ ___

9. Parte del gobierno estadounidense que funciona conjuntamente con el senado:

___ ___ ___ ___ ___ ___ ___ ___ ___

10. La persona que hace campaña para ganar algún puesto político:

___ ___ ___ ___ ___ ___ ___ ___ ___ ___

11. Lo que se ejecuta como innovación o mejora en el gobierno:

___ ___ ___ ___ ___ ___ ___ ___ ___

12. El que pertenece a cierta ciudad o cierto país:

___ ___ ___ ___ ___ ___ ___ ___ ___

13. Cuerpo militar:

___ ___ ___ ___ ___ ___ ___ ___

ESTRUCTURA I Talking about future events: The future tense

WB 14-3 | Las predicciones de Óscar Óscar piensa en cómo será su futuro y el futuro de las siguientes personas. Escribe lo que piensa Óscar usando el futuro. Sigue el modelo.

> **Modelo**   Yo / tomar una clase / trabajar para una organización política / el año que viene
> *Yo tomaré una clase y trabajaré para una organización política el año que viene.*

1. Yo / ir a Ecuador para encontrar a Marina / estudiar filosofía con ella / enamorarme de ella / olvidarme de mi novia en Chile

_____

_____

_____

_____

2. Marina / conocerme mejor / asistir a una clase de política contemporánea / querer cambiar de especialidad / decirme que me quiere

_____

_____

_____

_____

3. El novio de Marina / saber que Marina ya no lo quiere / escribirle muchas cartas de amor / hacer muchos esfuerzos para no perderla / tener que encontrar a una nueva novia

_____

_____

_____

_____

4. Marina y yo / irnos de Ecuador / volver a Chile / casarnos / tener cuatro hijos

_____

_____

_____

_____

WB 14-4 | Querido diario Marina también está pensando en Óscar y escribe varias de sus predicciones para el futuro. Para saber lo que escribe, completa los párrafos usando el futuro de los verbos apropiados de cada lista.

a. tener   volver   ahorrar   venir

Sé que algún día **1.** _____ a Chile. Esta vez mi mejor amiga, Carmen,

2. _____ conmigo. Creo que (yo) **3.** _____ más dinero

que ahora porque Carmen y yo lo **4.** _____ cada semana.

b. divertirse   visitar   escribir   alegrarse

Antes de salir para Chile, yo les **1.** _____ a mis otros amigos chilenos

para decirles que yo los **2.** _____. Estoy segura de que ellos

3. _____ de verme y que nosotros **4.** _____ mucho.

c. saber   hacer   tomar   poder   haber   ser

Carmen y yo **1.** _____ el viaje en la primavera. En esa temporada

2. _____ menos visitantes que ahora y los precios de los boletos

3. _____ más baratos. Yo **4.** _____ más de la política

contemporánea porque **5.** _____ más clases. Así

6. _____ hablar con Óscar sobre los asuntos políticos de Chile.

WB 14-5 | Te haces Walter Mercado Tú te has convertido en el famoso síquico latino, Walter Mercado, y ahora estás haciendo muchas predicciones para todo el mundo. Escribe tus predicciones.

1. El novio de mi mejor amiga le _____ (decir) que quiere salir conmigo.

2. Yo _____ (hacer) un viaje por las Américas.

3. El dueño del lugar donde vivo me _____ (cancelar) el contrato.

4. Mis padres _____ (ganar) la lotería.

5. Mis amigos y yo _____ (mudarnos) a Chile para vivir allí.

WB 14-6 | **Consulta con el oráculo** Carolina decidió preguntarle al oráculo sobre varias de sus predicciones para el futuro. Escribe sus preguntas. **¡OJO!** Recuerda que en las preguntas el sujeto va después del verbo. Sigue el modelo.

> Modelo   Borat / ser / presidente de Kazakhstan
> *¿Será Borat presidente de Kazakhstan?*

1. Hillary Clinton / estar / al lado de los conservadores

¿_____?

2. La dictadura de Cuba / seguir / después de Fidel Castro

¿_____?

3. Los gobiernos del mundo / terminar / la pobreza

¿_____?

4. Varios países del mundo / aprobar / más leyes para proteger la selva amazónica

¿_____?

5. Nosotros / tener / un mundo pacífico

¿_____?

VOCABULARIO   Las preocupaciones cívicas y los medios de comunicación

WB 14-7 | **Palabras revueltas** Lee las pistas y luego pon en orden las letras de estas palabras relacionadas con las preocupaciones cívicas y los medios de comunicación.

1. Dejar saber: farimnor _____

2. Protección: fenased _____

3. Tipo de protesta: galhue _____

4. Se leen en los periódicos: teporajers _____

5. estudiar a fondo: gainvstier _____

6. hacer más grande: autarmen _____

WB 14-8 | **Las últimas noticias** Esta mañana Juanita encontró el siguiente artículo en el periódico de su universidad. Dice que mañana varios estudiantes realizarán una manifestación para protestar en contra del aumento de la matrícula de la universidad. Completa el artículo con palabras apropiadas de la siguiente lista. Conjuga los verbos si es necesario.

protesta   informar   inflación   eliminar   corrupción   reducir   derechos civiles

desigualdad   huelga   prensa   reportaje   noticiero

Mañana cientos de estudiantes universitarios realizarán una **1.** _____ en contra del aumento de la matrícula, la cual subirá más del 200 por ciento el año que viene. Según **2.** _____ la administración de la universidad, el aumento es necesario debido a la **3.** _____ general que ha causado la subida de precios en todos los sectores de la economía. Sin embargo, los estudiantes creen que si el gobierno estatal *(state)*

4. _____ la 5. _____ que ha plagado *(plagued)* la

administración en los últimos años, podrán hasta 6. _____ el costo de la

educación para todos.

Los estudiantes señalan que el aumento de la matrícula constituirá una violación de los

7. _____ de los estudiantes y sólo creará más

8. _____ entre los ciudadanos.

Parece que los profesores apoyan a los estudiantes. Hernán González, portavoz de la Asociación de

Profesores Universitarios (APU), dice que los profesores están dispuestos a montar una

9. _____ y no volverán a trabajar hasta que el gobierno haga algo para evitar

el aumento de la matrícula. La manifestación será mañana a las diez de la mañana y Lola Sebastián,

representante de la 10. _____ universitaria, hará un

11. _____ en vivo para el 12. _____ de las seis

de la tarde.

ESTRUCTURA II Expressing conjecture or probability: The conditional

WB 14-9 | Si pudiera... Lidia Rodríguez está hablando con su amigo Pedro sobre cómo
sería la universidad si ella estuviera encargada *(were in charge)* de todas las decisiones
importantes de la universidad. Para saber lo que dice, forma oraciones en el condicional
usando los elementos dados. Sigue el modelo.

Modelo   los estudiantes / no pagar / ninguna matrícula
          Los estudiantes no pagarían ninguna matrícula.

1. los estudiantes / poder / obtener becas *(scholarships)* más fácilmente

_____

2. nosotros / no tener que / asistir a clases por las mañanas

_____

3. el rector de la universidad / salir / de la universidad

_____

4. los profesores / no darles / notas a los estudiantes

_____

5. todos los estudiantes / querer / asistir a esta universidad

_____

WB 14-10 | Paqui la periodista Paqui es reportera para un periódico hispano en California. Esta tarde va a entrevistar a uno de los candidatos para gobernador del estado. Ayúdale a elaborar la lista de preguntas, rellanando los espacios en blanco con una forma del **condicional** de los verbos indicados. **¡OJO!** Paqui usará la forma de usted con el candidato ya que es una situación formal y no lo conoce personalmente.

1. ¿_____ (Tener) Ud. algún problema en hablar abiertamente conmigo sobre su campaña?

2. ¿_____ (Decir) Ud. que la inmigración ilegal es un problema en el estado de California?

3. ¿_____ (Querer) Ud. aprobar una ley para hacer el inglés la lengua oficial del estado?

4. ¿Le _____ (gustar) hacer ilegal el aborto en este estado?

5. ¿_____ (Saber) Ud. si el otro candidato tiene más experiencia política que Ud.?

WB 14-11 | Imagínate Patricia soñó con *(dreamt)* que el presidente de la compañía Yahoo le dio a ella un puesto en su división de investigación en Santiago, Chile. Es un trabajo garantizado por cinco años con un salario de trescientos mil dólares al año. Se despertó y ahora piensa en cómo sería su vida si su sueño fuera *(were)* realidad. Escribe oraciones con el condicional.

1. Toda mi familia / estar / muy contenta

_____

2. Yo / mudarse / a Santiago de Chile

_____

3. Mi familia y yo / le donar / mucho dinero a la gente pobre de Latinoamérica

_____

4. Mi novio y yo / casarse / en una ceremonia en una playa privada de Chile

_____

5. Nosotros / no querer volver / a los Estados Unidos

_____

ESTRUCTURA III Making references to the present: The present perfect subjunctive

WB 14-12 | El día después de las elecciones María está leyendo el periódico en un café del centro el día después de las elecciones nacionales. Nota que todas las personas allí están opinando acerca de los resultados. Para saber qué dicen, completa las oraciones con la forma apropiada de los verbos en el presente perfecto del subjuntivo.

1. Me alegro de que mi candidato favorito _____ (ganar).

2. No puedo creer que los perdedores _____ (montar) una manifestación tan rápidamente.

3. ¡Nidia! ¡Es imposible que tú _____ (votar) por ese candidato! Es horrible.

4. Es dudoso que los candidatos _____ (ser) totalmente honestos con nosotros.

5. ¡Qué bueno que _____ (haber) tanta propaganda acerca de las elecciones! Así la gente reconoce la importancia de los asuntos políticos.

6. Es interesante que nosotros siempre _____ (tener) ideas políticas tan diferentes, pero seguimos siendo amigos.

WB 14-13 | El activista Carlos ha sido activista político por mucho tiempo. Para saber más de él cambia los verbos subrayados al presente perfecto del subjuntivo.

Modelo   Duda que los políticos siempre <u>quieran</u> lo mejor para el pueblo.
          hayan querido

1. Se alegra que los políticos lo <u>escuchen</u>.

_____

2. Le molesta que el cambio no <u>ocurra</u> rápidamente.

_____

3. Duda que el país <u>comprenda</u> completamente el tema de la inmigración.

_____

4. Le parece interesante que mucha gente no <u>vote</u> en las elecciones.

_____

5. No le gusta que las drogas <u>sigan</u> siendo un problema nacional.

_____

WB 14-14 | Foro abierto Kati Homedes ha invitado al público a un foro para discutir los temas más importantes del momento y para expresar sus opiniones. ¿Qué opina la señorita Homedes sobre los siguientes temas? Forma oraciones completas con los elementos dados, conjugando los verbos en el presente perfecto. Usa el subjuntivo cuando sea necesario.

Modelo   no pensar / los impuestos / subir / mucho durante los últimos años
          No pienso que los impuestos hayan subido mucho durante los últimos años.

1. dudar / los ciudadanos / estar / suficientemente activos en la política hasta ahora

_____

_____

2. estar segura / la inmigración ilegal / no causar / problemas graves para el estado

_____

_____

3. estar contenta / el presidente / preocuparse / tanto por las violaciones de los derechos humanos

_____

_____

4. creer / el gobierno / hacer / todo lo posible para eliminar el terrorismo nacional

_____

_____

5. no estar contenta / el público / decir / que no soy una buena candidata

_____

_____

WB 14-15 | **¿De verdad?** Durante una visita a Chile escuchas a dos amigos conversar en un café. Hablan de los Estados Unidos. Para saber cuánto saben de verdad, completa sus oraciones usando el presente perfecto o del indicativo o del subjuntivo. Luego, indica si sus oraciones son **ciertas** (C) o **falsas** (F). Sigue el modelo.

Modelo   Creo que en Estados Unidos _____ (decidir) adoptar el español como segunda
            lengua oficial del país.
            han decidido / F

1. No es cierto que los estudiantes universitarios de California _____ (estar) de huelga durante tres semanas.

_____   _____

2. Dudo que el presidente de los Estados Unidos _____ (eliminar) el ejército.

_____   _____

3. Me alegro de que el gobierno de los Estados Unidos _____ (reducir) la drogadicción en el país.

_____   _____

4. Es cierto que _____ (haber) menos inmigración a los Estados Unidos dentro de los últimos diez años.

_____   _____

5. Es posible que los estadounidenses _____ (hacer) ilegal el aborto.

_____   _____

BIENVENIDOS A CHILE

En este segmento del video, vas a aprender un poco sobre sobre Chile y la vida de sus ciudadanos. Los temas incluyen:

- la geografía
- la economía
- los recursos naturales
- la política
- las ciudades principales

WB 14-16 | En el segmento del video vas a escuchar muchos cognados que pueden facilitar tu comprensión. Algunos de estos cognados aparecen aquí. Trata de pronunciar cada palabra o frase y luego empareja los cognados con su definición en inglés.

1. _____ exportaciones
2. _____ minerales
3. _____ marxista
4. _____ soberanía
5. _____ cobre
6. _____ socialista
7. _____ industrialización
8. _____ ingreso
9. _____ comunista
10. _____ terrenos

a. communist
b. terrain/land
c. socialist
d. sovereignty
e. exports
f. revenue/income
g. copper
h. minerals
i. industrialization
j. Marxist

WB 14-17 | Después de ver el segmento del video, rellena los espacios en blanco con un cognado apropiado de la actividad **WB 14-16.**

1. Esta región es rica en minerales incluyendo el _____, los nitratos y el hierro.

2. La economía de Chile está basada en la explotación de _____.

3. La economía de Chile es una de las más fuertes y estables de toda Sudamérica, con un _____ per cápita de 12.900 dólares.

4. Chile logró la _____ sobre los _____ disputados.

5. El descubrimiento de importantes yacimientos de cobre, a principios del siglo XX, abriría el camino a la _____ y modernización del país.

6. Salvador Allende ganó las elecciones y fue el primer líder de un partido _____ en ser elegido presidente de un país por voto popular.

7. Bajo Alwyn la economía del país se ha fortalecido con aumentos en las _____ y reducciones en la deuda externa.

8. Ricardo Lagos, un _____, fue elegido presidente en enero del año 2000.

WB 14-18 | Después de ver el segmento del video otra vez, selecciona la mejor respuesta a las siguientes preguntas.

1. _____ ¿Con qué país o estado se compara el tamaño de Chile?
   a. Es casi el tamaño del estado de California.
   b. Es casi el doble del tamaño del país de Argentina.
   c. Es casi el tamaño del estado de Nuevo México.
   d. Es casi el doble del tamaño del estado de Montana.

2. _____ ¿Cómo se llama el desierto que está al norte del Chile?
   a. Atacama
   b. Cobre
   c. Valparaíso
   d. Concepción

3. _____ ¿Cuántos habitantes tiene la ciudad de Santiago?
   a. 55 millones
   b. 55.000
   c. 5.5 millones
   d. 15 millones

4. _____ ¿Cuáles son dos de los países vecinos de Chile?
   a. Bolivia y Paraguay
   b. Argentina y Uruguay
   c. Argentina y Perú
   d. Bolivia y Uruguay

5. _____ ¿Cuál de las oraciones es correcta?
   a. Chile tiene más gente indígena que hispana.
   b. En Chile el petróleo es la exportación más grande.
   c. Chile es el país más pequeño de Sudamérica.
   d. Chile tiene una de las economías más fuertes y estables de Sudamérica.

6. _____ ¿Por qué hubo guerra entre Chile, Argentina y Bolivia en el siglo XIX?
   a. por el gas natural
   b. por el acceso al Océano Pacífico
   c. por el control de la producción del vino
   d. por el cobre

7. _____ ¿Qué país ayudó en el asesinato de Salvador Allende?
   a. Argentina
   b. Perú
   c. España
   d. Estados Unidos

Nombre _____ Fecha _____

¡A ESCRIBIR!

Strategy: Writing from diagrams

In your textbook, you learned to write a paragraph about a current event or topic, based on information presented in charts, graphs, and diagrams, which offer specific information that can be readily understood and remembered. Written reports prepared by individuals in business, industry, government, and education often include diagrams, etc., and it is therefore important to learn how to interpret them and how to express the information they contain in a succinct and clear fashion.

Paso 1 In Chile, both the age at which people get married and the number of couples who live together before marriage has risen in the last 20 years. Do you believe there to be a similar trend among university-aged students in the U.S.? Do people in the U.S. marry at a later age or not marry at all more than before? Do people prefer to live together before marriage in the U.S.? Choose one of these questions and survey friends your age to find out their responses.

Paso 2 Organize the results you obtain from your survey in the form of a chart or table that can easily display the answer to the question.

Paso 3 Now, write a paragraph based on the results of the survey that you conducted. Write a sentence that indicates the result of the survey (i.e. what the majority of people said). Then mention the details of your survey. Explain why people responded the way they did. Finally, conclude your paragraph with a short statement that summarizes your results.

Paso 4 Read your paragraph and revise it for content and grammar. Write find draft below.

_____
_____
_____
_____
_____
_____
_____
_____
_____
_____

ATAJO 4.0

Functions: Comparing and contrasting; Comparing and distinguishing
Vocabulary: People; Relationships
Grammar: Comparisons

Autoprueba

VOCABULARIO

WB 14-19 | Políticamente hablando Emma le está enseñando a su prima algo de cómo son las elecciones para la presidencia de los Estados Unidos. Para saber lo que dice, rellena los espacios en blanco con una palabra apropiada de la siguiente lista. Conjuga los verbos si es necesario.

campaña	ciudadanos	debates	defender
dictadura	elegir	partidos políticos	republicanos
candidatos	conservadores	deber	democracia
ejército	liberales	paz	votar

a. Hay varios **1.** _____ en los Estados Unidos, pero los dos más populares

son los demócratas y los **2.** _____ . Los primeros tienden a ser

3. _____ , y los últimos normalmente son más **4.** _____ .

b. Cuando los **1.** _____ hacen su **2.** _____ , normalmente

tienen muchos **3.** _____ para discutir los temas importantes para los

4. _____ .

c. Ya que nuestro sistema de gobierno no es una **1.** _____ , sino una

2. _____ , nosotros **3.** _____ a nuestro presidente. Todas

las personas tienen el **4.** _____ de **5.** _____ en las elecciones.

d. Aparte de su trabajo como líder del país, el presidente también es el líder del

1. _____ . Así que el presidente también tiene que tratar de mantener la

2. _____ y **3.** _____ el país.

WB 14-20 | Las preocupaciones cívicas Empareja cada frase con su descripción.

1. _____ la defensa
2. _____ el noticiero
3. _____ la drogadicción
4. _____ la inflación
5. _____ los impuestos
6. _____ el reportaje
7. _____ la inmigración
8. _____ el terrorismo
9. _____ la manifestación
10. _____ la libertad de la prensa
11. _____ la revista
12. _____ el desempleo
13. _____ la huelga

a. el dinero que la gente tiene que pagarle al gobierno federal y estatal

b. la terminación de un embarazo

c. un informe periodístico

d. la falta de censura en cuanto a las publicaciones periodísticas

e. el aumento de precios y la reducción del valor del dinero

f. protección

g. falta de instrucción elemental para leer y escribir

h. acción de entrar a un país de otro país

i. presentación de las últimas noticias, normalmente por medio de la radio o la televisión

14. _____ el analfabetismo

15. _____ el aborto

j. publicación periódica sobre diferentes temas o sobre un tema específico

k. la dependencia de una sustancia química

l. actos violentos que tienen como objetivo crear miedo o inseguridad

m. la falta de trabajo

n. una reunión de la gente para expresar públicamente alguna opinión

o. acción de dejar de trabajar voluntariamente para lograr alguna meta

WB 14-21 | El primer día Lorena Magaña ganó las elecciones estudiantiles de su universidad y hoy es su primer día en este nuevo puesto. Su secretaria le ha dejado el siguiente mensaje para hablar del horario del primer día. Completa el mensaje, rellenando los espacios en blanco con la forma apropiada del futuro de los verbos entre paréntesis.

Hola, Lorena:

Hoy tú **1.** _____ (tener) muchas cosas que hacer. Tu primera reunión

2. _____ (comenzar) a las diez y **3.** _____ (ser) en la oficina del

rector de la universidad. Tu vicepresidente y otros miembros del senado **4.** _____

(venir) a buscarte a las nueve y media para acompañarte a la reunión. Ellos no

5. _____ (saber) que el rector **6.** _____ (querer) planear el

agenda para todo el año, pero no importa. Tú se lo **7.** _____ (decir) cuando los

acompañes a la reunión.

A la una **8.** _____ (haber) otra reunión, pero esta vez es con los estudiantes.

Ésta no **9.** _____ (durar) mucho tiempo.

A las tres de la tarde yo te **10.** _____ (ver) aquí en la oficina. Tenemos que hablar

de tu fiesta de inauguración y creo que **11.** _____ (poder) hacerlo a esa hora. ¡No te

preocupes! Yo **12.** _____ (hacer) todos los planes, pero sólo

necesito saber de ti algunos detalles importantes.

Bueno, sé que **13.** _____ (ser) una presidente excelente y que en tu primer día te

14. _____ (ir) súper bien.

Suerte, Ana María

WB 14-22 | Puros sueños David y Magali acaban de comprar dos boletos para la lotería. Ahora están conversando sobre sus planes para el dinero que piensan que van a ganar. Completa su conversación usando el condicional de los verbos indicados.

DAVID: ¿Qué **1.** _____ (hacer) tú con tanto dinero, Magali?

MAGALI: Yo **2.** _____ (viajar) a todos los países del mundo.

DAVID: Me **3.** _____ (gustar) acompañarte.

4. ¿_____ (Poder) ir yo?

MAGALI: ¡Cómo no! Nosotros **5.** _____ (salir) inmediatamente después de ganar.

DAVID: ¡Qué bueno! ¿Adónde **6.** _____ (ir) nosotros primero?

MAGALI: Pues mira, esto lo he pensado bastante. Primero **7.** _____ (tomar) un avión desde acá hasta Santiago de Chile. **8.** _____ (pasar) unas semanas viajando por Chile y ya que también **9.** _____ (querer) pasar unas semanas en Argentina, después **10.** _____ (volar) a Buenos Aires.

DAVID: Y después de eso, nosotros **11.** _____ (tener) que ir a Europa, ¿no?

MAGALI: ¡Claro que sí! ¡Espero que ganemos!

WB 14-23 | No lo creo. Raúl llama a Roberto por teléfono desde los Estados Unidos para contarle sobre su viaje a Estados Unidos. ¿Cómo reacciona Roberto a las cosas que le dice? Para saberlo, forma oraciones usando el presente perfecto del subjuntivo en las cláusulas subordinadas donde sea necesario.

1. ser imposible / tú quedarse / en hoteles de cuatro estrellas

_____

_____

2. no creer / tú y tu novia / conocer / al presidente de los Estados Unidos

_____

_____

3. estar seguro / tu novia / pasarlo bien / en Washington

_____

_____

4. no dudar / tú / participar / en tres manifestaciones políticas

_____

_____

5. no pensar / tu novia / decirte / que no quiere volver a Chile

_____

_____

Nombre _____ Fecha _____

 15 *Los avances tecnológicos: Uruguay*

VOCABULARIO Los avances tecnológicos

WB 15-1 | ¿Qué palabra es? Lee las pistas e identifica las palabras relacionadas con los aparatos electrónicos.

1. Usas un equipo de _____ para escuchar música.

2. Para hacer una llamada fuera de la casa usas un teléfono _____.

3. La antena _____ te lleva programas desde un _____.

4. Necesitas un _____ para recibir las llamadas cuando no estás en casa.

5. El _____ reemplazó el casete.

6. Para dejar de usar un aparato electrónico tienes que _____lo.

7. Para ver un programa de televisión después de su hora programada, tienes que _____lo.

8. Para conectar la electricidad a algún aparato electrónico, tienes que _____lo.

WB 15-2 | ¡Qué desastre! Alicia ya está harta de su compañera de casa, Marga, porque ella es adicta a los aparatos electrónicos. Ahora le está contando a su amigo cómo es Marga. Completa su conversación, rellenando los espacios en blanco con una palabra apropiada de la siguiente lista.

antena parabólica   desconectar   grabar   teléfono celular   contestador   encendido

prender   DVD   control remoto   funcionar   satélite   reproductor de DVD

ALICIA: Te juro, Leo, Marga es un desastre. Nunca sale de la casa porque siempre está

pegada a la televisión. Desde que compramos la **1.** _____ para

recibir los canales de **2.** _____, la pobre casi no se ha levantado

de su sillón.

LEO: Pues, ¿qué hace? ¿Se duerme en el sillón?

ALICIA: No, por lo menos no se duerme allí. Pero todo comienza a las diez de la mañana.

3. _____ la televisión e inmediatamente después, le mete un

4. _____ a el **5.** _____ para ver los

programas que perdió durante la noche anterior cuando dormía.

LEO: ¿Cómo?

ALICIA: ¡Ah! ¿No te lo dije? Sí, Marga **6.** _____ casi todas las telenovelas.

Claro, no las puede ver todas a la vez. Y bueno, cuando termina eso, empieza a

cambiar canales como loca con el **7.** _____. Nunca puedo ver

nada en la tele, porque está ella allí todo el tiempo.

LEO: ¡Qué lata! *(What a pain!)*

ALICIA: Pero, eso no es lo que más me molesta. Marga, como está tan ocupada durante el día,

nunca contesta el teléfono. Siempre deja que el **8.** _____ conteste, o simplemente **9.** _____ el teléfono porque no quiere que nadie

la moleste. ¿Te imaginas? Entonces nadie me puede dejar un mensaje.

LEO: Chica, yo en tu lugar, la botaría de la casa. Pero, una solución más inmediata sería

comprarte un **10.** _____ y dejarlo **11.** _____

todo el día por si te llaman tus amigos. ¿Qué te parece?

ALICIA: Ya tengo uno, el problema es que no me **12.** _____ bien. Creo que

necesito cambiarle las pilas *(batteries)*.

LEO: ¡Anda! ¡Ponle las pilas!

ESTRUCTURA I · Making statements in the past: Past (imperfect) subjunctive

To learn more about the **Subjunctive,** go to Heinle iRadio at www.thomsonedu.com/spanish.

WB 15-3 | Una carta al gerente Javier tuvo una mala experiencia hoy cuando fue a comprar un nuevo equipo de estéreo. Ahora le escribe una carta al gerente de la tienda para quejarse de esta experiencia. Ayúdale a completar la carta, rellenando los espacios en blanco con la forma apropiada del verbo en el imperfecto del subjuntivo.

Estimado Señor Gangas:

1. _____ (querer) informarle de una mala experiencia que tuve hoy cuando estaba en su

tienda con mi novia. Lo que quería yo era muy simple. Buscaba algún estéreo que **2.** _____

(tener) radio, que **3.** _____ (tocar) discos compactos y que **4.** _____ (ser)

barato. Punto. Pero su dependiente, Jorge Demalaleche, tenía otra idea. Él recomendaba que yo

5. _____ (mirar) las computadoras. Dijo que era necesario que yo **6.** _____

(comprar) un nuevo PC para que así mi novia y yo **7.** _____ (poder) escuchar la radio en

Internet y no **8.** _____ (necesitar) discos compactos. ¡Le dije que yo compraría el PC con

tal de que él me lo **9.** _____ (dar) al precio del estéreo barato que yo buscaba!

Pues, al señor Demalaleche, no le gustó para nada que yo le **10.** _____ (decir) eso y me

dijo que aunque las nuevas computadoras **11.** _____ (venderse) al mismo precio que los

estéreos, ¡no me vendería una! En ese momento le dije que antes de que (él) **12.** _____

(abrir) la boca una vez más, que era importante que **13.** _____ (hacer) un esfuerzo para

ser más cortés con nosotros. Entonces mi novia le dijo que podríamos ir a cualquier otra tienda para

comprar lo que buscábamos. El señor Demalaleche se puso más enojado y le dijo a mi novia que no

tenía miedo que nosotros **14.** _____ (irse) a otro lugar.

Señor Gangas, yo sé que el señor Demalaleche esperaba que nosotros **15.** _____ (gastar)

mucho dinero en su tienda, pero ésa no fue la manera de lograrlo. Quizás él **16.** _____

(deber) tomar un curso de cortesía. Yo, por mi parte, no volveré a su tienda.

Atentamente,
Javier Begaña

WB 15-4 | En el pasado ¿Cómo era la vida de Ana cuando vivía con sus padres? Termina cada oración con una frase apropiada, conjugando el verbo en el imperfecto del subjuntivo.

1. Mis padres nunca creían que yo _____ (portarse) bien en la escuela.

2. Era importante que mis amigos y yo no _____ (volver) a casa después de la medianoche.

3. Mi madre quería que yo _____ (buscar) un novio que fuera inteligente.

4. Mi familia iba de vacaciones a menos que nosotros no _____ (tener) dinero.

5. Mi padre nunca permitió que yo _____ (comprar) una moto.

WB 15-5 | ¡Qué buen día! Leticia y José están charlando con Luis sobre las fotos y los videos que sacaron hace dos semanas cuando unos amigos suyos se casaron. ¿Qué dicen? Forma oraciones completas con los elementos dados, usando el imperfecto del subjuntivo en la cláusula subordinada. Se indica si debes usar el pretérito o el imperfecto en la cláusula principal. Sigue el modelo.

Modelo: JORGE: yo / querer (imp.) que tú / sacar más fotos, Leticia
Yo quería que tú sacaras más fotos, Leticia.

1. LUIS: los novios / tener (imp.) miedo / Uds. llegar tarde

_____

_____

2. LETICIA: pues, nosotros / no creer (imp.) / el cura / dejarnos sacar fotos dentro de la iglesia

_____

_____

3. JOSÉ: sí, y nosotros / sólo querer (imp.) buscar / un lugar / ser bueno para sacar las fotos

_____

_____

4. LETICIA: ser (pret.) bueno / la boda / no empezar a tiempo

_____

_____

5. LUIS: ser (pret.) una lástima / el padre de Anita / no estar allí

_____

_____

6. LETICIA: sí, pero yo / alegrarse (pret.) / tú / servir de compañero para Anita, Luís

_____

_____

7. LUIS: a mí / gustarme (pret.) / todo el mundo / divertirse

_____

_____

8. JOSÉ: no haber (imp.) / nadie / irse / antes de las tres de la mañana

_____

_____

VOCABULARIO La computadora

WB 15-6 | De compras en Compuventa Mientras navegabas la Red, encontraste la siguiente oferta para una computadora en una tienda virtual. Mira el anuncio e identifica cada uno de los aparatos incluidos en el anuncio.

COMPUVENTA

www.compuventa.com.uy

¡Qué buena ganga!

¡Cómprelo ahora mismo!

¡TODO EL EQUIPO POR TAN SÓLO 10.640,00 PESOS!

1. _____   5. _____

2. _____   6. _____

3. _____   7. _____

4. _____   8. _____

Nombre _____ Fecha _____

WB 15-7 | Conectándose con Antel El proveedor uruguayo de Internet, Antel, necesita tu ayuda para completar su anuncio para su página web. Rellena los espacios en blanco con una palabra apropiada de la siguiente lista.

archivar	mensajes	disco duro
navegar	conexión	programar
quitar el programa	teletrabajar	estar conectado
Internet	salón de charla	
hacer click	correo electrónico	

¡Haga Antel su proveedor de Internet! Con Antel, usted puede **1.** _____

en línea las veinticuatro horas al día. Toda la familia puede **2.** _____ por

el **3.** _____ y recibir **4.** _____ por nuestro servicio de

5. _____. Además, Antel le ofrece su propio **6.** _____,

por el cual usted puede comunicarse en vivo con gente de todas partes del mundo. La

7. _____ que usted tendrá con Antel estará tan segura que usted podrá

8. _____ desde la casa y no necesitará ir al trabajo.

Sólo hace falta una computadora con un procesador de un mínimo de 800 Mhz y con por lo

menos 64 MB de memoria. No hace falta tener un **9.** _____ muy grande,

ya que usted puede **10.** _____ sus documentos en nuestro servidor; ¡Le

daremos 100 GB de espacio gratis!

Con Antel todo es fácil. No tiene que saber **11.** _____ la computadora,

sólo tiene que saber **12.** _____ sobre nuestro icono para empezar nuestro

servicio. Y al terminar su trabajo en línea, usted sólo tiene que **13.** _____

y ya está.

¡Conéctese hoy!

ESTRUCTURA II Taking about hypothetical situations: *If*-clauses

WB 15-8 | Viajes Nacho y Enrique fueron de viaje a Uruguay, pero las novias, Anita y Teresa, no los acompañaron. Ellas están en casa charlando sobre el viaje de los novios. Para saber lo que dicen, rellena los espacios en blanco con la forma apropiada de los verbos indicados. **¡OJO!** Vas a usar el imperfecto del subjuntivo y el condicional, pero tienes que saber dónde usar cada forma.

1. Si ellos no _____ (hablar) español, no _____

   (poder) comunicarse bien con la gente que encuentren allí, ni _____

   (gozar) mucho de su viaje.

2. Si estos dos chicos _____ (tener) más tiempo,

   _____ (quedarse) allí dos semanas más y _____

   (conocer) más las culturas indígenas.

3. Ellos dijeron que si _____ (llover) todos los días,

   _____ (volver) temprano.

4. Nacho me dijo que si _____ (estar) cerca de Argentina,

_____ (ir) a visitar a Hernán.

5. Si nosotras no les _____ (escribir) correos electrónicos, ellos

_____ (estar) enojados con nosotras y _____

(pensar) que hemos olvidado de ellos.

WB 15-9 | ¿Qué harían? Carlos y sus amigos están charlando sobre las posibilidades de montar un negocio virtual. Todos saben que en este momento no pueden hacerlo y por eso están hablando hipotéticamente. Para saber lo que dicen, forma oraciones hipotéticas con los elementos dados. Sigue el modelo.

> **Modelo** CARLOS Y TONI: si nosotros / tener dinero / montar una tienda virtual
> *Si tuviéramos dinero, montaríamos una tienda virtual.*

1. FERNANDO: si yo / saber más sobre diseño / poder ofrecer un servicio para diseñar páginas Web

_____

2. NIDIA Y LINDA: si nosotras / poder ir a Francia frecuentemente / establecer una tienda de perfumes franceses

_____

3. CARLOS: si Juan / estudiar negocios / poder ser nuestro gerente

_____

4. JUAN: Carlos, si tú / estar más al tanto con los negocios Web / poder ser millonario

_____

5. TONI: Si todos Uds. / no gastar tanto tiempo soñando / hacer algo más productivo

_____

BIENVENIDOS A URUGUAY

En este segmento del video, vas a aprender un poco sobre Uruguay y de la vida de sus ciudadanos. Los temas incluyen:

- la geografía
- la economía
- los recursos naturales
- la política
- las ciudades principales

WB 15-10 | En el segmento del video vas a escuchar muchos cognados que pueden facilitar tu comprensión. Algunos de estos cognados aparecen aquí. Trata de pronunciar cada palabra o frase y luego empareja los cognados con su definición en inglés.

1. _____ privilegiada   **a.** indices/indexes

2. _____ urbes   **b.** urban areas/cities

3. _____ noble   **c.** delight

4. _____ haciendas   **d.** noble

5. _____ aromática   **e.** disputed

6. _____ gratuito		f. aromatic
7. _____ deleite		g. gratuitous/free
8. _____ infusión		h. infusion/tea
9. _____ índices		i. haciendas/estates
10. _____ disputada		j. privileged

WB 15-11 | Después de ver el segmento del video, rellena los espacios en blanco con un cognado apropiado de la actividad **WB 15-10.**

1. Gracias a su _____ geografía y a su _____ ubicación, a 30 grados al sur del ecuador, Uruguay goza de un clima templado y agradable a lo largo del año.

2. Uruguay es un pueblo orgulloso de su vida democrática, de su sistema educativo que desde los niveles básicos hasta el profesional es _____ para todas las personas, de los altos _____ de seguridad tanto en las urbes como fuera de ellas.

3. Es aquí, precisamente en el campo y las _____, con sus grandes casas o estancias, donde nace el gaucho.

4. La ciudad de Colonia del Sacramento está ubicada cerca de la frontera con Argentina, en lo que por mucho tiempo fue una región _____ entre España y Portugal.

5. Y cómo olvidar el tango, esa desgarradora expresión de la sensibilidad uruguaya. Nació a principios del siglo XX en los suburbios de Montevideo y Buenos Aires y hoy gente de todo el mundo lo baila y lo escucha con _____.

WB 15-12 | Después de ver el segmento del video otra vez, selecciona la mejor respuesta a las siguientes preguntas.

1. _____ ¿Cuáles son los países vecinos de Uruguay?
   a. Argentina y Ecuador
   b. Paraguay y Portugal
   c. Brasil y Argentina
   d. Paraguay y Argentina

2. _____ ¿De qué ascendencia es la gente uruguaya?
   a. africana, china y española
   b. española, portuguesa e italiana
   c. argentina, española e indígena
   d. africana, española e italiana

3. _____ ¿Cuál es la capital de Uruguay?
   a. Montevideo
   b. Río de la Plata
   c. Buenos Aires
   d. Sacramento

4. _____ ¿Cuál es la principal actividad económica?
   a. el baile del tango
   b. la producción de mate
   c. la producción de carne de vaca
   d. la producción de carne de caballo

5. _____ ¿Quién es Eduardo Galeano?
   a. un famoso bailarín de tango
   b. el director de la sinfonía uruguaya
   c. un gaucho famoso
   d. un escritor uruguayo

¡A ESCRIBIR!

Strategy: Speculating and hypothesizing

In this section, you are going to use what you have learned to write about a hypothetical situation and make a projection about what might occur under particular circumstances. You will then outline some of the positive and/or negative consequences of this situation. This will involve speculating about the future and imagining possible outcomes that may arise from the hypothetical situation you select. Individuals in many professions prepare projections based on hypothetical situations. For example, marketing and advertising managers speculate about the success of their products, and individuals in government make projections about the effects of projects and programs.

Consider the situation of a university student:

Ojalá yo tuviera una computadora portátil. De momento, no poseo ninguna computadora, y estoy harto de hacer cola (stand in line) en los laboratorios de computadoras de la universidad. Si tuviera mi propia computadora portátil, podría navegar la Red o mirar mi correo electrónico en cualquier momento. Tendría más tiempo para estudiar o pasar con mis amigos porque no tendría que hacer cola en la universidad para usar una computadora. No importaría si estuviera en casa, en la universidad o en la casa de un amigo —siempre la tendría a mi lado. Sería mucho más fácil conectarme al Internet. También la podría llevar conmigo cuando estoy de vacaciones en casa de mis padres o en cualquier otro sitio.

Task: Preparing a projection

Paso 1 Think about how the world would be if there were no computers. Think about the following questions:

- In what ways would your life be easier?
- In what ways would your life be more difficult?
- Would people be different? How?
- How would the scientific world be different?
- What would international relations be like without the modes of communication that computers provide us?

Paso 2 Organize your ideas under a general topic and write a first draft of your essay.

Paso 3 Revise your first draft, checking the vocabulary and grammar. Make sure you have used the imperfect subjunctive and conditional with *if*-clauses correctly. When you have finished, write your second draft below.

_____

_____

_____

_____

_____

_____

_____

_____

_____

_____

_____

_____

_____

_____

_____

_____

_____

_____

_____

_____

_____

_____

_____

_____

_____

ATAJO 4.0

Functions: Expressing a wish or desire; Expressing conditions; Hypothesizing

Vocabulary: Dreams and aspirations; computers; Working conditions

Grammar: Verbs: *if*-clauses

Autoprueba

VOCABULARIO

WB 15-13 | **Los domingueros modernos** Juan y Delma van de viaje, pero antes de ir tienen que asegurarse de tener todos los aparatos electrónicos necesarios para el viaje. Completa su conversación, rellenando los espacios en blanco con palabras apropiadas de la siguiente lista.

antena parabólica	estéreo	grabadora de DVD
equipo	DVD	enchufado
videocámara digital	desconectar	teléfono celular
cámara digital	satélite	

DELMA: Juan, ¿tienes todo preparado para el viaje?

JUAN: Creo que sí, Delma. Déjame pensar… Sé que vamos a sacar muchas fotos así que ya

empaqué la **1.** _____ . Y para grabar en vivo lo que haremos,

empaqué también la **2.** _____ .

DELMA: Muy bien. Y empaqué el **3.** _____ por si nos llaman los vecinos

que vienen a cuidar la casa. ¿No te parece buena idea?

JUAN: Es una idea excelente. Sabes, no quiero perder el partido de fútbol este domingo así

que voy a meter un **4.** _____ en la **5.** _____

y a ponerla a grabar el partido.

DELMA: ¡Juan! ¡Eres imposible! Y no te olvides que el hotel adonde vamos tiene una

6. _____ y recibe todos los canales por

7. _____ . Ahora, dime, ¿vas a **8.** _____ la

computadora y el **9.** _____ de **10.** _____?

JUAN: Había pensado dejarlo **11.** _____ por si los vecinos, cuando

vengan a cuidar la casa, quieren escuchar música. ¿Qué piensas?

DELMA: Está bien, pero si se nos quema la casa va a ser tu culpa.

WB 15-14 | **¿Estás al tanto?** ¿Estás al tanto del mundo de la computadora? Empareja cada palabra con su definición para medir tu capacidad *(proficiency)*.

a. el teclado   **f.** la impresora

b. el disco duro   **g.** el correo electrónico

c. el ratón   **h.** el salón de charla

d. los altavoces   **i.** la pantalla

e. el escáner

_____ **1.** Lo pulsas para seleccionar diferentes opciones de un programa.

_____ **2.** Es el lugar donde guardas tus archivos en la computadora.

_____ **3.** Es un lugar en el ciberespacio donde te comunicas por la computadora con otras personas.

_____ **4.** Los usas para escuchar sonido emitido por la computadora.

_____ **5.** Es donde ves las imágenes en la computadora.

_____ **6.** Es un mensaje que se manda por la computadora.

_____ **7.** Lo usas para escribir con la computadora.

_____ **8.** La usas para imprimir imágenes de la computadora.

_____ **9.** Lo usas para pasar una foto o un documento a un formato electrónico.

WB 15-15 | Las instrucciones ¿Cuáles son las instrucciones que acompañan el nuevo programa que compró Jaime? Rellena los espacios en blanco con la palabra apropiada de la siguiente lista.

abrir el programa   navegar   pantalla   archivar

hacer click   página Web   quitar

Para **1.** _____, es necesario **2.** _____ sobre el icono

que aparece en su **3.** _____. Cuando el programa se abra, Ud. puede

empezar a trabajar en sus documentos. Antes de **4.** _____ el programa,

se le recomienda **5.** _____ los documentos directamente al disco duro.

Si Ud. necesita más instrucciones, las puede encontrar en nuestra **6.** _____.

De allí Ud. puede **7.** _____ a la sección que necesite.

WB 15-16 | Buenas amigas Carmen acaba de recibir un correo electrónico de una vieja amiga. Completa el mensaje, rellenando los espacios en blanco con la forma apropiada del imperfecto del subjuntivo.

Querida Carmen:

Cuando recibí tu email me alegré mucho de que tú **1.** _____ (recordarme).

Yo esperaba que nosotras **2.** _____ (hacer) contacto en algún momento porque éramos tan buenas amigas en la secundaria. Déjame contarte un poco de lo que he hecho en los últimos seis años. Me casé con Adolfo. ¿Te acuerdas de él? Cuando nos graduamos, mis padres no querían que nosotros **3.** _____ (casarse). ¿Te acuerdas? Pero eso fue porque deseaban que nosotros **4.** _____ (ir) a la universidad antes de que **5.** _____ (meternos) en una situación tan seria. No iba a casarme sin que mis padres me **6.** _____ (dar) su permiso, así que esperé y me casé después de graduarme.

Saqué mi título universitario y conseguí un trabajo inmediatamente. Tenía que ganar mucho dinero para que Adolfo **7.** _____ (poder) seguir sus estudios de informática.

Al principio fue difícil, pero después de poco tiempo estaba súper contenta de que él **8.** _____ (estudiar) porque sabía que iba a poder encontrar un buen trabajo cuando **9.** _____ (graduarse). ¡Y lo hizo! Ahora es el jefe de una compañía de computadoras.

Bueno, Carmen, ahora que me has localizado, escríbeme más y dime más de tu vida.

Un beso, Belén

WB 15-17 | ¿Qué harían? ¿Qué harían Juan y sus amigos en las siguientes situaciones? Forma oraciones hipotéticas con los elementos dados, usando el imperfecto del subjuntivo y el condicional.

1. si Juan / no tener que trabajar, / pasar todo su tiempo en la computadora

   _____

2. si Carlos y Marga / comprar una mejor computadora, / poder usar el Internet

   _____

3. si Tomás / no ser tan tímido, / poder conocer a más chicas en los salones de charla

   _____

4. si Nancy graduarse / con un título en informática, / ganar mucho dinero

   _____

5. si Óscar / ofrecerme un trabajo con su compañía, / yo cambiar de carrera

   _____

Lab Manual

¡Mucho gusto!

VOCABULARIO Saludos y despedidas

CD1,
Track 2
LM P-1 | Saludos y despedidas You will hear six brief dialogues. After listening to each one, identify the correct speakers and situations by writing the letter of the dialogue in the appropriate space below.

_____ **1.** Two students meeting each other for the first time.

_____ **2.** Two close friends saying "good-bye."

_____ **3.** A student addressing her professor.

_____ **4.** Two people of the same age saying "hello."

_____ **5.** A patient greeting his doctor.

_____ **6.** A daughter greeting her mother.

CD1,
Track 3
LM P-2 | ¿Qué dices? Respond to each statement you hear by choosing between the two replies that immediately follow it. Indicate your choice by selecting **a** or **b.**

1. a b   **2.** a b   **3.** a b   **4.** a b   **5.** a b   **6.** a b

CD1,
Track 4
LM P-3 | ¿Tú o Ud.? Listen to the following greetings. Decide if the speaker is addressing people in a formal or an informal manner by selecting **tú** or **Ud.**

1. tú Ud.   **2.** tú Ud.   **3.** tú Ud.   **4.** tú Ud.

ESTRUCTURA I Talking about yourself and others: Subject pronouns and the present tense of the verb *ser*

CD1,
Track 5
LM P-4 | El verbo *ser* You will hear sentences containing forms of the verb **ser.** Decide which subject pronoun corresponds to the sentences. Write the appropriate letter next to each pronoun.

_____ **1.** yo

_____ **2.** tú

_____ **3.** Ud.

_____ **4.** nosotros

_____ **5.** ella

_____ **6.** ellos

CD1,
Track 6 **LM P-5** | **¿Cómo son?** Say whether you agree (**sí**) or disagree (**no**) with the recorded statements. Write **sí** or **no** accordingly.

1. _____

2. _____

3. _____

4. _____

5. _____

CD1,
Track 7 **LM P-6** | **¿Cómo eres tú?** You will hear a total of six statements. Pick three that identify you and write down their corresponding letters in the blanks provided.

1. _____   4. _____

2. _____   5. _____

3. _____   6. _____

ASÍ SE DICE Identifying quantities: *Hay* and numbers 0–30

CD1,
Track 8 **LM P-7** | **Identificación** Match the statement you hear with its corresponding illustration. **¡OJO!** Pay close attention to the **hay** form.

1. _____   2. _____   3. _____

4. _____   5. _____   6. _____

CD1, Track 9 **LM P-8** | **Los números** Listen carefully to the following numbers. After repeating them aloud, write them in the spaces below first as numerals and then spelled out.

1. _____ _____

2. _____ _____

3. _____ _____

4. _____ _____

5. _____ _____

6. _____ _____

7. _____ _____

8. _____ _____

9. _____ _____

10. _____ _____

CD1, Track 10 **LM P-9** | **Las matemáticas** Listen carefully to the following math problems and write down the numerical responses in the spaces provided.

1. _____   4. _____

2. _____   5. _____

3. _____   6. _____

VOCABULARIO Palabras interrogativas

CD1, Track 11 **LM P-10** | **Interrogaciones** Listen carefully to the partial questions and choose the right interrogative word from the list. Identify your choice with the letter of the question that best corresponds to that interrogative word.

_____ 1. Cómo   _____ 6. Por qué

_____ 2. Cuál   _____ 7. Qué

_____ 3. Cuándo   _____ 8. Quién

_____ 4. Cuántos   _____ 9. Dónde

_____ 5. De dónde   _____ 10. Cómo

CD1, Track 12 **LM P-11** | **Información personal** Listen to the following statements and select the appropriate interrogative word. Make certain it agrees in gender and in number.

1. cuánta   cuánto   cuántos   cuántas

2. quién   quiénes

3. cuál   cuáles

4. cuánta   cuánto   cuántos   cuántas

5. cuál   cuáles

6. dónde   cuándo

CD1,
Track 13

LM P-12 | **¿Quién eres?** Answer the following questions posed by detective Austin, el «Poderoso». ¡OJO! Make sure you spell out the numbers!

1. _____
2. _____
3. _____
4. _____
5. _____
6. _____

RITMOS Y MÚSICA

LM P-13 | **La música** Listen to the song "Mami, me gustó *(I liked it)*" written by Arsenio Rodríguez and interpreted by Todos Estrellas. Then, indicate if the following statements about its content are **cierto** *(true)* or **falso** *(false)*.

1. _____ En la canción hay piano, trompetas y percusión.

2. _____ El ritmo es rápido, bueno para bailar.

3. _____ Hay una sola voz *(voice)* masculina.

4. _____ Esta canción es un ejemplo de la salsa.

5. _____ En la canción hay un solo de guitarra.

LM P-14 | **La letra** After listening to the song "Mami me gustó", choose the option that best applies to its lyrics.

1. a. En la canción hay palabras en inglés y en español.

   b. En la canción sólo hay palabras en español.

2. a. Es una canción de niños para la madre.

   b. Es una canción de un hombre para una mujer.

3. a. En la canción, al hombre le gustan *(he likes)* muchas cosas de la mujer.

   b. En la canción, al hombre le gusta sólo una cosa de la mujer.

4. a. La palabra "mami" en la canción es un término romántico para una mujer.

   b. La palabra "mami" en la canción es un término cómico para una mujer.

5. a. El coro de la canción dice "esa casa que me hiciste *(you did to me)*, mami, me gustó".

   b. El coro de la canción dice "esa cosa que me hiciste, mami, me gustó".

En una clase de español: Los Estados Unidos

VOCABULARIO En la clase

CD1, Track 14 **LM 1-1 | La clase de español de la profesora Muñoz** You will hear pairs of sentences based on the following illustration. After repeating each sentence aloud, select the one that best describes the illustration and select the corresponding letter.

1. a b   **2.** a b   **3.** a b   **4.** a b   **5.** a b   **6.** a b

CD1, Track 15 **LM 1-2 | ¿Es posible?** Mari is going to tell you who or what can be found either in a class-room or in a backpack. **¡OJO!** She sometimes exaggerates. Listen to what she says and select **a. es posible** or **b. es imposible** according to the statements she makes. Follow the model.

> Modelo   En la clase: la pizarra
> *a. es posible*

1. a. es posible   **b.** es imposible   **6. a.** es posible   **b.** es imposible

2. a. es posible   **b.** es imposible   **7. a.** es posible   **b.** es imposible

3. a. es posible   **b.** es imposible   **8. a.** es posible   **b.** es imposible

4. a. es posible   **b.** es imposible   **9. a.** es posible   **b.** es imposible

5. a. es posible   **b.** es imposible   **10. a.** es posible   **b.** es imposible

LM 1-3 | ¿De qué color es? Listen to the colors of the following objects. Repeat the colors after the speaker and write them in the spaces provided Then, answer the questions with the appropriate color.

1. El papel es _____.

   Es _____.

2. Los bolígrafos son _____.

   Son _____.

3. La mochila es _____.

   Es _____.

4. La pizarra es _____.

   Es _____.

5. Los escritorios son _____.

   Son _____.

ESTRUCTURA I Talking about people, things, and concepts: Definite and indefinite articles and how to make nouns plural

LM 1-4 | ¿Definido o indefinido? Choose the correct sentence from each set by selecting **a** or **b**. **¡OJO!** Pay close attention to the use of definite and indefinite articles.

1. a   b   **2.** a   b   **3.** a   b   **4.** a   b   **5.** a   b

LM 1-5 | ¡En plural! You will hear vocabulary words in the singular form. Write their plural forms in the spaces provided.

1. _____   5. _____

2. _____   6. _____

3. _____   7. _____

4. _____   8. _____

LM 1-6 | ¿Cuántas? ¿Cuántos? Answer the following questions in a complete sentence. Follow the model.

Modelo   ¿Cuántas computadoras hay en la clase?
           Hay una computadora en la clase.

1. _____

2. _____

3. _____

4. _____

5. _____

6. _____

VOCABULARIO Lenguas extranjeras, otras materias y lugares universitarios

CD1, Track 20 **LM 1-7** | **Los estudiantes internacionales de la profesora Muñoz** Listen to a brief description of eight international students in Professor Muñoz's class and complete the following sentences by stating their native language.

1. Felicitas Semprini habla _____.

2. Trini Whitmanabaum habla _____.

3. Miguel Paz d'Islilla habla _____.

4. Marilina Ribelina habla _____.

5. Kianu Tomasaki habla _____.

6. Stéphane Pagny habla _____.

7. Sergei Morosoff habla _____.

8. João do Maura habla _____.

CD1, Track 21 **LM 1-8** | **¿Qué cursos?** Listen again to **Track 20** and identify what courses each student studies. List their courses in the spaces provided below.

1. Felicitas Semprini estudia _____.

2. Trini Whitmanabaum estudia _____.

3. Miguel Paz d'Islilla estudia _____.

4. Marilina Ribelina estudia _____.

5. Kianu Tomasaki estudia _____.

6. Stéphane Pagny estudia _____.

7. Sergei Morosoff estudia _____.

8. João do Maura estudia _____.

CD1, Track 22 **LM 1-9** | **En mi universidad** Listen to the following university places. Then write the proper name of the corresponding building at your university. Follow the model.

Modelo   la clase de español
Hellems Hall 202

1. _____

2. _____

3. _____

4. _____

5. _____

6. _____

ESTRUCTURA II — Describing everyday activities: Present tense of regular -ar verbs

CD1, Track 23   **LM 1-10** | **¿Qué hacen?** *(What do they do?)* Listen to the sentences describing what each of the following people is doing. Then match the letter with the corresponding illustration.

1. _____

2. _____

3. _____

4. _____

5. _____

6. _____

CD1, Track 24 **LM 1-11 | Este semestre** Liliana is very excited about all of the things she and her friends are doing this semester; but who does what? Listen to each of her statements and then, choose who the subject of each sentence is. Follow the model:

Modelo   Descansas por la noche.
          b. tú

1. **a.** yo   **b.** mis compañeros y yo   **c.** la profesora

2. **a.** ellas   **b.** usted   **c.** mis amigas y yo

3. **a.** ustedes   **b.** la profesora   **c.** yo

4. **a.** mis compañeros   **b.** mi compañera de cuarto   **c.** tú

5. **a.** los profesores   **b.** yo   **c.** mi amigo

CD1, Track 25 **LM 1-12 | La vida de los estudiantes internacionales** Listen to a student's daily routine and compare it to your own by writing a sentence that describes your life. Follow the model.

Modelo   Sergei estudia mucho por la noche.
          Estudio mucho por el día.

1. _____

2. _____

3. _____

4. _____

5. _____

6. _____

CD1, Track 26 **LM 1-13 | Mi rutina semanal** *(weekly)* Fernando participates in many different activities during the week. Listen carefully as he describes his weekly routine. Match each activity with the corresponding day(s) of the week.

1. _____ canta en una banda   **a.** lunes

2. _____ toca la guitarra   **b.** martes

3. _____ dibuja en el parque   **c.** miércoles

4. _____ trabaja en la libería   **d.** jueves

5. _____ enseña música   **e.** viernes

                                      f. sábado

                                      g. domingo

ASÍ SE DICE   Telling time

CD1,
Track 27
LM 1-14 | Qué hora es? Match the time you hear with the corresponding times written below.

_____ **1.** 2:15 PM

_____ **2.** 8:30 AM

_____ **3.** 1:25 PM

_____ **4.** 8:45 PM

_____ **5.** 12:00 AM

_____ **6.** 10:45 PM

PRONUNCIACIÓN I   *a, e, i, o,* and *u*

CD1,
Track 28
Even though the letters **a, e, i, o, u**, and sometimes **y** are used to represent vowel sounds in both English and Spanish, the pronunciation of the vowel sounds is different. English vowels are generally longer than those in Spanish. In addition, English vowel sounds often merge with other vowels to produce combination sounds. As a general rule, pronounce Spanish vowels with a short, precise sound.

LM 1-15 | ¡Así suena! Listen and repeat.

a: armario   papel   lápiz   cuaderno   mochila

Hay tres lápices en la mochila.

e: reloj   mesa   secretaria   escritorio   pupitre

En la clase hay un reloj, un escritorio y veinte pupitres.

i: libro   mochila   cinta   silla   televisor

En la universidad hay sillas, libros y televisores.

o: consejero   bolígrafo   biblioteca   profesor   borrador

Hoy el profesor no necesita el borrador.

u: nueve   universidad   Ud.   alumnos   única

Un profesor de la universidad tiene nueve alumnos.

PRONUNCIACIÓN *h* and *ch*

CD1, Track 29

The letter **h** is the only silent letter in the Spanish alphabet; it is never pronounced: **historia**.

Ch is pronounced as in the English word *church:* **mochila**.

LM 1-16 | **¡Así suena!** Listen and repeat.

h: **h**istoria **h**oy **h**ola **h**amburguesa **H**éctor
Hoy **h**ay un examen en la clase de **h**istoria.
ch: mo**ch**ila o**ch**o **ch**ico dicio**ch**o pon**ch**o
El **ch**ico tiene o**ch**o pon**ch**os y mo**ch**ilas. ¡Son mu**ch**os!

RITMOS Y MÚSICA

LM 1-17 | **La música** Listen to the song "Cumbia de los muertos" by Ozomatli. Then, indicate if the following statements about its content are **cierto** *(true)* or **falso** *(false).*

1. _____ La música es triste, melancólica.

2. _____ Hay mucha percusión en la canción.

3. _____ Hay una voz principal y un coro.

4. _____ El ritmo no es muy bueno para bailar.

5. _____ La música es una mezcla *(mix)* de cumbia y reggae.

LM 1-18 | **La letra** After listening to the song "Cumbia de los muertos", choose the option that best applies to its lyrics.

1. **a.** La canción comienza en español y termina en inglés.
   b. La canción comienza en español, hay una parte en inglés y termina en español.

2. Una parte de la canción dice: "mira cómo baila mi mamá / bailando con mi hermano del pasado". ¿A qué se refiere *(refers to)*?
   a. a las madres y los hijos
   b. a los vivos y los muertos

3. **a.** En esta canción el pasado y el presente están en armonía *(harmony)*.
   b. En esta canción el pasado y el presente están en conflicto.

4. **a.** El autor de esta canción ve al pasado con melancolía.
   b. El autor de esta canción ve al pasado con alegría.

5. **a.** "Cumbia de los muertos" es una canción apropiada para un funeral.
   b. "Cumbia de los muertos" es una canción apropiada para el Día de los Veteranos en Estados Unidos.
   c. "Cumbia de los muertos" es una canción apropiada para el Día de los Muertos en México.

CD1, **LM 1-19** | **Comprensión** After watching the ¡**A ver!** video segment for Chapter 1, answer
Track 30 **cierto** *(true)* or **falso** *(false)* to the following statements.

1. _____   4. _____

2. _____   5. _____

3. _____   6. _____

CD1, **LM 1-20** | **Los amigos** Listen carefully to the following statements pertaining to the ¡**A ver!**
Track 31 video segment for Chapter 1. Link the sentence you hear with the person(s) to which it refers
by entering the appropriate letter in the space provided.

1. Javier _____

2. Alejandra _____

3. Antonio _____

4. Sofía _____

5. Valeria _____

CD1, **LM 1-21** | **¿Cuál es?** Choose the right word to complete the sentence pertaining to the
Track 32 video segment for this chapter.

1. filología — diseño

2. México — Texas

3. Valeria — Alejandra

4. va de compras — va a la playa

5. pasan — gastan

En una reunión familiar: México

VOCABULARIO La familia

CD2, Track 2 **LM 2-1 | Los miembros de la familia** Listen to each description and find the family relation to which it refers. Then, write the letter of the correct description next to it.

_____ **1.** mi tío   _____ **6.** mi abuelo

_____ **2.** mi hermana   _____ **7.** mi tía

_____ **3.** mi abuela   _____ **8.** mi padre

_____ **4.** mi madre   _____ **9.** mi hermano

_____ **5.** mis primos

CD2, Track 3 **LM 2-2 | Tu familia** Listen to the following sentences and select the response that best fits your family situation.

1. a b c   **3.** a b c   **5.** a b c

2. a b c   **4.** a b c   **6.** a b c

CD2, Track 4 **LM 2-3 | No es de la familia.** You will hear a list of family relationships in pairs. Repeat each pair and then write the pair that does not belong.

1. _____

2. _____

3. _____

4. _____

5. _____

6. _____

ASÍ SE DICE Indicating ownership and possession: Possession with *de(l)* and possessive adjectives

CD2, Track 5 **LM 2-4 | ¿Cómo son?** Juan Carlos is describing some family members. Complete his descriptions with the possessive adjectives that you hear. Follow the model below.

Modelo   Mi padre es paciente.
           Mi padre es paciente.

1. _____ hermanas son cómicas.

2. _____ padres son generosos.

3. _____ hermanos son responsables.

4. _____ novias son atléticas.

5. _____ abuelita es artística.

6. ¿Y _____ abuelita, es artística?

CD2, Track 6 **LM 2-5 | ¿Cómo se llaman?** Do you know the names of your classmates, professors, friends, pets, etc.? Answer the questions that you hear by filling in the possessive adjectives as well as the names. Follow the model.

> **Modelo** ¿Cómo se llaman tus abuelos?
> *Mis* abuelos se llaman *Alfonso y Alberto*.

1. _____ madre se llama _____.

2. _____ professor (o profesora) de español se llama _____.

3. _____ amigos se llaman _____ y _____.

4. _____ mascotas se llaman _____ y _____.

5. _____ madre se llama _____.

6. _____ compañero (o compañera) de clase se llama _____.

CD2, Track 7 **LM 2-6 | ¿De quién es?** Listen to the following questions and complete the answers. Follow the model.

> **Modelo** El bebé es del hermano de Jill. ¿De quién es el bebé?
> Es *del* hermano de Jill. Es *su* bebé.

1. Es _____ hermana de María. Es _____ nieto.

2. Es _____ padres de Tomás. Es _____ casa.

3. Son _____ Lupe y Miguel. Son _____ parientes.

4. Es _____ José y Simona. Es _____ libro.

5. Es _____ prima de Carolina. Es _____ fiesta.

6. Son _____ Julieta. Son _____ gatos.

ESTRUCTURA I Describing people and things: Common uses of the verb *ser*

CD2, Track 8 **LM 2-7 | ¿Qué son?** You will hear some sentences about family members and their professions. Complete the sentences that you hear by matching the items in the first column with the items in the second column.

1. Nosotras somos   a. piloto
2. Ellos son   b. doctor
3. Tú eres   c. hermanos
4. Mi hermano es   d. profesora
5. Yo soy   e. estudiantes

Nombre _____ Fecha _____

CD2,
Track 9

LM 2-8 | Identificación Listen carefully to each statement. Complete each statement with the correct form of the verb **ser** that you hear in the recording.

1. Tú _____ mi novio.

2. Roma _____ nuestra profesora.

3. Uds. _____ mis hermanos.

4. Mónica y yo _____ buenas amigas.

5. Yo _____ estudiante.

CD2,
Track 10

LM 2-9 | Las descripciones You will hear a description for each of the illustrations below. Match each one by writing the corresponding letter in the space provided.

1. _____

2. _____

3. _____

4. _____

5. _____

6. _____

CD2, Track 11   **LM 2-10** | **¡Así no son!** Below are six drawings representing Ángel's family. You will hear some descriptions that state the opposite of what each drawing represents. Match the drawings with the descriptions that state the opposite of what you see. Follow the model.

Modelo   *El tío Lito es delgado.*

1. _____

2. _____

3. _____

4. _____

5. _____

6. _____

CD2, Track 12 **LM 2-11** | **¡Así son!** Now you are going to listen to real descriptions of Ángel's family members. Write down the descriptive adjectives that you hear to complete the sentences. **¡OJO!** There are two adjectives per sentence.

1. Mis cuñados son _____ y _____.

2. Sus hijos son _____ y _____.

3. Mis tías son _____ y _____.

4. Mis hermanos son _____ y _____.

5. Mi padre es _____ y _____.

6. Mi madre es _____ y _____.

CD2, Track 13 **LM 2-12** | **¡Guapos y famosos!** Listen to the descriptions of the following celebrities. Match the descriptions with the celebrities.

1. _____ Oprah Winfrey

2. _____ Jodie Foster

3. _____ Arnold Schwarzenegger

4. _____ Danny DeVito

5. _____ Brad Pitt

6. _____ Nicole Kidman

VOCABULARIO Las nacionalidades

CD2, Track 14 **LM 2-13** | **¿De dónde son?** You will hear the names of ten famous people and their home countries. Complete the sentences by writing each person's nationality in the space provided.

Modelo   Penélope Cruz es de España.
          Penélope Cruz *es española*.

1. Gérard Depardieu _____

2. Antonio Banderas _____

3. Anna Kournikova _____

4. Gael García Bernal _____

5. Sting _____

6. Silvio Berlusconi _____

CD2, **LM 2-14** | **¿Qué lengua(s) hablan?** You will again hear the names of these famous people and
Track 15 their home countries. Complete the sentences with the language they most likely speak.

1. Gérard Depardieu habla _____.

2. Antonio Banderas habla _____.

3. Anna Kournikova _____.

4. Gael García Bernal habla _____.

5. Sting habla _____.

6. Silvio Berlusconi habla _____.

CD2, **LM 2-15** | **¿De qué nacionalidad?** You will hear the names of countries. For each country
Track 16 that you hear, write the nationality of the people who live in these countries.

Modelo   Brasil
          brasileños

1. _____

2. _____

3. _____

4. _____

5. _____

6. _____

ESTRUCTURA II Describing daily activities at home or at school:
Present tense of *-er* and *-ir* verbs

CD2, **LM 2-16** | **Mi suegra es una viuda alegre.** Listen to the story of a "happy widow" and fill in
Track 17 the blanks with the conjugated regular **-er** and **-ir** verbs you hear.

Mi suegra, Candela Sosa Noés, es una viuda alegre. Candela aún es joven—cincuenta

y un años—bastante atractiva y **1.** _____ mucho dinero. Personalmente,

2. _____ que **3.** _____ la vida loca. Mi esposa y yo siempre

4. _____ las cartas que ella **5.** _____ de diferentes lugares del mundo.

Candela es un idolo para sus nietos, Paqui y Tomasín. Paqui, la mayor, habla constantemente

de su moderna abuelita Candela que **6.** _____ wiski, baila salsa y ¡lleva bikini!

248   *Plazas*, Third Edition, Lab Manual

CD2,
Track 18

LM 2-17 | La vida loca de Candela You will hear a series of activities typical of Candela's life. After repeating each one, rewrite it using the corresponding change of subject. **¡OJO!** Pay special attention to the verb conjugations.

> Modelo   Candela recibe muchos regalos.
> Uds. *reciben muchos regalos.*

1. Nosotros _____.

2. Tus padres _____.

3. Sus amigas _____.

4. Tú _____.

5. Yo también _____.

ASÍ SE DICE   Counting to 100: Numbers from 30 to 100

CD2,
Track 19

LM 2-18 | Los números Spell out the numbers as you hear them.

1. _____

2. _____

3. _____

4. _____

5. _____

6. _____

CD2,
Track 20

LM 2-19 | La lotería You bought a lottery ticket with the numbers below. Listen to the audio to find out which winning numbers you have on your lottery ticket. As you hear the winning numbers called out, write down the numbers that match on your ticket. Did you win the lottery?

> Your lottery ticket: 80   58   45   32   61   79
>
> . . . And my matching numbers are . . . _____

CD2,
Track 21

LM 2-20 | Las edades Candela (the "happy widow") tells her friends' ages. Match her friends with their ages.

1. mi amigo Pedro   **a.** 54

2. mi amiga Lupe   **b.** 36

3. mis amigas Sonia y Silvia   **c.** 87

4. mis amigos Julio y Fernando   **d.** 99

5. mi amigo José   **e.** 48

6. mi amiga Ana   **f.** 63

PRONUNCIACIÓN I *r* and *rr*

CD2,
Track 22
To learn more about **r** and **rr,** go to Heinle iRadio at www.thomsonedu.com/spanish.

In Spanish there are two **r** sounds: the single **r** sound and the double **rr** sound. As you may have already noticed from the vocabulary words in this chapter and in previous chapters, the Spanish **r** is pronounced very differently from the English *r*. As a matter of fact, it has no equivalent in English. The single **r** is pronounced by flapping the tongue against the roof of the palate. The single **r** sound occurs when it is in the middle of a word, such as **prima** or **Karina.** When the **r** is placed at the beginning of a word, it has a double **r** sound, such as in the word **rubio** or **rojo.** To pronounce the double **r,** make your tongue vibrate behind the upper front teeth as you exhale. Try pronouncing the English word *thrive*. The vibration of the tongue in the *thr* sound is very close to the Spanish double **r** sound.

LM 2-21 | **¡Así suena!** Listen and repeat.

Single *r* sound: sob**r**ina; mo**r**ena; gene**r**osa; trabajado**r**es; pe**r**ezosos; libe**r**al.

Double *r* sound: **r**esponsable; **r**eservado; i**rr**esponsable; recibi**r**; bu**rr**ito; **r**ápido.

The two sounds combined: E**r**es una pe**r**sona inte**r**esante pe**r**o un poco a**rr**ogante y **r**ebelde.

PRONUNCIACIÓN II *d*

CD2,
Track 23
The Spanish **d** has two sounds. When the letter **d** is placed at the beginning of a word, such as in **Diego,** or after l or n such as in **Aldo** and **Fernando,** the sound resembles the English *d* as in *dog*. In these instances, the tongue touches the back of the front teeth rather than the gum ridge, as in English. When the **d** occurs between vowels, then the sound resembles the English *th* as in *that,* for example, in **tímido** or **humilde.**

To learn more about **d,** go to Heinle iRadio at www.thomsonedu.com/spanish.

LM 2-22 | **¡Así suena!** Listen and repeat.

The sound *d* at the beginning or after *l* and *n*: **d**ominicano; **d**eber; sal**d**o; man**d**o; **d**orado; cal**d**o

The sound *d* in the middle of a word: a**d**orno; gor**d**o; cana**d**iense; esta**d**ouni**d**ense; salva**d**oreño; apelli**d**o

The two sounds combined: **d**a**d**o; **d**e**d**o; **d**u**d**a; **d**on**d**e; **d**uen**d**e; **d**ormi**d**o

Nombre _____ Fecha _____

♪ RITMOS Y MÚSICA

LM 2-23 | Preguntas generales. Listen to the song "Labios compartidos" written by the Mexican group Maná, and select the answers that are the most appropriate.

1. Es una canción (song) de amor   Es una canción cómica
2. Es una salsa   Es pop moderno
3. La cantante (singer) es una mujer   El cantante es un hombre
4. El instrumento principal es el piano   El instrumento principal es la guitarra
5. El ritmo es lento   El ritmo es rápido
6. Es melancólica   Es alegre

LM 2-24 | ¿Reconoces palabras? Listen to the song "Labios compartidos" a second time, and select the words that you hear from the first 10 verses in the song.

1. amor lío   amor mío
2. si estás debajo   si estoy debajo
3. este es mi cielo   este es tu cielo
4. me tengo como un perro   me tienes como un perro
5. como un perro a tus pies como un perro a mis pies
6. vuelve a mi tu boca   vuelve a ti mi boca

CD2,
Track 24
LM 2-25 | **Comprensión** After watching the ¡**A ver!** video segment for Chapter 2, answer **cierto** *(true)* or **falso** *(false)* to the following statements.

1. _____

2. _____

3. _____

4. _____

5. _____

6. _____

LM 2-26 | **¿La familia de Alejandra?** In the video segment, Alejandra describes her family members to Sofi. Watch the scene of the video closely and complete the family descriptions below with the words that are missing.

SOFI: ¿Estas son fotos de tu familia en Colombia?

ALEJANDRA: Sí, mira. Estos son mi **1.** _____ y mi **2.** _____.

             Y en esta foto estamos mi **3.** _____ y yo. Y éstos son mis

             4. _____: Gitano y Lady.

SOFI: ¡Tu padre es **5.** _____ y tu madre es blanca de pelo negro y

             6. _____ como tú! Te pareces mucho a ella.

El tiempo libre: Colombia

VOCABULARIO Los deportes y los pasatiempos

CD2, Track 25 **LM 3-1 | Los deportes, los pasatiempos y las actividades culturales** Do you remember the Incredible Juanjo? He enjoys all sports, leisure-time and cultural activities. Listen carefully and select the correct response indicating whether the activity you hear is a sport (**un deporte**), a leisure-time activity (**un pasatiempo**), or a cultural activity (**una actividad cultural**) by putting an **x** under the appropriate heading.

Modelo   ver la tele
          un pasatiempo

	un deporte	un pasatiempo	una actividad cultural
1.			
2.			
3.			
4.			
5.			
6.			
7.			
8.			
9.			
10.			

CD2, Track 26 **LM 3-2 | Adivina, adivina** You will hear two clues. Select the activity associated with them and write in the letter of the correct response in the space provided.

_____ **1.** la natación

_____ **2.** sacar fotos

_____ **3.** bailar

_____ **4.** jugar al tenis

_____ **5.** visitar un museo

_____ **6.** andar en bicicleta

CD2, Track 27 **LM 3-3 | Mis actividades favoritas** Listen to the following sentences. Repeat each one and indicate whether they are true (**cierto**) or false (**falso**) according to your daily routine by writing **cierto** or **falso** in the space provided.

1. _____   3. _____   5. _____

2. _____   4. _____   6. _____

Expressing likes and dislikes: *Gustar* + infinitive and *gustar* + nouns

CD2,
Track 28

LM 3-4 | **¿Qué les gusta?** Listen to the descriptions based on the six illustrations below. Identify each description with the illustration and write the letter in the appropriate space.

1. _____

2. _____

3. _____

4. _____

5. _____

6. _____

CD2,
Track 29

LM 3-5 | **Gustos son gustos.** You will hear a series of activities or actions. Match them with the famous people that usually perform them by placing the correct letter in the space provided.

1. A Serena Williams y a mí _____.

2. A Penélope Cruz y a ti _____.

3. A Shakira y a Juanes _____.

4. A Eric Clapton _____.

5. A mí _____.

6. A David Beckham _____.

CD2,
Track 30

LM 3-6 | **Los gustos de tu familia** Listen to the statements and complete them according to your family's likes and dislikes. Follow the model.

Modelo   tu padre / ver películas
          A mi padre *le gusta ver películas.*

1. A mí _____.

2. A mis hermanos _____.

3. A mi madre _____.

4. A mi padre _____.

5. A mi tío y a mí _____.

6. A mi novio(a) _____.

VOCABULARIO Los lugares

CD2,
Track 31

LM 3-7 | **¿Dónde vas?** Tell where you go to do the things you hear. Follow the model.

Modelo   comprar papel
papelería

1. _____

2. _____

3. _____

4. _____

5. _____

6. _____

CD2,
Track 32

LM 3-8 | **Encuentra el lugar** Listen as Pepe, who is new in town, talks about what he likes to do. As he tells you, point him to the place he can go to fulfill his wishes. Match his statement to the correct picture by writing in the letter.

la oficina de correos

A

la piscina

B

la plaza

C

el museo

D

el restaurante

E

el banco

F

1. _____

2. _____

3. _____

4. _____

5. _____

6. _____

ESTRUCTURA II
Expressing plans with *ir*: *Ir a* + destination and *ir a* + infinitive

CD2,
Track 33

LM 3-9 | Los polos opuestos se atraen *(Opposites attract)* Gabriel and his girlfriend Silvia are soulmates. Although they like doing things together, their favorite activities don't always coincide. Listen to the dialogue so you may later complete activity LM3-10.

CD2,
Track 34

LM 3-10 | ¿Qué van a hacer las almas gemelas? After listening to the dialogue, what do you think these soulmates will do? Follow the model.

> Modelo   dar una fiesta
> *Ella va a dar una fiesta.*

1. _____
2. _____
3. _____
4. _____
5. _____
6. _____

CD2,
Track 35

LM 3-11 | ¿Quién tiene razón? How would you reply to your soulmate's proposition? Write your response in a complete sentence following the model.

> Modelo   Vamos al museo.
> *No, yo no voy al museo.*
> o   *Sí, vamos al museo.*

1. _____
2. _____
3. _____
4. _____
5. _____
6. _____

ESTRUCTURA III	Describing leisure-time activities: Verbs with irregular *yo* forms

CD2, Track 36 **LM 3-12 | Más actividades** Listen closely to the following activities and their letters. Match each letter to the drawing. Follow the model.

Modelo   la familia
              ver la televisión

1. tú _____

3. los novios _____

2. Laura _____

6. mis amigos y yo

4. el disc jockey _____

5. yo _____

_____

LM 3-13 | Lo que la gente hace Using the drawings in activity **LM3-12**, write a complete sentence conjugating the verb. Follow the model.

Modelo   la familia
         La familia ve la televisión.

1. _____
2. _____
3. _____
4. _____
5. _____
6. _____

LM 3-14 | ¿Qué haces tú? You will hear a series of statements by someone who is trying to impersonate you. Indicate whether what's being said is true (**cierto**) or false (**falso**) by writing **cierto** or **falso** in the space provided.

1. _____   4. _____
2. _____   5. _____
3. _____   6. _____

ASÍ SE DICE   Expressing knowledge and familiarity: *Saber, conocer,* and the personal *a*

LM 3-15 | ¿Saber o conocer? Listen to the following statements. Choose the correct one by writing **a** or **b** in the space provided.

1. _____   4. _____
2. _____   5. _____
3. _____   6. _____

LM 3-16 | ¿Cuál es? Listen to each sentence carefully and write the infinitive form of the verb used (**saber** or **conocer**) in the space provided.

1. _____   4. _____
2. _____   5. _____
3. _____   6. _____

Nombre _____ Fecha _____

CD2, **LM 3-17** | *¿**Saber** o **conocer**? **Esa es la cuestión*** Listen carefully to each set of sentences
Track 41 and select the correct one by writing **saber** or **conocer** in the space provided.

1. _____

2. _____

3. _____

4. _____

5. _____

6. _____

ASÍ SE DICE Talking about the months, seasons, and the weather

CD2, **LM 3-18** | **¿Qué estación es?** Listen to the following months and choose the season to which
Track 42 they belong in the Northern Hemisphere. Follow the model.

   Modelo   marzo
            b. primavera

1. a. invierno   b. primavera   c. verano   d. otoño

2. a. invierno   b. primavera   c. verano   d. otoño

3. a. invierno   b. primavera   c. verano   d. otoño

4. a. invierno   b. primavera   c. verano   d. otoño

5. a. invierno   b. primavera   c. verano   d. otoño

6. a. invierno   b. primavera   c. verano   d. otoño

CD2, **LM 3-19** | **¿Qué tiempo hace?** Listen to the questions related to the weather. Choose the
Track 43 most logical expression from the following three: **hace fresco, hace calor, hace frío**. Follow
the model.

   Modelo   ¿Qué tiempo hace en Canadá en invierno?
            Hace frío.

1. _____

2. _____

3. _____

4. _____

5. _____

6. _____

PRONUNCIACIÓN I Diphthongs: *ia, ie, io,* and *iu*

CD2,
Track 44
The letter **i** (and also **y**) placed before the vowels **a, c, o,** and **u** sound like the English words *yacht, yet, yoke,* and *you*.

 To learn more about **Diphthongs,** go to Heinle iRadio at www.thomsonedu.com/spanish.

LM 3-20 | **¡Así suena!** Listen and repeat.

ia: famil**ia**   estud**ia**   Amal**ia**   residenc**ia**   universitar**ia**

Amal**ia** es estud**ia**nte y vive en la residenc**ia** universitar**ia**, no con su famil**ia**.

ie: f**ie**sta   b**ie**n   par**ie**ntes   t**ie**ne   v**ie**ne

¡Qué b**ie**n! Mis par**ie**ntes v**ie**nen a la f**ie**sta.

io: Anton**io**   Jul**io**   nov**io**   felicitac**io**nes   qu**io**sco

Anton**io** y Jul**io** compran per**ió**dicos en el qu**io**sco.

iu: v**iu**da   c**iu**dad   or**iu**nda   vent**iu**no   d**iu**rna

El día vent**iu**no, la v**iu**da va a venir a la c**iu**dad.

PRONUNCIACIÓN II Diphthongs: *ua, ue, ui,* and *uo*

CD2,
Track 45
The letter **u** before the vowels **a, e, i/y,** and **o** sound like the English words *quit, quartz,* and *quench*.

 To learn more about **Diphthongs,** go to Heinle iRadio at www.thomsonedu.com/spanish.

LM 3-21 | **¡Así suena!** Listen and repeat.

ua: c**ua**dernos   Ed**ua**rdo   c**ua**tro   G**ua**dalupe   g**ua**pa

G**ua**dalupe es la más g**ua**pa para Ed**ua**rdo.

ue: b**ue**na   p**ue**s   P**ue**rto Rico   Man**ue**l   esc**ue**la

P**ue**s, Man**ue**l es un b**ue**n estudiante en P**ue**rto Rico.

ui/y: c**ui**dar   r**ui**nas   m**uy**   c**ui**tas   s**ui**cidio

Antonio está en la r**ui**na y sus c**ui**tas le hacen
pensar en el s**ui**cidio.

uo: c**uo**ta

La c**uo**ta de la casa es muy alta.

RITMOS Y MÚSICA

LM 3-22 | La música Listen to the song "Fíjate bien" by Juanes. Then, indicate if the following statements about its content are **cierto** *(true)* or **falso** *(false)*.

1. _____ La voz de Juanes en esta canción es muy cómica y alegre.

2. _____ Uno de los instrumentos usados en esta canción es el acordeón.

3. _____ En esta canción usan la guitarra eléctrica, pero no la guitarra acústica.

4. _____ Una parte de la canción es similar a una transmisión de radio.

5. _____ El ritmo de esta canción es similar al tango.

LM 3-23 | La letra After listening to the song "Fíjate bien" by Juanes, choose the option that best applies to its lyrics.

1. Parte del coro de la canción dice: "fíjate bien donde pisas *(step on)* / fíjate cuando caminas". ¿Cuál es otra manera de decir "fíjate bien"?

   a. mira con atención

   b. escucha con atención

2. **a.** El tema principal de esta canción es el peligro de las minas *(landmines)*.

   b. El tema principal de esta canción es el peligro de las drogas *(drugs)*.

3. **a.** Esta canción habla de la importancia de los pies *(feet)*.

   b. Esta canción habla de la importancia de la vida.

4. **a.** La letra de esta canción es humorística.

   b. La letra de esta canción es política.

5. Según *(According to)* esta canción, ¿a quién afecta este problema? *(Mark all that apply.)*

   a. los viejos   **c.** los niños

   b. la radio   **d.** la televisión

CD2,
Track 46
LM 3-24 | **Comprensión** After watching the **¡A ver!** video segment for Chapter 3, answer **cierto** *(true)* or **falso** *(false)* to the following statements.

a. _____

b. _____

c. _____

d. _____

e. _____

f. _____

CD2,
Track 47
LM 3-25 | **Los deportes** Listen carefully to the following statements pertaining to the video segment for this chapter. Identify the sentence you hear with the person(s) to whom it refers by entering the corresponding letter in the space provided.

1. Alejandra _____

2. Valeria _____

3. Javier _____

4. Antonio _____

5. Sofía _____

6. Valeria _____

4 | *En la casa: España*

VOCABULARIO La casa

CD3,
Track 2 **LM 4-1** | **La casa de Doña Rosa** You will listen to a series of statements describing Doña Rosa's house. Repeat each statement. Look at the drawing and indicate whether the descriptions that you hear are **cierto** *(true)* or **falso** *(false)*.

1. _____
2. _____
3. _____
4. _____
5. _____
6. _____
7. _____

CD3,
Track 3

LM 4-2 | **Un robo en el condominio** Take a look at the illustrations before and after the burglary. The police make an inventory of the items that are missing. Listen to the missing items and write them down. Follow the model.

> Modelo   ¿Qué falta *(What is missing)* en el baño?
> En el baño no está *el espejo*.

1. En la sala no están _____
2. En la habitación no están_____
3. En la cocina no está _____
4. En el estudio no están _____

264   *Plazas*, Third Edition, Lab Manual

CD3,
Track 4 **LM 4-3** | **¿Dónde están?** Listen and indicate in which part of the house you would find each thing. Choose from the list provided. You will use some answers more than once. Follow the model.

Modelo   el armario
Está en *la habitación.*

la cocina   la habitación   la sala   el baño

1. Está en _____.
2. Está en _____.
3. Está en _____.
4. Está en _____.
5. Está en _____.
6. Está en _____.

CD3,
Track 5 **LM 4-4** | **¿Cuál es?** Match the descriptions listed below with the appliances that you hear mentioned in your audio program. Write the names of the appliances in the spaces provided next to their descriptions. Follow the model.

Modelo   Se utiliza para secar la ropa.
la secadora

1. Se pone la comida dentro *(inside):* _____
2. Se utiliza por la mañana temprano: _____
3. Se ponen los platos sucios en el interior: _____
4. Se utiliza para calentar la comida: _____
5. Se utiliza para limpiar la alfombra: _____

Describing household chores and other activities:
Present tense of stem-changing verbs $(e \rightarrow ie; o \rightarrow ue; u \rightarrow ue; e \rightarrow i)$

LM 4-5 | Diferencias irreconciliables Listen to a conversation between Pilar and Alvaro, a newlywed couple. Each has different preferences and hobbies. Pay attention to the irregular verbs and complete the sentences with the verbs that you hear.

   1. ALVARO: ¿Qué _____ hacer ahora?

   2. PILAR: Ahora _____ leer un libro.

   3. ALVARO: Yo no _____ estar en silencio. ¿_____ hablar?

   4. PILAR: ¿Qué _____?

   5. ALVARO: ¡Nada! ¡No _____ importancia!

LM 4-6 | ¿Quién lo hace? Listen to the sentences and write down who does the actions described in the audio. Choose from the list below. Follow the model.

    Modelo   Vienen a clase con los exámenes.
                  los profesores

    los profesores   los bebés   un mal estudiante   un buen estudiante   una madre   nosotros

   1. _____

   2. _____

   3. _____

   4. _____

   5. _____

   6. _____

LM 4-7 | ¿Dónde se hace? Listen to the sentences and write down where one can do the activities described in the audio. Choose from the list below. Follow the model.

    Modelo   Los camareros sirven la comida.
                  en los restaurantes

    en mi cama   en el estante   en el casino   en el restaurante   en la sala   en la biblioteca

   1. _____

   2. _____

   3. _____

   4. _____

   5. _____

   6. _____

ASÍ SE DICE — Expressing physical conditions, desires, and obligations: Expressions with the verb *tener*

CD3, Track 9 **LM 4-8 | ¿Cómo reaccionas?** Listen to the following situations and choose from the list below to indicate what your logical reaction would be.

Modelo   Estoy en Alaska en diciembre.
Tengo frío.

tengo sueño   tengo paciencia   tengo calor   tengo miedo   tengo hambre   tengo celos

1. _____
2. _____
3. _____
4. _____
5. _____
6. _____

CD3, Track 10 **LM 4-9 | ¿Cómo estoy?** You will hear six situations. Listen to the audio and choose the most logical situations to complete the sentences below. Write the letter of each situation, rather than the whole sentence.

Modelo   No tengo ganas de venir a clase cuando
a. [hay un exámen]

1. Tengo miedo de hablar con el profesor cuando _____ .
2. Tengo ganas de mirar la tele cuando _____ .
3. Tengo miedo de perder cuando _____ .
4. Tengo ganas de beber un gran vaso de agua cuando _____ .
5. No tengo paciencia cuando _____ .
6. No tengo ganas de estudiar cuando _____ .

CD3, Track 11 **LM 4-10 | Las obligaciones** Before going on a trip, your Spanish roommate asks you to do some chores in the apartment. First, listen to the list of things you must do, and then, to make sure that you understand what you were told to do, translate into English the chores that you must perform. Write your translations in the spaces below.

Modelo   Tienes que limpiar el horno.
You must clean the oven.

1. _____
2. _____
3. _____
4. _____
5. _____
6. _____

VOCABULARIO Los quehaceres domésticos

CD3,
Track 12

LM 4-11 | **¡Te toca a ti!** You will hear a list of household chores. Write the chores that each person listed below needs to do.

	Pepita	Ramón	Lola	Jorge
1.				
2.				
3.				
4.				
5.				
6.				
7.				

CD3,
Track 13

LM 4-12 | **¿Quién lo hace?** Write the name of the person that you see in the drawing for each house chore that you hear.

Modelo   saca la basura
           Ana

1. _____
2. _____
3. _____
4. _____
5. _____
6. _____

CD3,
Track 14

LM 4-13 | **¿En qué parte de la casa?** Based on the house chores that you hear, write where the people in the drawing do these house chores.

1. _____
2. _____
3. _____
4. _____
5. _____
6. _____

Expressing preferences and giving advice: Affirmative *tú* commands

CD3, Track 15 **LM 4-14** | **Los seis consejos de oro** Since Francisco moved out of the house to go to college, his mom has been reminding him constantly of all those things he ought to do. Listen to the sentence and write the verbs that you hear in the imperative mood.

Modelo   Escribe muchos correos electrónicos.
          Escribe.

1. _____

2. _____

3. _____

4. _____

5. _____

6. _____

CD3, Track 16 **LM 4-15** | **¿Qué tengo que hacer?** Listen to what you must do today. Match the commands that you hear with the sentences below. Follow the model.

Modelo   Los platos están sucios.
          a. [Lava los platos.]

_____ 1. Las plantas están secas.

_____ 2. No tienes paciencia.

_____ 3. La cama no está hecha.

_____ 4. No hay nada en la nevera.

_____ 5. Llegas tarde a clase.

_____ 6. La puerta está abierta.

CD3, Track 17 **LM 4-16** | **¡No oigo bien!** Luisito is a naughty little boy. When he is told is told what do and what not to do, he pretends that he does not hear well. Rephrase the commands using **Tienes que** followed by what Luisito must do or must not do.

Modelo   ¡Saca la basura, Luisito!
          Tienes que sacar la basura.

1. Tienes que _____.

2. Tienes que _____.

3. Tienes que _____.

4. Tienes que _____.

5. Tienes que _____.

6. Tienes que _____.

Nombre _____ Fecha _____

CD3, Track 18 **LM 4-17** | **¿Dónde están? ¿Cómo están?** Listen to the following sentences that will tell you where the people pictured below are located and how they feel physically or emotionally. Match each sentence you hear with an illustration and write how each person feels.

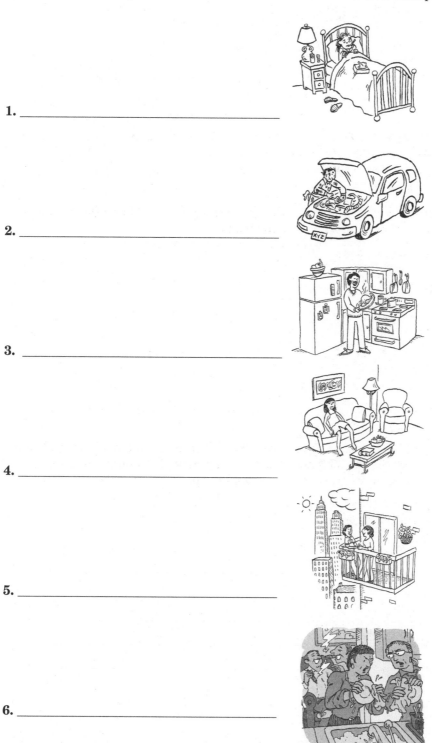

1. _____

2. _____

3. _____

4. _____

5. _____

6. _____

LM 4-18 | **¿Cómo estás cuando... ?** Indicate how you feel when you are facing certain situations by writing **cierto** (true) or **falso** (false) based on the statements that you will hear. When the statements are false, correct the statement.

Modelo   Cuando no hablas con tu novia estás contento.
Falso. Estoy triste.

1. _____
2. _____
3. _____
4. _____
5. _____
6. _____

LM 4-19 | **Un espión *(Peeping Tom)* en el condominio** Miguel, Francisco's roommate, lives directly across from the Casa de Troya. With his telescope he can watch what the neighbors are doing this instant. Match what he sees with the drawings by placing the appropriate letter in the blank.

1. _____

2. _____

3. _____

4. _____

5. _____

Nombre _____ Fecha _____

ASÍ SE DICE — Counting from 100 and higher: Numbers from 100 to 1,000,000

CD3,
Track 21
LM 4-20 | Los números Francisco is moving out, and he is selling his furniture. As people ask for the prices for each item, pay close attention to the prices so that you can write them below in both numeric and written form.

Modelo   El espejo cuesta cien euros.
         100   cien

numeric form   **written form**

1. _____   _____

2. _____   _____

3. _____   _____

4. _____   _____

5. _____   _____

6. _____   _____

PRONUNCIACIÓN   *s, ce, ci,* and *za, zo, zu*

In most of peninsular Spain (except in Andalucía, in the Canarias, and the Baleares), the letter combination **ci, ce, za, zo,** and **zu** are pronounced like the English sound *th* as in *those*. The pronunciation of the letter **s** is also stronger and is similar to the English *s* as in *snake*.

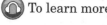 To learn more about **c, s,** and **z,** go to Heinle iRadio at www.thomsonedu.com/spanish.

CD3,
Track 22
LM 4-21 | ¡Así suena! Listen and repeat.

ce: **C**ecilia, es ne**c**esario ha**c**er la **c**ena.

ci: La **c**ocina de la ve**c**ina está en una residen**c**ia de an**c**ianos.

za: Mi **za**pato lo hizo un **za**patero.

ze: **Z**enón es un Dios Griego.

zi: La **z**innia es una flor muy **z**íngara.

zo: El **zo**o está en una **zo**na con **zo**rros.

zu: ¡El **z**umo es a**z**ul!

s: La ca**s**a de **S**ilvia e**s** e**s**tupenda y está **s**iempre **s**úper limpia.

LM 4-22 | La música The song "Bulería" by David Bisbal is a variation of flamenco. After listening to this song, identify the correct answers.

1. ¿Cuál es el instrumento más utilizado en esta canción?
   a. la guitarra   **b.** el piano   **c.** la trompeta

2. ¿Quién canta esta canción?
   a. un hombre   **b.** una mujer   **c.** unos hombres

3. ¿Además de (*in addition to*) los instrumentos, qué sonidos reconoces en esta canción?
   a. palmadas (*clapping*) **b.** taconeo (*rhythmic stomping of heels*)   **c.** claquet (*tap dance*)

4. ¿Cómo es el ritmo de la canción?
   a. lento   **b.** rápido

5. ¿Qué influencias musicales tiene esta canción?
   a. rusas   **b.** árabes   **c.** japonesas

LM 4-23 | La letra Listen to the song a second time and select the words or phrases that you hear in the song from the list provided.

1. (Beginning of the song)
   a. pienso   **b.** prefiero   **c.** quiero

2. (Beginning of the song)
   a. ten   **b.** ven   **c.** pon

3. (Beginning of the song)
   a. más y más   **b.** mar y mar   **c.** mal y mal

4. (Middle of the song)
   a. veo con tus labios (*lips*)   **b.** bebo con tus labios   **c.** viajo con tus labios

5. (Middle of the song)
   a. yo no soy nadie   **b.** yo no soy nunca   **c.** yo no soy nada

6. (End of the song)
   a. de rodillas (*on my knees*) te lo digo   **b.** de rodillas te lo pido **c.** de rodillas te lo sirvo

🅳🆅🅳 ¡A VER!

LM 4-24 | ¿Qué tienen los cuartos? In the video segment from Chapter 4, the actors describe the bedrooms. Watch and listen to this segment and complete the bedroom descriptions below with the words that are missing.

Hay tres **1.** _____. Hay un cuarto con **2.** _____ **3.** _____ cerca del

4. _____. ¿ Tiene **5.** _____? No, pero tiene dos camas, un **6.** _____,

un **7.** _____ y muchas **8.** _____.

CD3,
Track 23 **LM 4-25 | ¿Cierto o falso?** Identify if the following statements from this video segment are true **(cierto)** or falso **(falso)**.

1. cierto   falso

2. cierto   falso

3. cierto   falso

4. cierto   falso

5. cierto   falso

6. cierto   falso

CD3,
Track 24 **LM 4-26 | ¿Qué son?** Listen to the definitions of the food items that appear in the video segment for Chapter 4 and select the correct word.

1. salchichas	café	palomitas de maíz
2. refrescos	jalapeños	paté
3. jugo	agua	té
4. agua	café	enlatados
5. jalapeños	salchichas	palomitas de maíz
6. mejillones	paté	salchichas

Nombre _____ Fecha _____

5 | La salud: Bolivia y Paraguay

VOCABULARIO El cuerpo humano

CD3, Track 25 **LM 5-1 | Una lección de anatomía** Listen and repeat as you hear different parts of the body. Label each body part on the drawing.

1. _____
2. _____
3. _____
4. _____
5. _____
6. _____
7. _____
8. _____
9. _____
10. _____
11. _____
12. _____

CD3, Track 26 **LM 5-2 | ¿Dónde están?** As you hear the names of different parts of the human body, write them in the columns and blanks provided according to where they would be found in the body.

En la cara	En el pecho	En las piernas
1. _____	4. _____	7. _____
2. _____	5. _____	8. _____
3. _____	6. _____	9. _____

CD3, Track 27 **LM 5-3 | Asociaciones** Listen to each word and write in the part of the human body with which you associate it.

1. _____
2. _____
3. _____
4. _____
5. _____
6. _____

CD3,
Track 28
LM 5-4 | La rutina diaria de Tomás. You will hear a series of daily activities. Match them with the illustrations below by writing each activity in the blank provided.

1. _____

2. _____

3. _____

4. _____

5. _____

6. _____

CD3,
Track 29
LM 5-5 | El matrimonio Dardo Chávez Listen to the dialogue between Dr. Carlos Dardo Chávez and his wife Doctor Nilda Calviño Guner, a dentist. Then write all the reflexive verbs you hear in the correct column. Follow the model. ¡OJO! There are 13 verbs.

Modelo   Dra. Calviño Guner: Me ducho.
          Dr. Calviño Guner: *Se ducha.*

Dra. Calvino Guner   Dr. Dardo Chávez

_____   _____

_____   _____

_____   _____

_____   _____

_____   _____

_____   _____

Nombre _____ Fecha _____

CD3, Track 30

LM 5-6 | **¿Cómo se dice?** Listen to the detailed description of what Drs. Dardo Chávez and Calviño Guner do, and then write in the appropriate letter in the space provided.

_____ **1.** Se acuestan tarde.

_____ **2.** El Dr. Dardo se afeita.

_____ **3.** Se despiertan muy temprano.

_____ **4.** La Dra. Calviño se pone la ropa después de bañarse.

_____ **5.** El Dr. Dardo no se pinta.

_____ **6.** La Dra. Calviño se peina todos los días.

_____ **7.** No se cuidan.

ASÍ SE DICE	Talking about things you have just finished doing: *Acabar de* + infinitive

CD3, Track 31

LM 5-7 | **¿Qué acaban de hacer?** Listen to the following activities and write down how each individual in question just finished completing them. Follow the model.

Modelo   Tomás se levanta de la cama
Tomás acaba de levantarse.

1. _____

2. _____

3. _____

4. _____

5. _____

CD3, Track 32

LM 5-8 | **¿Qué pasa antes?** You will hear a sentence stating an activity about to take place. Please indicate which activity most likely was recently completed just before. Follow the model.

Modelo   Va a levantarse.
Acaba de despertarse y se va a levantar.

1. _____

2. _____

3. _____

4. _____

5. _____

6. _____

VOCABULARIO La salud

CD3, Track 33 **LM 5-9 | Doctora, ¿qué tengo?** Listen to the patient's symptoms and recommend a treatment. Write in the letter for the treatment you consider necessary.

_____ **1. a.** Necesita tomar jarabe y descansar.

      b. Necesita dejar de hacer ejercicio.

_____ **2. a.** Necesita hacer ejercicio y comer bien.

      b. Necesita guardar cama, beber muchos líquidos y tomar aspirina.

_____ **3. a.** Necesita tomar Pepto Bismol y cuidar su dieta.

      b. Necesita ir al hospital inmediatamente.

_____ **4. a.** Necesita unas medicinas y descanso.

      b. Necesita bañarse y acostarse temprano.

CD3, Track 34 **LM 5-10 | ¿Qué le duele?** Fran overdoes it sometimes. Everything hurts! Listen to her and mark what part of her body is in pain.

_____ **1.** Le duele la garganta.

_____ **2.** Le duele la cabeza.

_____ **3.** Le duele el estómago.

_____ **4.** Le duele la mano.

_____ **5.** Le duelen los ojos.

_____ **6.** Le duelen las piernas.

ESTRUCTURA II Describing people, things, and conditions: *Ser* versus *estar*

CD3, Track 35 **LM 5-11 | ¿Cómo es?** Listen to the description of Dr. Calviño Guner. Pay special attention to the uses of **ser** and **estar.** Write in the missing verbs as you hear them.

1. _____ la doctora Calviño Guner. 2. _____ de Bolivia.

3. _____ boliviana. 4. _____ dentista. 5. _____

casada. 6. _____ baja. Hoy 7. _____ el 16 de febrero y

8. _____ mi cumpleaños. Esta noche hay una fiesta para mí. La fiesta

9. _____ en mi casa.

En este momento 10. _____ en mi casa. Mi casa 11. _____ en

Monteros. Monteros 12. _____ en Bolivia. 13. _____ muy contenta.

14. _____ bailando y comiendo en la fiesta.

CD3,
Track 36
LM 5-12 | Sobre la Dra. Calviño Guner Answer the questions using the correct forms of **ser** and **estar.**

1. _____
2. _____
3. _____
4. _____
5. _____
6. _____

ESTRUCTURA III   Pointing out people and things: Demonstrative adjectives and pronouns

CD3,
Track 37
LM 5-13 | ¿Qué quieres, *ésa, ésta o aquélla*? Answer each question by replacing the demonstrative adjective with the demonstrative pronoun. Follow the model.

Modelo   ¿Prefieres esas pastillas?
          Sí, prefiero ésas.

1. _____
2. _____
3. _____
4. _____
5. _____
6. _____

PRONUNCIACIÓN *p* and *t*

CD3,
Track 38
The letters **p** and **t,** when placed at the beginning of a word, are pronounced with more strength in English than in Spanish. In English, the sound is stronger like in *Peter* or *Tom*.

In Spanish, however, the sound of these two letters is softer; it is very similar to the *p* in *spill* and to the *t* in *still*.

To learn more about the letters **p** and **t,** go to Heinle iRadio at www.thomsonedu.com/spanish.

LM 5-14 | ¡Así suena! Listen, repeat, and write what you hear.

1. _____
2. _____
3. _____
4. _____

♪ RITMOS Y MÚSICA

LM 5-15 | La música Listen to the song "Tambores paganos" by Pukaj Wayra. Then, indicate if the following statements about it are **cierto** *(true)* or **falso** *(false)*.

1. _____ "Tambores paganos" es una canción instrumental porque no tiene letra.

2. _____ El ritmo de esta canción es similar al ritmo de la salsa y el merengue.

3. _____ "Tambores paganos" es un ejemplo de una canción típica de la zona andina de Latinoamérica.

4. _____ Esta canción es de tradición indígena.

5. _____ En "Tambores paganos" usan instrumentos acústicos y eléctricos.

LM 5-16 | Los instrumentos As you listen to "Tambores paganos" by Pukaj Wayra, indicate whether the following instruments are used in this song. Mark **"sí"** if they are used, and **"no"** if they are not used.

1. la flauta   sí   no

2. la trompeta   sí   no

3. la quena *(bamboo flute)*   sí   no

4. el charango *(small lute)*   sí   no

5. el piano   sí   no

6. el tambor *(drums)*   sí   no

🄳🅅🄳 ¡A VER!

CD3, Track 39 **LM 5-17 | ¿Cierto o falso?** After watching the **¡A ver!** video segment for Chapter 5, answer true **(cierto)** or false **(falso)** to the following statements.

1. _____

2. _____

3. _____

4. _____

5. _____

6. _____

CD3, Track 40 **LM 5-18 | ¿Quiénes son?** You will hear six statements. Match each one with the right person by writing the correct letter in the space provided.

1. Javier _____   4. Sofía _____

2. Víctor _____   5. Antonio _____

3. Alejandra _____   6. Valeria _____

6 ¿Quieres comer conmigo esta noche? Venezuela

VOCABULARIO La comida

CD4,
Track 2
LM 6-1 | ¡Qué hambre tengo! Place your order according to what you hear. Make sure you match the food/beverage with the illustrations below.

1. _____

2. _____

3. _____

4. _____

5. _____

6. _____

CD4,
Track 3
LM 6-2 | En El Criollito The Santos family is at the *El Criollito* restaurant for lunch. Pay attention to what they order, and check off each item as you hear it.

_____ una sopa de verduras   _____ el pollo asado

_____ las chuletas de cerdo en salsa de tomate   _____ unos refrescos

_____ las arepas   _____ el flan casero

LM 6-3 | ¡Buen provecho! Listen to different food categories and write a food item of your choice that belongs to that category. Do not repeat a food item!

> Modelo   los entremeses
> *las arepas*

1. _____

2. _____

3. _____

4. _____

5. _____

6. _____

ESTRUCTURA I   Making comparisons: Comparatives and superlatives

LM 6-4 | Comparando alimentos Listen to the following comparisons regarding food habits. Select the symbols below to indicate if what you hear is a comparison of equality, inequality, or a superlative. Symbols: = **(tan)**   – **(menos)**   + **(más)**   ↑ **(mejor)**   ↓ **(peor)**

> Modelo   Los colombianos beben menos café que los argentinos.
> –

1. = – + ↑ ↓
2. = – + ↑ ↓
3. = – + ↑ ↓
4. = – + ↑ ↓
5. = – + ↑ ↓
6. = – + ↑ ↓

LM 6-5 | ¿Qué serán? Listen to the following comparative descriptions and select the word that corresponds best with the description that you hear.

1. las chuletas   los calamares   la langosta

2. la carne de res   el pavo   el pollo

3. la banana   la naranja   la manzana

4. el aceite   el agua   el café

5. el vino   el té   la leche

6. la cerveza   el vino   el jugo

CD4,
Track 7

LM 6-6 | Tú, ¿qué crees? Listen to the following statements about eating habits and indicate if the statements that you hear are **cierto** *(true)* or **falso** *(false)*.

1. cierto   falso

2. cierto   falso

3. cierto   falso

4. cierto   falso

5. cierto   falso

6. cierto   falso

VOCABULARIO En el restaurante

CD4,
Track 8

LM 6-7 | Definiciones Listen to the following definitions and choose the words or expressions that best match the definitions that you hear.

1. ¡Buen provecho!   ¡Salud!   ¡Cómo no!

2. la propina   la cuenta   las bebidas

3. los postres   el menú   la especialidad de la casa

4. ligero   caliente   fresco

5. ¡Salud!   ¡Yo quisiera!   ¡No puedo más!

6. Te invito.   Estoy satisfecho. Estoy a dieta.

CD4,
Track 9

LM 6-8 | En el restaurante Rosa and Luis are at a restaurant. Listen to the dialogue and fill in the blanks with the words that you hear.

EL CAMARERO: ¡Buenos días! ¿Qué **1.** _____ comer?

ROSA: Yo **2.** _____ algo **3.** _____. Estoy a

               4. _____. Una sopa de mariscos, por favor.

LUIS: Voy a comer pescado con la ensalada de la casa.

EL CAMARERO: ¿Algo para **5.** _____?

LUIS: Unas arepas.

EL CAMARERO: Aquí tienen, ¡buen **6.** _____!

CD4,
Track 10

LM 6-9 | ¿Cómo esta? Listen to Alberto's questions about the food his mother has prepared. Answer his questions using the vocabulary from this section. Do not repeat the same words more than twice and be logical!

Modelo   —Mamá, ¿cómo está el helado?
         —¡Está rico!

1. ¡Está _____!

2. ¡Está _____!

3. ¡Están _____!

4. ¡Está _____!

5. ¡Están _____!

6. ¡Está _____!

CD4,
Track 11

LM 6-10 | Un día muy ocupado Marina will tell you all about her day yesterday. Match what she says with the illustrations below.

1. _____

2. _____

3. _____

4. _____

5. _____

CD4,
Track 12

LM 6-11 | ¿Es cierto? Marina's husband Gabriel thinks he knows what Marina did yesterday. For each statement he makes about Marina's day, select **cierto** *(true)* or **falso** *(false)*. Look at the pictures in the previous activity to help you select your answer.

1. cierto   falso
2. cierto   falso
3. cierto   falso
4. cierto   falso
5. cierto   falso
6. cierto   falso

CD4,
Track 13
LM 6-12 | **¿Y tú?** Marina wants to know if you did the same things she did. Select **sí** or **no** to answer her questions.

1. sí   no

2. sí   no

3. sí   no

4. sí   no

5. sí   no

6. sí   no

ESTRUCTURA III | Giving detailed descriptions about past events: More verbs with stem changes in the preterite

CD4,
Track 14
LM 6-13 | **Una romántica indigestión** Olga and Roberto went out to dinner. However, Roberto ate too much and got sick! Listen to what happened, and fill in the blanks with the verbs in the preterite that you hear.

Roberto 1. _____ muchos, pero muchos camarones y a Olga el camarero le

2. _____ carne de res asada. A Roberto le 3. _____ mucho los

camarones y 4. _____ kilos. Los dos se 5. _____ mucho pero él

6. _____ una horrible indigestión.

CD4,
Track 15
LM 6-14 | **¿Cierto o falso?** Listen to each statement based on the story you just heard in the previous activity, and indicate if it's **cierto** *(true)* or **falso** *(false)*.

1. cierto   falso

2. cierto   falso

3. cierto   falso

4. cierto   falso

5. cierto   falso

6. cierto   falso

CD4,
Track 16
LM 6-15 | **Tus amigos** Listen to the questions about your friends who went to a restaurant yesterday, and answer them conjugating the verbs provided in the preterite.

Modelo   ¿Qué prefirieron beber tus amigos?
           (preferir beber vino tinto) *Prefirieron beber vino tinto.*

1. (dormir)

_____

2. (pedir cervezas)

_____

3. (sonreir a las chicas guapas)

_____

4. (vestirse muy elegantemente)

_____

5. (reirse mucho)

_____

6. (despedirse a las diez)

_____

PRONUNCIACIÓN _m, n,_ and _ñ_

CD4, Track 17 The consonants **m** placed in all positions of a word and **n** before **b, v, f, m** are pronounced like the English _m_ in _men:_ **más**, **morir**, **amor**, and **invertido** [i-**m**-vertido], **anfiteatro** [a-**m**-fiteatro], **inmenso** [i-**m**-enso].

Before the letters k and g, the letter _n_ is pronounced like the _in_ sound in _sink_ and/or _sing:_ **angustia** [an-gustia], **pongo** [pon-go], **kanguro** [kan-guro].

In all other instances, **n** is pronounced like the English _n_ as in _no!:_ **nube**, **nieto**, **Anita**, **honor.**

The letter **ñ** is similar to the sound _ni_ in _onion:_ **Muñoz, España, niño.**

To learn more about the letters **n,** and **ñ,** go to Heinle iRadio at www.thomsonedu. com/spanish.

LM 6-16 | **¡A escribir!** Listen and repeat the list of words that have the sounds that you just learned. Then, fill in the missing words.

Letter **m:**

1. mamá, comida, _____

2. mucho, _____, camarones

3. _____, champiñón, mantequilla

Letter **n:**

4. nuevo, cena, _____

5. un poco, _____, una empanada

6. jamón, mineral, _____

Letter **ñ:**

7. español, _____, año

8. _____, pequeña, niña

RITMOS Y MÚSICA

LM 6-17 | La música Listen to the song "Amparito" by Maracaibo 15. Then, indicate if the following statements about its content are **cierto** *(true)* or **falso** *(false)*.

1. El ritmo es rápido y bueno para bailar.

2. El instrumento predominante en esta canción es la guitarra.

3. El ritmo de la canción es rápido al principio, pero es lento al final.

4. Hay un cantante masculino y un coro.

5. El coro solamente repite el título de la canción.

LM 6-18 | La letra After listening to "Amparito", choose the option that best applies to its lyrics.

1. **a.** Amparito es una chica colombiana.

   b. Amparito es una chica venezolana.

2. **a.** El cantante dice que conoció a Amparito en Cartagena.

   b. El cantante dice que conoció a Amparito en Barranquilla.

3. **a.** "Amparito" es una canción de un viaje que hizo un hombre por Colombia.

   b. "Amparito" es una canción del amor de un hombre por una mujer.

4. **a.** El cantante no pudo casarse *(get married)* con Amparito porque ella se fue para Cartagena.

   b. El cantante no pudo casarse *(get married)* con Amparito porque ella se fue para Barranquilla.

5. **a.** Según *(According to)* la letra, a Amparito le gusta bailar con un venezolano.

   b. Según la letra, a Amparito le gusta bailar con un colombiano.

¡A VER!

CD4,
Track 18

LM 6-19 | **¿Comprendiste?** After watching the first scene in the video segment for Chapter 6, **¿Quieres ir de compras conmigo?** listen to the statements based on the video and indicate if they are **cierto** *(true)* or **falso** *(false)*.

1. cierto   falso

2. cierto   falso

3. cierto   falso

4. cierto   falso

5. cierto   falso

6. cierto   falso

LM 6-20 | **Vale como cocinera** Watch the video segment for Chapter 6 again, as Valeria recalls her horrible cooking experience. Then fill in the blanks with the verbs in the preterite. Do not use the subtitles!

La cena **1.** _____ todo un desastre. Los chiles se me **2.** _____. El queso que **3.** _____ estaba muy salado. Le **4.** _____ mucho picante a la salsa. Estaba todo horrible, pero a pesar de todo, Antonio **5.** _____ muy cortés y se **6.** _____ todo un chile relleno.

7 | *De compras: Argentina*

VOCABULARIO La ropa

CD4,
Track 19
LM 7-1 | La ropa You will hear the name of an article of clothing twice. First repeat it, and then write its letter under the correct illustration.

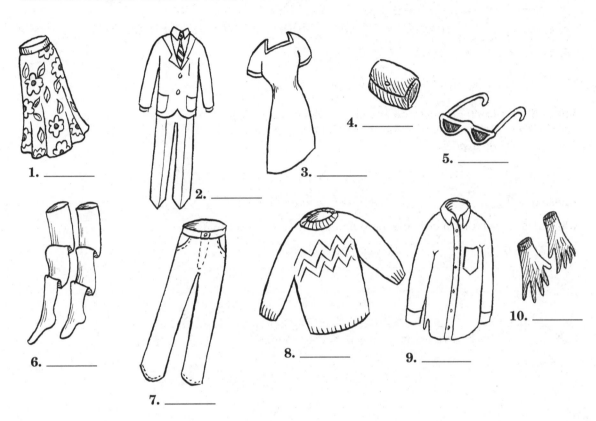

1. _____   2. _____   3. _____   4. _____   5. _____

6. _____   7. _____   8. _____   9. _____   10. _____

CD4,
Track 20
LM 7-2 | ¿Qué me pongo? One of your friends is asking you what to wear for each situation. Listen to the questions and answer by writing the most appropriate clothing item. Follow the model.

Modelo   ¿Qué me pongo para ir a la piscina?
             el traje de baño

1. _____

2. _____

3. _____

4. _____

5. _____

6. _____

LM 7-3 | Los famosos y la ropa You're listening to an online broadcast of interviews with the stars on the red carpet minutes before the Oscar ceremony. Pay attention to what they're wearing and indicate if it is **posible** or **imposible.**

1. posible   imposible   4. posible   imposible

2. posible   imposible   5. posible   imposible

3. posible   imposible   6. posible   imposible

ASÍ SE DICE	Making emphatic statements: Stressed possessive adjectives and pronouns

LM 7-4 | ¿De quién es? ¿De quiénes son? Listen to the sentence and then rewrite it using a pronoun as shown in the model.

Modelo   Los pantalones son de Pepe.
Son suyos. o *Son los suyos.*

1. _____

2. _____

3. _____

4. _____

5. _____

6. _____

LM 7-5 | ¡No! Your friend thinks that everything belongs to him. Tell him he is wrong by indicating the correct stressed pronoun. Follow the model.

Modelo   ¡Es mi libro!
¡No es el tuyo! o *¡No es tuyo!*

1. _____

2. _____

3. _____

4. _____

5. _____

6. _____

LM 7-6 | ¿A qué te refieres? You will hear stressed pronouns. Depending on the form and gender of the stress pronoun that you hear, write a possible clothing item.

Modelo   ¡Son las mías!
¿A qué te refieres?
A las sandalias o *las gafas de sol,* o *las botas;* etc.

1. ¿A qué te refieres?

_____

2. ¿A qué te refieres?

_____

3. ¿A qué te refieres?

_____

4. ¿A qué te refieres?

_____

5. ¿A qué te refieres?

_____

6. ¿A qué te refieres?

_____

ESTRUCTURA I	Talking about singular and/or completed events in the past: Verbs irregular in the preterite

CD4, Track 25 **LM 7-7** | **Un día de compras en Buenos Aires** Listen to the story about a husband and wife who go shopping. Complete the story by filling in the blanks with the irregular verbs in the preterite tense.

1. Ayer mi esposo y yo _____ de compras.

2. _____ ir a una de las boutiques de la calle Florida.

3. Mi esposo _____ conmigo.

4. Me _____ un vestido muy bonito en una tienda.

5. Pero no _____ comprarlo.

6. ¡Mi esposo y yo no _____ la cartera!

CD4, Track 26 **LM 7-8** | **Más sobre las compras** The sentences that you just heard in the previous activity each had an irregular verb in the preterite. Identify the infinitive of the irregular preterite verbs. Choose the correct infinitive from the choices below.

1. ir   ser   estar

2. saber   poder   querer

3. decir   venir   tener

4. poder   poner   querer

5. poner   poder   saber

6. querer   tener   traer

CD4, Track 27 **LM 7-9** | **¡Yo también!** Listen to what the following people did last week. You did exactly the same things! For each statement, write the same activity in the first-person singular. Follow the model.

Modelo   Ayer Amalia se puso el traje de baño para ir a la playa.
                ¡Yo también, *me puse* el traje de baño!

1. ¡Yo también, _____ de compras!

2. ¡Yo también, _____ de Rosarito!

3. ¡Yo también, _____ comer en un restaurante argentino!

4. ¡Yo también, _____ hacer la tarea!

5. ¡Yo también, _____ en el cine!

6. ¡Yo también, _____ un regalo!

VOCABULARIO De compras

CD4,
Track 28 **LM 7-10 | Definiciones** Listen to the items and choose the closest definitions from the choices.

1. es para pagar

   es para probarse

   es para llevar

2. es importante para rebajar

   es importante para probarse

   es importante para mostrar

3. cuando algo cuesta más

   cuando algo cuesta menos

   cuando algo no cuesta

4. cuando se paga con tarjeta

   cuando se paga con descuento

   cuando se paga con dinero en monedas y billetes

5. es la persona que depende

   es la persona que trabaja en una tienda

   es la persona que trabaja en las rebajas

6. es similar a ver

   es similar a cambiar

   es similar a gastar

CD4,
Track 29 **LM 7-11 | Expresiones idiomáticas** For each idiomatic expression that you hear, match the equivalent expression and indicate its letter.

1. _____ Es algo que no es nada caro. Es muy barato.

2. _____ Ropa que está muy «in» y que todo el mundo lleva.

3. _____ Es para preguntar si la ropa o los zapatos van bien o mal.

4. _____ Es cuando la ropa o los zapatos no son de la talla o del número apropiados.

5. _____ Es lo que se dice al dependiente antes de pagar.

6. _____ Es para preguntar si uno se puede poner ropa o zapatos en una tienda.

CD4,
Track 30 **LM 7-12 | En la tienda** Listen to the questions that clients ask in a store, and select the most logical answer from the choices listed below.

1. Le quedan divinamente.

   Te quedan divinamente.

   Te quedan baratas.

2. Me debe una talla 54.

   Me debe 10.000 bolívares.

   Me debe 54 por ciento.

3. Claro que sí, pruébeselo.

   Claro que sí, pruébeselos.

   Claro que sí, pruébeselas.

4. Sí, son muy grandes.

   Sí, tengo unos zapatos para Ud.

   Sí, tengo su número.

5. Sí, están en rebajas.

   Sí, están en efectivo.

   Sí, están de su talla.

6. Sí, puede llevarse otras gafas.

   Sí, puede ver con las gafas.

   Sí, hacen juego con sus ojos.

ESTRUCTURA II Simplifying expressions: Direct object pronouns

CD4, Track 31 **LM 7-13 | ¿Qué tal las compras?** Your friend is curious to know how your shopping day went. Listen to the questions and choose the correct answer. **¡OJO!** Pay attention to the pronouns!

> **Modelo** ¿Te probaste un vestido?
> *Me lo probé.*

1. Me lo compré.   Me los compré.   Me las compré.

2. Me la llevé.   Me las llevé.   Me los llevé.

3. Me la probé.   Me las probé.   Me los probé.

4. Lo cambié.   La cambié.   Los cambié.

5. La compré.   Las compré.   Lo compré.

6. Me la llevé.   Me las llevé.   Me los llevé.

CD4, Track 32 **LM 7-14 | ¡Especifica!** Now your friend tells you about her day at the mall. She does not specify what she bought, tried on, and exchanged. Depending on the pronoun that you hear, choose the correct item. Follow the model.

> **Modelo** Me lo probé.
> *el impermeable*

1. el collar   los chalecos   la bufanda

2. los vaqueros   la pulsera   el abrigo

3. el traje   las sandalias   la camisa

4. la gorra   el cinturón   los guantes

5. los calcetines   la falda   las blusas

6. los sombreros   el anillo   la chaqueta

CD4, Track 33 **LM 7-15 | ¿Quién?** Listen to the sentences, paying attention to the object pronouns. Then choose from the list below to indicate the person to whom each pronoun refers. Follow the model.

> **Modelo** No me queda bien.
> *yo*

1. vosotros   ellos   nosotros

2. nosotros   ellas   vosotros

3. ellas   él   ellos

4. ella   usted   tú

5. yo   ustedes   tú

6. él   ella   ellas

CD4, Track 34 — **LM 7-16 | Cuando Valeria Mazza era niña.** Listen to the famous Argentine model, Valeria Mazza. Identify the verbs in the imperfect tense and write them in the spaces provided.

Cuando **1.** _____ niña **2.** _____ ser modelo. No

3. _____ que las modelos **4.** _____ que hacer tantos

sacrificios. Por ejemplo, no **5.** _____ que las modelos duermen y comen poco

y trabajan tanto. Pero **6.** _____ decidida a afrontar las dificultades, y así

empecé: con mucha fuerza de voluntad.

CD4, Track 35 — **LM 7-17 | La niñez de Crystal** Listen to Crystal's childhood years in Argentina. Write the conjugated verbs that you hear and indicate whether they are in the imperfect or the preterite tense.

1. pretérito   imperfecto _____

2. pretérito   imperfecto _____

3. pretérito   imperfecto _____

4. pretérito   imperfecto _____

5. pretérito   imperfecto _____

6. pretérito   imperfecto _____

CD4, Track 36 — **LM 7-18 | ¿Y tú niñez?** Answer the following questions by conjugating the verbs that you hear in the preterite or the imperfect tense. Then select the choice that best applies to you.

1. De pequeño, *(yo)* _____

   un ángel   un demonio

2. Mis padres me _____

   eres muy malo(a)   eres muy bueno(a)

3. (Yo) _____

   de vacaciones a la playa   de vacaciones a la montaña

4. (Yo) _____

   a la pelota *(ball)*   a las muñecas *(dolls)*

5. Mi pasatiempo favorito _____

   mirar la tele   practicar deportes

6. (Yo) _____ en

   los Estados Unidos   Europa

Nombre _____ Fecha _____

PRONUNCIACIÓN I *c* and *qu*

CD4,
Track 37

The letter **c** can be pronounced with two different sounds: a hard sound and a soft sound.
When the letter **c** is combined with the vowels **a (ca)**, **o (co)**, **u (cu)**, the sound is hard (like
the English *k*): **c**orbata, **c**amisa, **c**uñado. When the letter **c** is combined with the vowels **e (ce)**
and **i (ci)** the sound is soft: co**c**ina, **ci**ta, él di**c**e, abe**c**edario. In Spain, the softer sound is pronounced like **z** and in Latin America like **s**.

If you wonder about the Spanish letter **k** (also pronounced like the **c** in **ca**, **co**, **cu**), it only
appears in very few words in Spanish: **k**ilo, **k**angurú.

The letters **qu** combined with **i** and **e** are pronounced like the sound **k**: **Qui**to, **qui**ero, ¿**qu**é tal?

 For more information, visit Heinle iRadio at www.thomsonedu.com/spanish.

LM 7-19 | ¡Así suena! Listen to a list of words with the soft **c** sound and the hard **c** sound.
For each word, indicate if the **c** sound that you hear is soft or hard.

1. soft hard	**4.** soft hard
2. soft hard	**5.** soft hard
3. soft hard	**6.** soft hard

PRONUNCIACIÓN II *l, ll,* and *y*

CD4,
Track 38

The letter **l** in Spanish is pronounced like the English *l*: **L**ola, ca**l**or, ca**l**cetines.

The sound **ll** is pronounced like the English *y* as in *yet*: Me **ll**amo, **ll**evo, **ll**ueve, ca**ll**e.

However, Argentinians and Uruguayans pronounce it like the English *z* as in *measure*.

The letter **y** is like the English *y* as in *yet*: Re**y**es, ma**y**or. However, when it is placed at the
end of a word, it is pronounced like the English sound *ee* as in **Lee**: so**y** [so-**ee**], vo**y** [vo-**ee**],
ho**y** [o-**ee**].

LM 7-20 | ¡Así suena! Listen and repeat.

l: salsa   chile   enchilada   guacamole   frijoles

ll/y: tortilla   pollo   paella   Guillermo   Yolanda

LM 7-21 | ¡A escuchar! Identify the sounds of **l** and **ll/y** in the words that you hear.

CD4,
Track 39

1. l ll/y	**4.** l ll/y
2. l ll/y	**5** l ll/y
3. l ll/y	**6.** l ll/y

RITMOS Y MÚSICA

LM 7-22 | La música Listen to the song "Santa María (del Buen Ayre)" by the group *Gotan
Project*. Then, indicate if each of the following statements about its content is **cierto** *(true)* or
falso *(false)*.

1. Se escucha el sonido de grillos *(crickets)*.

2. Hay solamente dos voces: una voz masculina y una voz femenina.

3. El ritmo es similar al flamenco.

4. El instrumento predominante es la guitarra.

5. Es una canción folclórica; no es muy moderna.

LM 7-23 | **La letra** After listening to the song "Santa María (del Buen Ayre)", choose the option that best applies to its lyrics.

1. a. La música es simple; lo importante es la letra.

 b. No hay mucha letra; es mayormente instrumental.

2. a. La cantante menciona dos ritmos típicos de Argentina: el tango y la milonga.

 b. La cantante menciona dos ritmos típicos de Argentina: el tango y la zamba.

3. a. La cantante dice "este tango es para ti".

 b. La cantante dice "este tango es para vos".

4. a. El cantante dice "la puerta de Santa María del Buen Ayre".

 b. El cantante dice "el puerto de Santa María del Buen Ayre".

5. a. El cantante menciona la ciudad de Buenos Aires en la canción.

 b. El cantante menciona la ciudad de Rosario en la canción.

DVD **¡A VER!**

LM 7-24 | **¡Sofía está pasada de moda!** While watching the video segment for Chapter 7, fill in the blanks to complete Sofía's description of her clothing collection.

SOFÍA: Mis **1.** _____ los tengo desde que salí del colegio y

 todavía me quedan. Mis playeras de algodón, un **2.** _____ de

 playa, mis shorts, dos **3.** _____, la **4.** _____;

 el **5.** _____, unos **6.** _____ y mis sandalias

 que ya conoces.

CD4, **LM 7-25** | **¿Sí o no?** Watch the video segment again and indicate if the statements that you
Track 40 hear are true (**sí**) or not (**no**).

1. sí   no   **4.** sí   no

2. sí   no   **5.** sí   no

3. sí   no   **6.** sí   no

CD4, **LM 7-26** | **¿Quién lo dice?** Watch the video clip one last time and identify who says the
Track 41 statements that you hear.

1. Alejandra   Sofía   **4.** Alejandra   Sofía

2. Alejandra   Sofía   **5.** Antonio   Javier

3. Alejandra   Sofía   **6.** Javier   Antonio

8 | *Fiestas y vacaciones: Guatemala y El Salvador*

VOCABULARIO Fiestas y celebraciones

CD5,
Track 2

LM 8-1 | ¿Qué haces ese día? Listen to the descriptions of a celebration, a holiday, or an occurence and indicate what you do that day.

_____ 1. ¡Me asusto!

_____ 2. Lo paso bien.

_____ 3. Doy una fiesta.

_____ 4. Les digo: «¡Felicitaciones!»

_____ 5. Me pongo triste.

_____ 6. Lo paso muy mal (me preocupo mucho).

CD5,
Track 3

LM 8-2 | Días festivos Listen to the name of holidays and write their English translations.

1. _____

2. _____

3. _____

4. _____

5. _____

6. _____

CD5,
Track 4

LM 8-3 | ¿Quién hace qué? Listen to the story. Then read the questions and write the name of the person from the list provided below to indicate who does the following things or reacts the following way.

Ana   Patricia   Victoria   Juan

1. ¿Quién da una fiesta sorpresa? _____

2. ¿Quién se reúne con su familia? _____

3. ¿Quién se pone un disfraz? _____

4. ¿Quién hace un pastel el 24 de diciembre? _____

5. ¿Quién le desea muchas felicidades a su hermana? _____

6. ¿Quién tiene una celebración de cumpleaños? _____

ASÍ SE DICE | Inquiring and providing information about people and events: Interrogative words

CD5,
Track 5

LM 8-4 | Identifica la palabra interrogativa You will hear a series of questions. Listen to the questions and write the equivalent interrogative in English. Follow the model.

Modelo   ¿Adónde vas esta tarde?
          where

1. _____

2. _____

3. _____

4. _____

5. _____

6. _____

CD5,
Track 6
LM 8-5 | Respuesta correcta Listen to the questions and choose the correct answer from the two choices provided below. Write the letter that corresponds to the correct answer.

1. _____ **a.** Son de Manuela.   **b.** Es de Manuela.

2. _____ **a.** Está muy bueno.   **b.** Es una tarta de chocolate.

3. _____ **a.** Porque me gusta tener dos.   **b.** Pagué trescientos dólares para la televisión.

4. _____ **a.** Es de Ricardo.   **b.** Es Ricardo.

5. _____ **a.** Es una profesora de Guatemala.   **b.** Es la profesora Rodríguez.

6. _____ **a.** Hay treinta estudiantes.   **b.** Hay un estudiante muy simpático.

CD5,
Track 7
LM 8-6 | ¿Cuál es la pregunta? You will hear some answers. Based on the model, write logical questions for each answer.

    Modelo   Estudio español para trabajar en Guatemala.
                 ¿Para qué estudias español?

1. _____

2. _____

3. _____

4. _____

5. _____

6. _____

ESTRUCTURA I Narrating in the past: The preterite vs. the imperfect

CD5,
Track 8
LM 8-7 | Preguntas personales Listen to the following questions about your childhood. If the question is based on something that already happened, write **pretérito.** If the question is based on a repeated or a habitual event, write **imperfecto.** Follow the model.

    Modelos   ¿Ibas a la playa de vacaciones cuando tenías nueve años?
                 imperfecto

1. _____

2. _____

3. _____

4. _____

5. _____

6. _____

CD5,
Track 9
LM 8-8 | ¡Contéstame! Listen once again to the questions in activity **LM 8-9** and answer them.

1. _____

2. _____

3. _____

4. _____

5. _____

6. _____

CD5, Track 10 **LM 8-9** | **¿Qué pasó con Patricia y Victoria?** Listen to the story of Victoria and Patricia. They are vacationing on the Guatemalan coast. For each sentence choose the correctly conjugated verb from the two choices provided. Then write the verbs, conjugated as you hear them. Follow the model.

Modelo   Victoria y Patricia celebraron Semana Santa en la costa.
celebraron

1. _____   se ponía   se puso

2. _____   tenían   tenía

3. _____   fue   fueron

4. _____   había   hubo

5. _____   nadaban   nadaron

6. _____   estaba   estaban

VOCABULARIO La playa y el campo

CD5, Track 11 **LM 8-10** | **¡De vacaciones!** Listen to the following descriptions of places to go on vacation and write the letter that best describes each place.

_____ **1.** la playa   _____ **4.** el balneario

_____ **2.** la montaña   _____ **5.** la costa

_____ **3.** el campo   _____ **6.** el mar

CD5, Track 12 **LM 8-11** | **¿Posible o imposible?** Listen to the following statements and write in Spanish if they are possible (**posible**) or impossible (**imposible**).

1.   4.

2.   5.

3.   6.

CD5, Track 13 **LM 8-12** | **¿Dónde?** Listen to the following activities and write down the most logical places where they can be done. Choose from the list provided.

en el lago en la playa en la montaña en el campo en el balneario en el mar

1. _____

2. _____

3. _____

4. _____

5. _____

6. _____

CD5,
Track 14
LM 8-13 | **¡No estoy de acuerdo!** Listen to the following statements and write the contrary using affirmative or negative expressions as appropriate.

1. _____
2. _____
3. _____
4. _____
5. _____
6. _____

CD5,
Track 15
LM 8-14 | **¿Qué ves?** Look at the drawing and answer the following questions with the most logical affirmative or negative expressions.

1. _____
2. _____
3. _____
4. _____
5. _____
6. _____

CD5,
Track 16
LM 8-15 | **¡Nunca y nadie!** Listen to the sentences and answer negatively using **nunca** or **nadie** accordingly. Choose from the two choices.

1. _____ **a.** Nunca voy al gimnasio. **b.** No voy con nadie al gimnasio.

2. _____ **a.** Nadie me ve fuera de las clases. **b.** No veo a nadie fuera de las clases.

3. _____ **a.** No hablo nunca cuando duermo.   **b.** No hablo con nadie.

4. _____ **a.** Nunca tomo el sol.   **b.** Nadie toma el sol.

5. _____ **a.** No voy a la playa con nadie.   **b.** Nunca voy a la playa.

6. _____ **a.** No llamo a nadie por la mañana.   **b.** Nadie llama a mi casa por las mañanas.

ASI SE DICE   Talking about periods of time since an event took place: *Hace* and *hace que*

CD5, Track 17   **LM 8-16 | ¡El tiempo vuela (Times flies)!** Listen to **abuelita** going over the main events in her life. Write down the amount of time that has passed for each event. Follow the model.

> Modelo   Ya hace dos años que me mudé a la casa de retiro.
> La abuelita se mudó a la casa de retiro *hace dos años*.

1. El esposo de la abuelita murió _____.

2. _____ que la abuelita duerme mal por la noche.

3. El primer nieto de la abuelita nació _____.

4. La abuelita conoció a su segundo esposo _____.

5. _____ que la abuelita no trabaja.

6. La abuelita vendió su casa _____.

CD5, Track 18   **LM 8-17 | La nostalgia** Silvia Sepúlveda is very romantic. She thinks about her husband Julio, and wonders about a few things. Look at the drawings and identify the answers based on Silvia's thinking. Write down the answers.

1. _____
2. _____
3. _____
4. _____
5. _____
6. _____

LM 8-18 | **Hablando de tiempo** Respond to the questions you hear in complete sentences.

1. _____
2. _____
3. _____
4. _____
5. _____
6. _____

PRONUNCIACIÓN I *x*

CD5, Track 20

In Spanish, the letter called **equis** is not very common at the beginning of a word, and it is pronounced like an **s**, as in **xenófobo.** Between two vowels it is pronounced like the English *x,* as in *exam*. However, when it is before a consonant, **x** is pronounced almost like an **s**, as in **extranjero.** In Mexico, **x** sounds like a **j** even if the word is written with an **x.** For example, **México** is written with an **x** but pronounced like a **j: Méjico.** In Spain, numerous words, such as **Javier** and **Jiménez,** used to be spelled with an **x (Xavier, Ximénez)**, but these words have changed their spelling, transforming **x** into a **j.** Only in Latin America have some words kept the **x** spelling (but **j** pronunciation): for example, **México.**

To learn more about the letter **x,** go to Heinle iRadio at www.thomsonedu.com/spanish.

LM 8-19 | **¡Así suena!** Listen, repeat, and write.

x: (between two vowels)

1. _____

x: (before a consonant)

2. _____

x: (initial position)

3. _____

x: (in Mexico)

4. _____

x: (in different positions)

5. _____

x: (in a sentence in different positions)

6. _____

304   *Plazas*, Third Edition, Lab Manual

PRONUNCIACIÓN II La entonación

CD5, Track 21 When we ask a question, the intonation changes—it rises or it falls—depending on the expected answer.

- In Spanish, the intonation rises if the expected answer to the question is affirmative or negative:
¿Tiene Victoria su traje de baño?
¿Se reúne Juan con su familia en Navidad?
¿Hay olas en el mar?

- The intonation also rises if the expected answer confirms something in the question:
Toño es el novio de Patricia, ¿cierto?
San Salvador es la capital de El Salvador, ¿no?
Guatemala está al sur de México, ¿verdad?

- However, the intonation falls if the questions are requesting information:
Por favor, ¿me puede decir qué hora es?
Me gustaría alquilar un velero. ¿Cuánto cuesta una hora?

LM 8-20 | ¿Pregunta o respuesta? Indicate whether what you hear is a question or an answer. Pay particular attention to the intonation. Then, select the arrow pointing up or the arrow pointing down to show if the intonation rises or falls.

1. pregunta respuesta ↑↓
2. pregunta respuesta ↑↓
3. pregunta respuesta ↑↓
4. pregunta respuesta ↑↓
5. pregunta respuesta ↑↓
6. pregunta respuesta ↑↓

RITMOS Y MÚSICA

LM 8-21 | La música Listen to "Mojado", a song by Ricardo Arjona. **Mojado** means *wet* and is a term that is used to refer to an undocumented immigrant. After listening to this song, please indicate if each of the following statements about its content is **cierto** *(true)* or **falso** *(false)*.

1. Se escucha el sonido del acordeón.
2. El ritmo de la canción es lento al principio, pero cambia en la mitad *(middle)*.
3. Toda la canción consiste en la voz de Ricardo Arjona y el sonido de su guitarra.
4. Es una canción alegre, cómica.
5. Esta canción es un tango.

LM 8-22 | La letra After listening to "Mojado", choose the option that best applies to its lyrics.

1. a. Otra palabra para "el mojado" en esta canción es "el ilegal"
   b. Otra palabra para "el mojado" en esta canción es "el indocumentado"
2. a. Al principio de la canción, Arjona habla de un inmigrante que se va de su país y cruza la frontera.
   b. Al principio de la canción, Arjona habla de un inmigrante que es deportado y debe volver a su país.

3. Parte del coro de la canción dice: "Por qué el mojado precisa (necesita) / comprobar *(to prove)* con visas que no es de Neptuno?". ¿Qué mensaje quiere dar Arjona con estas palabras?

    a. Los inmigrantes que no tienen visas son como extraterrestres y deben volver a su planeta.

    b. Los inmigrantes que no tienen visas son personas iguales a todos.

4. **a.** La letra de la canción habla de los inmigrantes mexicanos.

    b. La letra de la canción habla de los inmigrantes en general.

5. **a.** Según *(According to)* la canción, la vida de un inmigrante ilegal es triste y difícil.

    b. Según la canción, la vida de un inmigrante ilegal está llena *(full)* de oportunidades para hacer de sus sueños *(dreams)* realidad.

DVD **¡A VER!**

CD5, Track 22   **LM 8-23** | **¿Cierto o falso?** After watching the **¡A ver!** video segment for Chapter 8, write **cierto** *(true)* or **falso** *(false)* in response to the following statements.

1. _____
2. _____
3. _____
4. _____
5. _____
6. _____

CD5, Track 23   **LM 8-24** | **¿Quién lo dice?** Watch the **¡A ver!** video segment for Chapter 8 a second time, and listen to the statements in order to identify the characters who say these statements. Write the names of the appropriate characters in the spaces provided below.

1. ¿Alejandra o Valeria? _____
2. ¿Alejandra o Valeria? _____
3. ¿Alejandra o Valeria? _____
4. ¿Alejandra o Sofi? _____
5. ¿Valeria o Sofi? _____
6. ¿Javier o Antonio? _____

De viaje por el Caribe: La República Dominicana, Cuba y Puerto Rico

VOCABULARIO Viajar en avión

CD5, Track 24 | **LM 9-1** | **Un viaje en avión** You will hear some statements about Patricia and her sister, two students from the University of Colorado who studied abroad at the University of Puerto Rico in San Juan last semester. Put the sentences in a logical order by entering the letter that corresponds to each one in the space provided.

1. _____   4. _____

2. _____   5. _____

3. _____   6. _____

CD5, Track 25 | **LM 9-2** | **¡Ésa no!** Listen to the words associated with flights and traveling. First, repeat each word or expression that you hear. Next, write the word or expression that does not belong in the group in the space provided.

1. _____.

2. _____.

3. _____.

4. _____.

5. _____.

6. _____.

CD5, Track 26 | **LM 9-3** | **Tus preferencias cuando viajas en avión** You are planning your next vacation. At the travel agency, the agent, in order to find the ideal place for you, asks that you fill out a form indicating your preferences. Select your preferences: **sí, no,** or **es posible.**

1. sí   no   es posible   4. sí   no   es posible

2. sí   no   es posible   5. sí   no   es posible

3. sí   no   es posible   6. sí   no   es posible

ESTRUCTURA I Simplifying expressions: Indirect object pronouns

CD5,
Track 27 **LM 9-4 | ¿A quién le sucede?** Ester Carranza is assisting her clients at the travel agency. Listen to what she does for each client, and select the option with the indirect object pronoun that best reflects Ester's actions. Write its letter in the space.

1. _____   4. _____

2. _____   5. _____

3. _____   6. _____

CD5,
Track 28 **LM 9-5 | ¿Quién es responsable?** Identify the individual that carries out the action you hear by entering the correct letter in the space provided.

1. el agente de viajes _____

2. el piloto _____

3. mi amigo _____

4. el asistente de vuelo _____

5. la madre _____

6. el oficial de aduana _____

CD5,
Track 29 **LM 9-6 | Un viaje especial** Julio and Gloria went to the Caribbean on a romantic getaway. Listen to what they did, and answer the questions following the model.

Modelo   Julio y Gloria trajeron fotos para mí.
          ¿A quién le trajeron fotos Julio y Gloria?
          Me trajeron fotos a mí.

1. _____.

2. _____.

3. _____.

4. _____.

5. _____.

6. _____.

ESTRUCTURA II Simplifying expressions: Double object pronouns

CD5,
Track 30 **LM 9-7 | ¿Qué hicieron?** Answer each travel-related question by selecting a logical response from the list below. **¡OJO!** Pay special attention to the use of double pronouns in the answers.

1. Se los dimos a nuestros padres. _____

2. Se las mandaron a sus amigas desde la República Dominicana. _____

3. Se lo mandé a Visa para pagar nuestro viaje al Caribe. _____

4. Me lo abroché durante el vuelo. _____

5. Se lo enseñaste al oficial de aduana. _____

6. Se lo dio al asistente de vuelo. _____

CD5, Track 31 **LM 9-8** | **¡Qué bien se lo pasa uno en el Caribe!** Listen to each sentence carefully. Then, replace the direct and indirect objects in the sentences with direct and indirect object pronouns and write them down in the space provided. Follow the model.

> Modelo Mi amigo compró el boleto para mí.
> ***Me lo* compró.**

1. _____ _____ enseñaron.

2. _____ _____ recomendó.

3. _____ _____ prestaron.

4. _____ _____ regaló.

5. _____ _____ ofreció.

6. _____ _____ escribimos.

CD5, Track 32 **LM 9-9** | **Abreviando** Abreviate each statement you hear by replacing the subjects and the objects with their respective pronouns. Write the sentences in the blanks provided. Follow the model.

> Modelo Julio y Gloria trajeron fotos para mí.
> *Me las trajeron.*

1. _____.

2. _____.

3. _____.

4. _____.

5. _____.

6. _____.

VOCABULARO El hotel

CD5, Track 33 **LM 9-10** | **En el hotel** Manny and Teri are spending their honeymoon in a hotel in La Habana. Listen to their story and write the letters in the spaces to put their statements in logical order.

1. _____   4. _____

2. _____   5. _____

3. _____   6. _____

CD5, Track 34 **LM 9-11** | **¿Qué recuerdas de los recién casados?** Listen to the following statements about the newlyweds Manny and Teri. Show how much you know about their honeymoon by answering **cierto** (*true*) or **falso** (*false*) to the following sentences.

1. _____   4. _____

2. _____   5. _____

3. _____   6. _____

LM 9-12 | ¿Qué parte del hotel es? Listen to the definitions and choose the correct vocabulary word by entering its corresponding letter in the space provided.

1. la llave _____

2. la recepción _____

3. un baño privado _____

4. la cama doble _____

5. un hotel lujoso _____

6. la reserva _____

ASÍ SE DICE Giving directions: Prepositions of location, adverbs, and relevant expressions

LM 9-13 | ¿Dónde están? Study the map below. As you hear the locations described, indicate where things are located by selecting the correct direction.

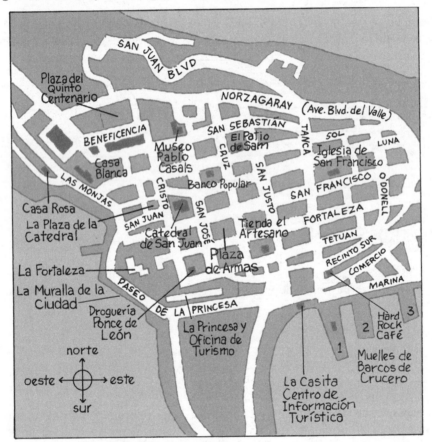

1. norte   sur   este   oeste

2. norte   sur   este   oeste

3. norte   sur   sureste   suroeste

4. norte   sur   sureste   suroeste

5. norte   sur   sureste   suroeste

6. norte   sur   este   oeste

CD5, Track 37

LM 9-14 | ¿Cómo llego? You are lost in San Juan and you forgot your map at the hotel. You ask a local for directions. As reference the local will show you a map identical to the one in activity **LM 9-13.** Listen to the directions and then select which itinerary the directions are for. Enter the appropriate number in the space provided.

1. _____ De la Droguería Ponce de León al Museo Pablo Casals.

2. _____ Del Hard Rock Café a la Plaza del Quinto Centenario.

3. _____ De La Casita Centro de Información Turística a la Muralla de la Ciudad.

4. _____ De los Muelles de Barcos de Crucero a la Casa Blanca.

5. _____ De la Iglesia de San Francisco a la Catedral de San Juan.

6. _____ Del Banco Popular a la Plaza de la Catedral.

ESTRUCTURA III Giving directions and expressing desires: Formal commands and negative *tú* commands

CD5, Track 38

LM 9-15 | Durante un vuelo Listen to the instructions that the flight attendant Silvia Vargas is giving to the passengers on the plane. Identify each command with the corresponding drawing.

1. _____

2. _____

3. _____

4. _____

5. _____

CD5, **LM 9-16** | **Las promociones para viajes especiales** Tere is listening to the radio when she
Track 39 hears a commercial from the travel agency Caribetel. Listen to the commercial at least twice
and then write down the commands in the spaces provided.

1. _____   7. _____

2. _____   8. _____

3. _____   9. _____

4. _____   10. _____

5. _____   11. _____

6. _____   12. _____

CD5, **LM 9-17** | **En el aeropuerto** Verónica and Juan are at the airport. They are both very excited
Track 40 about going to Aguadilla, Puerto Rico, but Verónica is so afraid of flying that she is giving
orders to Juan constantly telling him what not to do. ¡**OJO!** She is so nervous that some of
her commands make no sense! First listen to the affirmative commands and then write them
in the negative form.

1. _____.

2. _____.

3. _____.

4. _____.

5. _____.

6. _____.

PRONUNCIACIÓN I *j*

CD5, The Spanish **j** has a sound somewhat like the *h* in *hill,* but harder. It is never pronounced
Track 41 like the English *j* in *jet.*

LM 9-18 | **¡Así suena!** Repeat and write each sentence.

1. _____.

2. _____.

3. _____.

4. _____.

PRONUNCIACIÓN II *g*

CD5, The Spanish **g** before an **e** or **i** is pronounced like the **j** in **Juan**. In all other cases, **g** is
Track 42 pronounced like the *g* in *go.*

To learn more about **g, gu,** and **ga,** go to Heinle iRadio at www.thomsonedu.com/spanish.

LM 9-19 | **¡Así suena!** Repeat and write each sentence.

1. _____.

2. _____.

3. _____.

4. _____.

5. _____.

6. _____.

CD5,
Track 43

LM 9-20 | **¡Así suena!** Repeat and write each sentence.

1. _____.

2. _____.

3. _____.

4. _____.

RITMOS Y MÚSICA

LM 9-21 | **La música** Listen to the song "Guavaberry" by Juan Luis Guerra. Then, indicate if the following statements about its content are **cierto** *(true)* or **falso** *(false)*.

1. La canción comienza con un solo de percusión.

2. El ritmo no es constante; cambia varias veces.

3. Hay un cantante masculino y un coro.

4. El ritmo de la canción es rápido y bueno para bailar.

5. "Guavaberry" es un ejemplo del reggae dominicano.

LM 9-22 | **La letra** After listening to the song "Guavaberry", choose the option that best applies to its lyrics.

1. **a.** Según la letra de esta canción, la guavaberry es una comida.
   b. Según la letra de esta canción, la guavaberry es una bebida.
   c. Según la letra de esta canción, la guavaberry es una planta.

2. **a.** El cantante dice que quiere vivir en San Diego de Macorís.
   b. El cantante dice que quiere vivir en San Juan de Macorís.
   c. El cantante dice que quiere vivir en San Pedro de Macorís.

3. **a.** El cantante dice que se siente feliz cuando sale *(rises)* el sol.
   b. El cantante dice que se siente feliz cuando baila.
   c. El cantante dice que se siente feliz cuando está con una mujer.

4. **a.** El cantante dice que le gusta bailar en la calle.
   b. El cantante dice que le gusta bailar en la playa.
   c. El cantante dice que le gusta bailar en el parque.

5. **a.** La letra de esta canción es toda en inglés.
   b. La letra de esta canción es toda en español.
   c. La letra de esta canción es en inglés y español.

CD5, **LM 9-23 | Comprensión** After watching the video segment for Chapter 9, answer **cierto**
Track 44 *(true)* or **falso** *(false)* to the following statements.

1. _____   4. _____

2. _____   5. _____

3. _____   6. _____

CD5, **LM 9-24 | ¿Consejos para Javier o para Valeria?** You will hear a person giving advice to
Track 45 Javier and Valeria. Listen to each sentence, and then decide if the advice is intended for
Javier or for Valeria, based on what happened in the **¡A ver!** video segment.

1. Javier   Valeria

2. Javier   Valeria

3. Javier   Valeria

4. Javier   Valeria

5. Javier   Valeria

Las relaciones sentimentales: Honduras y Nicaragua

VOCABULARIO | Las relaciones sentimentales

CD6, Track 2 **LM 10-1 | ¿Qué definición es?** Listen to the definitions about relationships. In the spaces provided write the letters that correspond to the definitions.

_____ **1.** los recién casados   _____ **4.** la luna de miel

_____ **2.** el ramo   _____ **5.** la boda

_____ **3.** los invitados   _____ **6.** el divorcio

CD6, Track 3 **LM 10-2 | Tú, ¿qué piensas?** Listen to the sentences and fill in the missing words in the following sentences. Then, give your opinion by writing one of the following expressions in the space provided.

Estoy de acuerdo. or **No estoy de acuerdo.**

1. No creo en el amor _____. ¡Es imposible!

_____

2. _____ es una institución anticuada y muy tradicional.

_____

3. Muchas veces _____ no es fácil.

_____

4. El _____ a alguien y que sea recíproco es una sensación muy bonita.

_____

5. Vivir en pareja y no _____ es la mejor situación.

_____

6. Después de muchos años de matrimonio, sólo hay _____ y no amor.

_____

CD6, Track 4 **LM 10-3 | ¿Cúal no pertenece?** Listen to the following word sequences and write the word that does not belong to each group.

1. _____

2. _____

3. _____

4. _____

5. _____

6. _____

Describing recent actions, events, and conditions: The present perfect tense

CD6, Track 5 **LM 10-4 | Eva en una boda** Eva went to her cousin's wedding last week. Listen to her story and complete the sentences with verbs you hear in the present perfect.

1. Primero, los invitados _____ en la iglesia.

2. La solista _____ el «Ave María» de Schubert.

3. Después del «Ave María», la novia _____ con su padre a la iglesia.

4. Las madres se _____ a llorar al ver a la novia entrar en la iglesia.

5. Los novios _____ «sí, quiero».

6. Los novios se _____ al terminar la ceremonia religiosa.

CD6, Track 6 **LM 10-5 | ¿Qué ha hecho Eva ayer?** Listen to what Eva did yesterday before her cousin's wedding. Then match each sentence with its English translation by writing the correct letter.

1. _____ In the morning, Eva and her mother have gone to try on their dresses.

2. _____ After that, they have bought flowers for their dresses.

3. _____ Eva has come back home in the afternoon.

4. _____ Eva has read her fashion magazine.

5. _____ Eva has eaten with her parents.

6. _____ After dinner, Eva has seen a movie.

CD6, Track 7 **LM 10-6 | ¿Y los demás?** Now listen to what the other members in the family have done before the wedding. Pay attention to the verbs, because you will have to conjugate the verbs that you hear to agree with different family members (subjects) that appear below. The verbs that you hear are all conjugated in the third-person singular, "Eva".

Modelo   Eva ha descansado en el sofá.
         Sus padres *han descansado en el sofá.*

1. Sus hermanos _____ a la abuela a casa.

2. Nosotros _____ a la peluquería.

3. Tú _____ una botella de champán.

4. Ustedes _____ por teléfono con el novio.

5. Yo _____ mucho con toda la familia.

6. Usted _____ que el día de la boda será muy divertido.

ASÍ SE DICE | Describing reciprocal actions: Reciprocal constructions with *se, nos* and *os*

CD6, Track 8 **LM 10-7 | ¿Es recíproco?** You will hear some statements about Victoria and Juan's relationship. Follow the model below and change each sentence into a reciprocal action.

> Modelo   Victoria mira a Juan con cariño.
> *Se miran.*

1. _____
2. _____
3. _____
4. _____
5. _____
6. _____

CD6, Track 9 **LM 10-8 | El contrario** You are going to hear sentences that describe Juan y Victoria's relationship. Find a term in the list below that states the opposite of what the statements say. Make sure that you conjugate the verbs to agree with **Juan** and **Victoria**.

> casarse   quererse   enojarse   comprenderse   contradecirse   abrazarse

1. _____
2. _____
3. _____
4. _____
5. _____
6. _____

CD6, Track 10 **LM 10-9 | ¿Qué hacen?** Listen to the statements that describe what the people are doing. Choose the English translation that best corresponds with the Spanish description. Write the letters in the spaces provided.

1. _____ We kiss each other.
2. _____ We give each other gifts.
3. _____ You speak to each other on the phone.
4. _____ They write to each other.
5. _____ You scream at each other.
6. _____ We hold hands.

VOCABULARIO La recepción

CD6, Track 11 **LM 10-10 | Sinónimos** Listen to the definitions and the synonyms of the vocabulary. Write down the appropriate letter of the definition or the synonym next to each word listed below.

_____ 1. terminar

_____ 2. asistir

_____ 3. la pareja

_____ 4. la orquesta

_____ 5. el banquete

_____ 6. acompañar

CD6, Track 12 **LM 10-11 | Más definiciones** You will hear five words related to banquets and receptions. For each word, select the definition that corresponds to it by writing the correct letter in the space provided. Follow the model.

Modelo   a. felicitar
          Decir: ¡«Felicidades»! _____ *a* _____

1. hacer ruido *(noise)* con las manos _____

2. las personas que vienen a la fiesta _____

3. tomar, obtener un objeto; por ejemplo, el ramo de la novia _____

4. una persona que lleva ropa muy elegante _____

5. expresar buenos deseos antes de beber champán *(champagne)* o vino _____

CD6, Track 13 **LM 10-12 | ¿Pudo ocurrir así?** Listen to the following statements about a wedding reception. Decide if the statements describe something that could have happened or not; write **sí** if the event could have happened or **no** if it could not have happened. Be logical!

1. _____   2. _____   3. _____

4. _____   5. _____   6. _____

ASÍ SE DICE Qualifying actions: Adverbs and adverbial expressions of time and sequencing of events

CD6, Track 14 **LM 10-13 | ¿Cómo?** Qualify Victoria and Juan's actions with the most logical adverbs. Follow the model.

Modelo   Victoria llama a Juan. frecuente
          frecuentemente

1. _____   4. _____

2. _____   5. _____

3. _____   6. _____

CD6, **LM 10-14 | ¡Radio Chismes Increíbles!** Listen to the program **Radio Chismes** (Gossips)
Track 15 **Increíbles** about the rich and famous, and write how the celebrities did what they did. Use
the adverbs of frequency based on what you hear in the sentences. Follow the model.

Modelo Julia Roberts ha tenido a su tercer hijo con un parto difícil.
Julia Roberts ha tenido a su tercer hijo *difícilmente*.

1. Jennifer Aniston salió del aeropuerto de Los Ángeles _____.

2. Angelina Jolie ha adoptado a su sexto niño _____.

3. Paris Hilton ha estado en la cárcel _____.

4. Britney Spears se ha afeitado la cabeza una tercera vez _____.

5. Madonna ha bebido cocktails _____.

6. Gwyneth Paltrow se ha vestido _____.

CD6, **LM 10-15 | ¡Para mí, no!** You have different opinions from your friend. Listen to your friend's
Track 16 opinions and write the contrary, using the opposite adverbs. Write only the adverbs instead
of the whole sentence. The adverbs that you will hear are the equivalents of: *well, best, poorly,
a little, late, always,* etc.

1. _____
2. _____
3. _____
4. _____
5. _____
6. _____

ESTRUCTURA II Using the Spanish equivalents of *who, whom, that,*
and *which:* Relative pronouns

CD6, **LM 10-16 | ¿Cuál es?** Listen to the sentences and write down the relative pronouns that you
Track 17 hear from the list below. Follow the model.

que   quien   con quien   a quien   lo que

Modelo La mujer que te mira es mi hermana.
que

1. _____   2. _____   3. _____

4. _____   5. _____   6. _____

CD6, **LM 10-17 | Identificación** You are going to hear sentences with relative pronouns. Identify
Track 18 the English relative pronoun that corresponds to each Spanish relative pronoun.

Modelo Los novios que se besan son mis primos.
who

1. _____   4. _____
2. _____   5. _____
3. _____   6. _____

LM 10-18 | Oraciones incompletas Listen to the beginning of the sentences and complete them in a logical way. Follow the model.

> Modelo   Lo que más quiero en el mundo es...
> *ser feliz / tener buena salud / tener un buen trabajo / etc.*

1. _____

2. _____

3. _____

4. _____

5. _____

6. _____

PRONUNCIACIÓN I: Review of accents

One easy rule to remember is that all words ending in **–ión** have a written accent on the **o**; for example, **atención** and **información.** The voice always rises with the accent, emphasizing its placement on the **ó.** Listen to the following words ending in **–ión** and repeat: **interrogación, acumulación, constitución, argumentación, legión.**

All interrogative words have a written accent mark as well. The voice rises with the accent.

Listen to the following interrogative words and repeat: **¿Cómo estás hoy? ¿Qué tal estás hoy? ¿Por qué fumas tanto? ¿Cuándo llegas a casa?**

Now, compare **¿Por qué fumas tanto?** (interrogative) with **Porque me gusta** (affirmative statement). Do you hear the difference? Listen and repeat: **¿Por qué no vienes a clase? Porque estoy cansado.**

Some words have a written accent mark and are pronounced accordingly to distinguish one word from another: for example, **sí** and **si.** Listen and repeat: **¡Sí, quiero! Si te casas conmigo, serás muy feliz.**

To learn more about **Accents,** go to Heinle iRadio at www.thomsonedu.com/spanish.

LM 10-19 | ¿Puedes distinguir? Of the two options presented, write the words that you hear.

1. si   sí   _____

2. por qué   porque   _____

3. que   qué   _____

4. se   sé   _____

5. cuándo   cuando   _____

6. como   cómo   _____

PRONUNCIACIÓN II   Review of pronunciation of vowels

CD6,
Track 21

The vowel **a:** The Spanish **a** sounds like the English *a* in the word *father*.

mar   palabra   caja   puerta   mesa

The vowel **e:** The Spanish **e** sounds like the English *e* found in the word *get*.

Pepe   duele   meter   leer   pese

The vowel **i:** The Spanish **i** sounds like the English sound *ee* in the word *India*.

Lili   Pili   mili   tía   mía   pistola

The vowel **o:** The Spanish **o** sounds like the English *o* in *mother*.

por   amor   olor   agosto   oído

The vowel **u:** The Spanish **u** sounds like the English *oo* found in *choose*.

mula   muela   tutú   luz   suena

LM 10-20 | **¡Así suena!** Repeat and write the words you hear.

1. _____   4. _____

2. _____   5. _____

3. _____   6. _____

RITMOS Y MÚSICA

LM 10-21 | **La música** Listen to the song "La Danza del Cielo" by Nicaragua Libre. Then, indicate if the following statements about its content are **cierto** *(true)* or **falso** *(false)*.

1. Esta canción tiene muchos cantantes.

2. "La Danza del Cielo" es una canción folclórica nicaragüense.

3. El ritmo es alegre, festivo.

4. "La Danza del Cielo" es un ejemplo del merengue centroamericano.

5. En la canción usan instrumentos acústicos tradicionales y también instrumentos eléctricos modernos.

LM 10-22 | **Los instrumentos** As you listen to "La Danza del Cielo", indicate whether the following instruments are used in this song. Mark **sí** if they are used, and **no** if they are not used.

1. La marimba   sí   no

2. El tambor *(drums)*   sí   no

3. Las maracas   sí   no

4. La guitarrilla *(small guitar)*   sí   no

5. La quena *(bamboo flute)*   sí   no

CD6,
Track 22
LM 10-23 | **¿Cierto o falso?** Watch the **¡A ver!** video segment from Chapter 10 and tell if the statements that you hear are true (**cierto**) or false (**falso**).

1. _____   4. _____

2. _____   5. _____

3. _____   6. _____

CD6,
Track 23
LM 10-24 | **¿Quién lo dice?** Watch the video clip again, and pay attention to the end of the segment, where Valeria and Antonio are talking. Indicate who says each statement.

1. ¿Valeria o Antonio? _____

2. ¿Valeria o Antonio? _____

3. ¿Valeria o Antonio? _____

4. ¿Valeria o Antonio? _____

5. ¿Valeria o Antonio? _____

6. ¿Valeria o Antonio? _____

Nombre _____ Fecha _____

El mundo del trabajo: Panamá

VOCABULARIO Profesiones y oficios

CD6, Track 24 **LM 11-1 | ¿Profesión u oficio?** Listen carefully to the following items and indicate whether they are professions or trades by selecting the correct choice.

1. profesión / oficio	**4.** profesión / oficio	**5.** profesión / oficio
2. profesión / oficio	**3.** profesión / oficio	**6.** profesión / oficio

CD6, Track 25 **LM 11-2 | Las profesiones** Listen to the descriptions. Match the descriptions that you hear with the appropriate professions below and write in the corresponding letter.

_____ **1.** el (la) fotografo(a)   _____ **4.** el (la) periodista

_____ **2.** el (la) contador(a)   _____ **5.** el (la) programador(a)

_____ **3.** el (la) jefe   _____ **6.** el (la) traductor(a)

CD6, Track 26 **LM 11-3 | ¿A quién llamas?** Listen to each situation and decide which person you would call by selecting the appropriate illustration. Make certain you write in the letter corresponding to the situation, as well as the name of the professional in question.

1. _____   **2.** _____   **3.** _____

4. _____   **5.** _____

ESTRUCTURA I | Making statements about motives, intentions, and periods of time: *Por* vs. *para*

CD6,
Track 27 **LM 11-4** | **¿Cuál de las dos?** Listen to each pair of sentences containing the prepositions **por** and **para**. Decide which one is correct by selecting the appropriate letter.

1. a / b   **2.** a / b   **3.** a / b   **4.** a / b   **5.** a / b   **6.** a / b

CD6,
Track 28 **LM 11-5** | **¿*Por o para*?** Listen to the dialogue carefully and decide which prepositions you need to use. Select the correct ones.

1. por / para   **4.** por / para

2. por / para   **5.** por / para

3. por / para   **6.** por / para

CD6,
Track 29 **LM 11-6** | **Más decisiones** Listen to the following incomplete statements. Complete each sentence by choosing the appropriate preposition and writing it in the space provided.

1. _____   **4.** _____

2. _____   **5.** _____

3. _____   **6.** _____

VOCABULARIO | La oficina, el trabajo y la búsqueda de un puesto

CD6,
Track 30 **LM 11-7** | **Buscando trabajo** You are at an employment agency looking for a job. For the agency to match your qualifications with the right position, you must fill out a form indicating your preferences. Give your opinion (**sí, no,** or **no es importante**) after hearing each statement.

1. sí   no   no es importante   **4.** sí   no   no es importante
2. sí   no   no es importante   **5.** sí   no   no es importante
3. sí   no   no es importante   **6.** sí   no   no es importante

CD6,
Track 31 **LM 11-8** | **Cosas de trabajo** Match the definition with its appropriate term. Write the letter of the definition in the space.

_____ **1.** pedir un aumento   _____ **4.** solicitar un puesto

_____ **2.** la impresora   _____ **5.** de tiempo completo

_____ **3.** contratar   _____ **6.** despedir

CD6,
Track 32 **LM 11-9** | **¿Qué hacer primero?** Listen to the necessary steps one must take in preparation for that perfect job. Place the statements in chronological order by writing in their letters in the spaces provided.

1. _____   **4.** _____

2. _____   **5.** _____

3. _____   **6.** _____

ESTRUCTURA II | Expressing subjectivity and uncertainty: The subjunctive mood

LM 11-10 | El jefe de mis pesadillas (*nightmares*) Julián had a dream that his boss was great; however, that is not the case. When Julián woke up he remembered how awful his boss is. Listen to what Julián says about his boss. Then indicate whether you agree (**Estoy de acuerdo.**) or disagree (**No estoy de acuerdo.**) that these traits make his boss awful to work for.

1. Estoy de acuerdo. No estoy de acuerdo.

2. Estoy de acuerdo. No estoy de acuerdo.

3. Estoy de acuerdo. No estoy de acuerdo.

4. Estoy de acuerdo. No estoy de acuerdo.

5. Estoy de acuerdo. No estoy de acuerdo.

6. Estoy de acuerdo. No estoy de acuerdo.

LM 11-11 | ¿Qué le recomiendas a Julián? Poor Julián is so tired of his awful boss that he comes to you for advice. Listen to the options and choose the one that will improve Julián's situation. Select the appropriate letters.

1. a / b   4. a / b

2. a / b   5. a / b

3. a / b   6. a / b

LM 11-12 | ¿Qué te parece? You will hear a series of situations pertaining to the workplace. Offer your perspective or opinion by using the subjunctive to complete the sentences below.

1. Recomiendo que _____.

2. Deseo que _____.

3. No dudo que _____.

4. Es necesario que _____.

5. Es probable que _____.

6. Es posible que _____.

VOCABULARIO Las finanzas personales

CD6,
Track 36

LM 11-13 | ¡Empareja! Listen to the following definitions and match them with the appropriate term. Write the letter of the definition in the space provided.

_____ **1.** el préstamo   _____ **4.** la cuenta de ahorros

_____ **2.** las facturas   _____ **5.** la cuenta corriente

_____ **3.** la tarjeta de crédito   _____ **6.** el cajero automático

CD6,
Track 37

LM 11-14 | Asociaciones Listen to the following expressions and select the one that does not belong in the sequence. Write it in the space provided.

1. _____

2. _____

3. _____

4. _____

5. _____

6. _____

CD6,
Track 38

LM 11-15 | La administración de tu dinero Answer the following questions with complete sentences.

1. _____

2. _____

3. _____

4. _____

5. _____

6. _____

ESTRUCTURA III   Expressing desires and intentions: The present subjunctive with statements of volition

CD6,
Track 39

LM 11-16 | El trabajo ideal Listen to the ideal job description. Pay close attention to the use of the subjunctive and write the subjunctive phrase in the spaces provided.

1. _____

2. _____

3. _____

4. _____

5. _____

6. _____

CD6, Track 40 **LM 11-17 | ¡Ese es!** Choose the correct form in order to complete the sentence correctly.

1. que se divierta / que se divierte

2. que me da / que me dé

3. que te aumenta / que te aumente

4. que no les pide / que no les pida

5. que vayan / que van

6. que escribe / que escriba

CD6, Track 41 **LM 11-18 | El empleo de mis sueños** Listen to the prompts and respond according to your preferences with regard to the perfect job. Pay close attention in using the present subjunctive.

1. _____

2. _____

3. _____

4. _____

5. _____

6. _____

♪ RITMOS Y MÚSICA

LM 11-19 | La música Listen to the song "Pablo Pueblo" by Rubén Blades. Then, indicate if each of the following statements about its content is **cierto** (true) or **falso** (false).

1. Hay una voz principal masculina y un coro de voces femeninas.

2. El coro no canta mucho, sólo repite las mismas palabras.

3. El ritmo es lento y melancólico.

4. Se escucha el sonido de las trompetas y la percusión, típico de la música centroamericana.

5. En esta canción, Rubén Blades no usa ni el piano ni la guitarra.

LM 11-20 | La letra After listening to the song "Pablo Pueblo", choose the option that best applies to its lyrics.

1. **a.** La letra de esta canción trata un tema serio.
   b. La letra de esta canción trata un tema cómico.

2. **a.** El tema principal de esta canción es la vida en un pequeño pueblo.
   b. El tema principal de esta canción es la vida de la gente pobre.

3. **a.** Pablo Pueblo está contento y es optimista.
   b. Pablo Pueblo está triste y decepcionado.

4. **a.** Pablo Pueblo es un hombre que no tiene mucho dinero.
   b. Pablo Pueblo es un hombre que no tiene trabajo.

5. **a.** Pablo Pueblo vive en un barrio donde hay basura en las calles.
   b. Pablo Pueblo vive en un barrio donde llueve mucho.

CD6,
Track 42

LM 11-21 | **Comprensión** After watching the video segment for Chapter 11, decide if the recorded statements are **cierto** *(true)* or **falso** *(false)*.

1. _____

2. _____

3. _____

4. _____

5. _____

6. _____

CD6,
Track 43

LM 11-22 | **¿Quién fue?** Decide which of the five characters in the video is responsible for the action you hear.

1. Sofía   Valeria   Antonio   Javier   Alejandra

2. Sofía   Valeria   Antonio   Javier   Alejandra

3. Sofía   Valeria   Antonio   Javier   Alejandra

4. Sofía   Valeria   Antonio   Javier   Alejandra

5. Sofía   Valeria   Antonio   Javier   Alejandra

6. Sofía   Valeria   Antonio   Javier   Alejandra

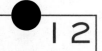

12 | *El medio ambiente: Costa Rica*

VOCABULARIO La geografía rural y urbana

CD7,
Track 2 **LM 12-1 | ¿Rural o urbana?** Listen to the words from the vocabulary. Identify the words pertaining to urban or rural geography. Write **rural** or **urbana** according to the vocabulary term that you hear. Follow the model.

Modelo   la fábrica
           urbana

1. _____   4. _____

2. _____   5. _____

3. _____   6. _____

CD7,
Track 3 **LM 12-2 | ¿Es posible o imposible?** Listen to the following statements and decide if each one is possible or impossible. Write **Es posible.** or **No es posible.** depending on the information given.

1. _____   4. _____

2. _____   5. _____

3. _____   6. _____

CD7,
Track 4 **LM 12-3 | ¿Dónde están?** Listen to the following words pertaining to urban or rural geography. Next to the choices provided, write the most logical place where each may be found.

1. el bosque, la carretera, la metrópolis, la basura _____

2. la fábrica, la selva, la colina, el tráfico _____

3. el arroyo, el bosque, la finca, la metrópolis _____

4. la basura, la tierra, la selva, el ruido _____

5. la catarata, la colina, la basura, los rascacielos _____

6. la basura, la selva, el bosque, la carretera _____

ESTRUCTURA I | Expressing emotion and opinions: Subjunctive following verbs of emotion, impersonal expressions, and *ojalá*

CD7, Track 5 **LM 12-4 | Y tú, ¿qué opinas?** You will hear statements made by six people who lead very different lives. Listen carefully, and express your opinion or reaction to each of one. You should use verbs of emotion (**me alegro de que, me molesta que, me sorprende que,** etc.) or impersonal expressions (**es bueno que, es necesario que, es mejor que,** etc.) in your reponses. Follow the model.

> Modelo Siempre utilizo el transporte público.
> *Es bueno que tú utilices el transporte público.*

1. _____
2. _____
3. _____
4. _____
5. _____
6. _____

CD7, Track 6 **LM 12-5 | Sugerencias** Listen to your friend's opinions regarding lifestyles. Respond to her opinions by commenting on the way she lives. Follow the model.

> Modelo Es una lástima no vivir en una metrópolis.
> *Es una lástima que tú no vivas en una metrópolis.*

1. _____
2. _____
3. _____
4. _____
5. _____
6. _____

CD7, Track 7 **LM 12-6 | ¡Ojalá!** Your best friend just found a job in a big metropolitan area. Listen to the statements in the present tense, and then wish your friend the very best in the big city. Begin each of your sentences with the expression **ojalá** + *subjunctive*. Follow the model.

> Modelo La vida en una gran metrópolis te gusta.
> *¡Ojalá que la vida en una gran metrópolis te guste!*

1. _____
2. _____
3. _____
4. _____
5. _____
6. _____

VOCABULARIO La conservación y la explotación

CD7, Track 8 **LM 12-7** | **¿Qué palabra es?** You will listen to some definitions. Write the letter of the appropriate definition with each word.

_____ **1.** destruir   _____ **3.** reforestar   _____ **5.** recoger

_____ **2.** el petróleo   _____ **4.** acabar   _____ **6.** el aire

CD7, Track 9 **LM 12-8** | **¿Verdad o mentira?** The president of the country is speaking about conservation and exploitation. Listen carefully to the president's message and select either **verdad** or **mentira** depending on the statements. **¡OJO!** Be logical!

1. _____   **3.** _____   **5.** _____

2. _____   **4.** _____   **6.** _____

CD7, Track 10 **LM 12-9** | **¿Es posible o es imposible?** Listen to the following statements regarding the environment and select either **es posible** or **es imposible** depending on the statements.

1. _____   **3.** _____   **5.** _____

2. _____   **4.** _____   **6.** _____

CD7, Track 11 **LM 12-10** | **¡Adivina!** Listen to the descriptions of animals or insects. Based on the descriptions, guess which animal or insect being described.

1. _____   **3.** _____   **5.** _____

2. _____   **4.** _____   **6.** _____

ESTRUCTURA II — Expressing doubts; or uncertainty and hypothesizing: The subjunctive with verbs; or expressions of doubt and uncertainty; and adjective clauses

CD7, Track 12 **LM 12-11** | **¿Indicativo o subjuntivo?** Listen to the sentences and write the verbal mode that you hear: **indicativo** or **subjuntivo.** Follow the model.

Modelo   Creo que hay mucha contaminación en las grandes metrópolis.
           indicativo

1. _____   **3.** _____   **5.** _____

2. _____   **4.** _____   **6.** _____

CD7, Track 13 **LM 12-12** | **¡Lo contrario!** You are going to listen again to the statements in activity LM 12-11. Following the model, write the opposite of what you hear.

Modelo   Creo que hay mucha contaminación en las grandes metrópolis.
           No creo que haya mucha contaminación en las grandes metrópolis.

1. _____

2. _____

3. _____

4. _____

5. _____

6. _____

LM 12-13 | Dudas y certezas Your best friend is going to express his doubts and certainties regarding the environment. Listen to his statements and write the verbs that you hear, explaining why they are in the subjunctive or the infinitive, by also writing: **duda** *(doubt)* or **certeza** *(certainty).*

Modelo   Pienso buscar un trabajo en la conservación de energía.
          buscar (certeza)

1. _____   4. _____

2. _____   5. _____

3. _____   6. _____

♪ RITMOS Y MÚSICA

LM 12-14 | La música Listen to the song "Muchacha y Luna" by the group Malpaís from Costa Rica. Then, indicate if the following statements about its content are **cierto** *(true)* or **falso** *(false).*

1. Es una canción folclórica; no es muy moderna.

2. Es mayormente *(mostly)* instrumental; no tiene mucha letra.

3. Los instrumentos principales son el violín y el piano.

4. Hay más de un cantante.

5. El ritmo es rápido, bueno para bailar.

LM 12-15 | La letra As you listen to the song "Muchacha y Luna", notice all the references to nature in its lyrics. Can you identify all of them? Circle the ones you hear in the song.

el arroyo	el viento	el aire	la colina
la catarata	la tierra	los bosques	el río
pájaro	tortuga	mariposa	los árboles

💿 ¡A VER!

LM 12-16 | ¿Cierto o falso? Watch the **¡A ver!** video segment for Capítulo 12 and listen to the statements. For each statement write **cierto** or **falso.**

1. _____   4. _____

2. _____   5. _____

3. _____   6. _____

LM 12-17 | ¿Quién lo dice? Watch the video segment a second time and indicate who says the following statements.

1. ¿Sofi o Valeria? _____

2. ¿Sofi o Alejandra? _____

3. ¿Sofi o Alejandra? _____

4. ¿Antonio o Javier? _____

5. ¿Valeria o Alejandra? _____

6. ¿Antonio o Javier? _____

El mundo del espectáculo: Perú y Ecuador

VOCABULARIO Programas y películas

CD7,
Track 17

LM 13-1 | Las artes y los medios de comunicación Listen to the titles and match them with the most logical category from the list below. Write the corresponding letter next to each category.

_____ **1.** la película romántica   _____ **4.** el programa de realidad

_____ **2.** el programa deportivo   _____ **5.** el pronóstico del tiempo

_____ **3.** la película extranjera   _____ **6.** el drama

CD7,
Track 18

LM 13-2 | ¿Qué opinas? You are a movie critic / TV program reviewer. Indicate your opinion regarding the shows or movies that you hear by selecting what best describes how you feel.

1. Me aburre.   Me molesta.   Siempre lo (la) miro.   No me gusta.

2. Me aburre.   Me molesta.   Siempre lo (la) miro.   No me gusta.

3. Me aburre.   Me molesta.   Siempre lo (la) miro.   No me gusta.

4. Me aburre.   Me molesta.   Siempre lo (la) miro.   No me gusta.

5. Me aburre.   Me molesta.   Siempre lo (la) miro.   No me gusta.

6. Me aburre.   Me molesta.   Siempre lo (la) miro.   No me gusta.

CD7,
Track 19

LM 13-3 | Tus preferencias Complete each sentence according to your preferences.

1. _____

2. _____

3. _____

4. _____

5. _____

6. _____

ESTRUCTURA I | Talking about anticipated actions: Subjunctive with purpose and time clauses

CD7,
Track 20

LM 13-4 | Ponte hipotético(a) Listen carefully to each statement and select the most logical conjunction to complete the sentence. Follow the model.

Modelo   La madre les permite ver el programa a sus hijos (sin que / con
           tal de que) hagan la tarea.
           con tal de que

1. para que / con tal de que   **4.** aunque / tan pronto como

2. para que / sin que   **5.** Después de que / En caso de que

3. cuando / a menos que   **6.** a menos que / en caso de que

CD7,
Track 21 **LM 13-5** | **¿Subjuntivo o indicativo?** Listen and repeat the sentences that you hear. Then, decide if the verbs should be in the subjunctive or indicative. Select your choice accordingly.

1. ve / vea

2. calmas / calmes

3. son / sean, ven / vean

4. canta / cante

5. podemos / podamos

6. preparo / prepare

CD7,
Track 22 **LM 13-6** | **¡Ah! Las probabilidades...** Listen carefully to each sentence. Complete the sentences logically, using the subjunctive when necessary.

1. _____.

2. _____.

3. _____.

4. _____.

5. _____.

6. _____.

VOCABULARIO Las artes

CD7,
Track 23 **LM 13-7** | **¡El arte y eso es todo!** Listen to the forms of art and match them to the illustrations below by entering the corresponding letter in the space provided.

1. _____

2. _____

3. _____

4. _____   5. _____   6. _____

CD7, Track 24 **LM 13-8 | ¿Qué género? ¿Qué artista? ¿Qué obra?** Listen to the names of the following personalities and their works. Place them in the correct categories by writing the letters in the spaces provided.

1. la arquitectura, el arquitecto, el edificio _____

2. la pintura, el pintor, la obra maestra _____

3. la escultura, el escultor, la estatua _____

4. la autora, la novela _____

5. el escritor de teatro, el teatro, la obra de teatro _____

6. la música, la cantante _____

CD7, Track 25 **LM 13-9 | Cuéntanos de ti** Answer the following questions orally first. Then write your answers in the spaces provided.

1. _____.
2. _____.
3. _____.
4. _____.
5. _____.
6. _____.

ESTRUCTURA II Talking about unplanned or accidental occurrences: No-fault *se* construction

CD7, Track 26 **LM 13-10 | ¿A quién le pasó?** Listen to the sentences and repeat them. Then match each sentence with the appropriate drawing. Write the corresponding letter in the space provided.

1. _____   2. _____   3. _____

4. _____

5. _____

6. _____

CD7,
Track 27 **LM 13-11** | **¡No es culpa tuya!** Listen to the following sentences and write the expressions with **se** that are the most logical. Follow the model.

> Modelo   No puedes beber leche porque tu hermana acabó la botella de leche.
> *Se acabó la botella de leche.*

1. _____.
2. _____.
3. _____.
4. _____.
5. _____.
6. _____.

CD7,
Track 28 **LM 13-12** | **¿Qué está pasando aquí?** Listen carefully. Match the action you hear with the corresponding illustration by writing the letters in the spaces provided.

1. _____

2. _____

3. _____

4. _____

5. _____

6. _____

ESTRUCTURA III | Describing completed actions and resulting conditions: Use of the past participle as adjective

CD7, Track 29 **LM 13-13 | ¿Cómo están?** Match the past participle below with the sentence you hear by writing the corresponding letter of the sentence in the space provided.

1. cerrado _____

2. abiertas _____

3. muertos _____

4. cancelado _____

5. escrita _____

6. resuelto _____

CD7, Track 30 **LM 13-14 | ¿Quién fue?** Transform each sentence that you hear with **por** + *the agent of the action*. Follow the model.

Modelo   el cuadro La artista pintó el cuadro.
        El cuadro fue pintado por la artista.

1. *La Gioconda* _____.

2. *Los heraldos negros* _____.

3. América _____.

4. La Sagrada Familia _____.

5. El concierto _____.

6. *La casa de los espíritus* _____.

LM 13-15 | La versión de Simon y Garfunkel Listen to Simon & Garfunkel's version of the song "El Cóndor Pasa". Then, indicate if each of the following statements is **cierto** *(true)* or **falso** *(false)*.

1. La letra es en inglés.

2. La letra de la canción habla de los cóndores *(vultures)* en la zona andina.

3. Se escuchan instrumentos acústicos y eléctricos.

4. El ritmo cambia en la mitad de la canción.

5. Los instrumentos principales son el charango y la flauta. (Lee la sección *Ritmos y música* en el *Encuentro cultural* si no estás seguro[a]).

LM 13-16 | La versión del grupo Inca the Peruvian Ensemble Now, listen to the version of the same song by Inca the Peruvian Ensemble. Then, indicate if each of the following statements is **cierto** *(true)* or **falso** *(false)*.

1. La letra es en español.

2. Es una canción folclórica.

3. El ritmo es exactamente igual que la versión de Simon y Garfunkel.

4. Los instrumentos principales son el charango y la flauta.

5. El ritmo en la primera parte de la canción es más lento que en la segunda parte.

DVD ¡A VER!

CD7,
Track 31 **LM 13-17 | Comprensión** After watching the **¡A ver!** video segment for Chapter 13, answer **cierto** *(true)* or **falso** *(false)* to the following statements.

1. _____   4. _____

2. _____   5. _____

3. _____   6. _____

CD7,
Track 32 **LM 13-18 | ¿Qué chica fue?** Decide which of the three roommates is responsible for the action you hear. Select the correct response.

1. Sofía   Valeria   Alejandra

2. Sofía   Valeria   Alejandra

3. Sofía   Valeria   Alejandra

4. Sofía   Valeria   Alejandra

5. Sofía   Valeria   Alejandra

6. Sofía   Valeria   Alejandra

14 | *La vida pública: Chile*

VOCABULARIO La política y el voto

CD8,
Track 2

LM 14-1 | Definiciones Listen to the definitions and match them with the correct vocabulary words by writing the appropriate letter in the space provided.

1. el congreso _____   4. el ejército _____

2. el dictador _____   5. el presidente _____

3. la democracia _____   6. la ley _____

CD8,
Track 3

LM 14-2 | ¡Aquí no! In each case, you will hear three vocabulary words. Write the one that does not belong.

1. _____

2. _____

3. _____

4. _____

5. _____

6. _____

CD8,
Track 4

LM 14-3 | ¿Sinónimos o antónimos? You will hear five pairs of words or phrases. For each pair decide if they are **sinónimos** (of similar meaning) or **antónimos** (of opposite meaning).

1. **a.** sinónimos   **b.** antónimos

2. **a.** sinónimos   **b.** antónimos

3. **a.** sinónimos   **b.** antónimos

4. **a.** sinónimos   **b.** antónimos

5. **a.** sinónimos   **b.** antónimos

6. **a.** sinónimos   **b.** antónimos

ESTRUCTURA I Talking about future events: The future tense

CD8,
Track 5

LM 14-4 | Predicciones para mañana The university newspaper, *Informed Students*, is making some predictions about the upcoming student elections. Identify the verbs in the future tense by writing them in the space provided.

1. _____

2. _____

3. _____

4. _____

5. _____

6. _____

CD8, Track 6

LM 14-5 | ¿Qué pasará mañana? Virginia is asking some questions of her friend, Natalia, who is one of the candidates for the student body presidency. She wants to know what will happen in the future elections. Match the question with the appropriate future tense by entering the letter in the space provided.

1. cambiarás _____

4. tendrás _____

2. votarás _____

5. sabrás _____

3. estarás _____

6. te pondrás _____

CD8, Track 7

LM 14-6 | ¿Y tu futuro? You will hear some questions pertaining to your future. Answer them in complete sentences making certain you use the correct form of the future tense in Spanish.

1. _____

2. _____

3. _____

4. _____

5. _____

6. _____

VOCABULARIO Las preocupaciones cívicas y los medios de comunicación

CD8, Track 8

LM 14-7 | En el futuro, ¿qué pasará? Lilí can predict the future with her cards. Listen to her predictions and select **Es bueno** or **Es malo** according to what Lilí sees in the cards.

1. Es bueno. Es malo.

4. Es bueno. Es malo.

2. Es bueno. Es malo.

5. Es bueno. Es malo.

3. Es bueno. Es malo.

6. Es bueno. Es malo.

CD8, Track 9

LM 14-8 | ¿Qué palabra es? Listen to the definitions and match each one to the correct word by writing in the letter in the space.

1. el analfabetismo _____

4. los impuestos _____

2. el Internet _____

5. el aborto _____

3. el desempleo _____

6. la huelga _____

CD8, Track 10

LM 14-9 | ¿Quién lo hace? You will hear six terms. Match each one to the word with which it is most closely connected.

1. la revista

2. el presidente

3. la manifestación

4. el ejército

5. el dictador

6. los ciudadanos

ESTRUCTURA II Expressing conjecture or probability: The conditional

CD8, Track 11 **LM 14-10 | Si yo fuera *(were)* presidente** Natalia thinks there are many things wrong with the current government of her country. Listen to her as she points them out, and then complete each statement with what you *would do* differently if you were president. Follow the model.

> **Modelo** El gobierno no respeta los derechos humanous
> Pero si yo fuera presidente, el gobierno *respetaría* los derechos humanos.

1. Pero si yo fuera presidente, los impuestos _____ bajos.

2. Pero si yo fuera presidente, no _____ guerras.

3. Pero si yo fuera presidente, la prensa _____ objetivamente.

4. Pero si yo fuera presidente, los políticos _____ la verdad.

5. Pero si yo fuera presidente, muchos ciudadanos _____ empleo.

CD8, Track 12 **LM 14-11 | Especulaciones** You will hear some questions. Write down your answers according to the model.

> **Modelo** ¿Dónde irían los estudiantes ayer por la mañana?
> *Los estudiantes irían a la universidad.*

1. _____

2. _____

3. _____

4. _____

CD8, Track 13 **LM 14-12 | ¡Con educación, por favor!** Alex is a small child who does not yet have proper manners. You will hear him make a statement; change his command into a more gentle request by using the conditional. Write each reworked request in the space provided, and then repeat each one. Follow the model.

> **Modelo** ¡Camarero, quiero agua!
> *Camarero, querría agua, por favor.*

1. _____

2. _____

3. _____

4. _____

5. _____

6. _____

ESTRUCTURA III — Making references to the present: The present perfect subjunctive

CD8, Track 14

LM 14-13 | Un discurso Natalia and her party have won the student elections, and she is giving her victory speech. Following the model, identify the present perfect subjunctive verb forms she uses to express her feelings, and write them in the spaces provided.

> Modelo   Estoy muy contenta que mi partido haya ganado las elecciones.
> *haya ganado*

1. _____   4. _____

2. _____   5. _____

3. _____   6. _____

CD8, Track 15

LM 14-14 | ¿Cómo te sientes? Listen to the following statements pertaining to U.S. politics and government. Provide your reaction by selecting the appropriate verb or expression. Remember to conjugate the infinitive in the present perfect subjunctive.

1. Me alegro / Dudo / Es interesante
   que George W. Bush _____ (ganar) las elecciones.

2. Me preocupa / Me molesta / Es una lástima
   que el ex candidato a la presidencia y ex vicepresidente de la nación, Al Gore,
   _____ (hacer) una película sobre los problemas del medio ambiente titulada
   «Una verdad inconveniente».

3. No creo / Espero / Es malo
   que todos los supermercados del país _____ (comenzar) la huelga por un aumento de sueldo.

4. Estoy triste / Estoy alegre / Es bueno
   que el Presidente _____ (decir) que la guerra continuará.

5. Dudo que / Es bueno que / Es una lastima que un 80% de los ciudadanos _____ (participar) en las elecciones.

6. Lamentablemente, no es cierto / no creo / es importante
   que no _____ (disminuir) ni el desempleo ni el crimen.

CD8, Track 16

LM 14-15 | ¿Contento(a) o triste? What makes you happy? What makes you sad? Start your sentences with **estoy contento(a) que** or **estoy triste que** to express what makes you happy or sad. Base your answers on the indications that your hear. Write the verbs in the present subjunctive. Follow the model.

> Modelo   mis padres / tener trabajo siempre
> *Estoy contento(a) que mis padres hayan tenido trabajo siempre.*

1. _____

2. _____

3. _____

4. _____

5. _____

6. _____

RITMOS Y MÚSICA

LM 14-16 | La música Listen to the song "Me gustan los estudiantes" written by Violeta Parra. Then, indicate if each of the following statements about its content is **cierto** *(true)* or **falso** *(false)*.

1. El instrumento predominante en esta canción es la guitarra.

2. El ritmo es constante durante toda la canción, no cambia abruptamente.

3. El ritmo es rápido y bueno para bailar, como la salsa o el merengue.

4. Hay más de un cantante.

5. La música y la voz de esta canción son simples; lo importante es la letra.

LM 14-16 | La letra After listening to the song "Me gustan los estudiantes", choose the option that best applies to its lyrics.

1. **a.** Es una canción con un tema social y político.
   b. Es una canción con un tema cómico y sarcástico.

2. **a.** En los primeros ocho versos, dice que le gustan los estudiantes porque no se asustan (no tienen miedo) de la policía.
   b. En los primeros ocho versos, dice que le gustan los estudiantes porque no obedecen (no respetan) a la policía.

3. Después, dice que los estudiantes «rugen *(roar)* como los vientos». ¿A qué se refiere?
   a. Los estudiantes sólo se quejan de todo.
   b. Los estudiantes protestan y expresan sus opiniones.

4. Más tarde, menciona a diferentes profesiones y dice «¡vivan los especialistas!». ¿Cuál es el mensaje que quiere dar?
   a. que los estudiantes deberían buscar trabajo
   b. que la educación universitaria es importante

5. ¿A qué estudiantes se aplica mejor la letra de esta canción?
   a. a todos los estudiantes, incluso los pre-escolares
   b. a los estudiantes de la escuela primaria
   c. a los estudiantes de la universidad

CD8, **LM 14-18** | **Comprensión** After watching the **¡A ver!** video segment for Chapter 14, answer
Track 17 **cierto** *(true)* or **falso** *(false)* to the following statements.

1. _____
2. _____
3. _____
4. _____
5. _____
6. _____

CD8, **LM 14-19** | **¿Quién fue?** Identify the action, thought, or situation with the character to
Track 18 whom it pertains by selecting the character's name.

1. Sofía	Valeria	Alejandra	Javier	Antonio
2. Sofía	Valeria	Alejandra	Javier	Antonio
3. Sofía	Valeria	Alejandra	Javier	Antonio
4. Sofía	Valeria	Alejandra	Javier	Antonio
5. Sofía	Valeria	Alejandra	Javier	Antonio
6. Sofía	Valeria	Alejandra	Javier	Antonio

Los avances tecnológicos: Uruguay

VOCABULARIO Los avances tecnológicos

CD8, Track 19 **LM 15-1 | ¡Ay, la tecnología!** Listen to the following statements from Minia's technologically challenged friend. Help her out by writing the letter of the correct response in the space provided.

1. Tiene instalado un reproductor de MP3. _____

2. Eso es porque es un televisor plasma. _____

3. Necesitas un reproductor de DVD. _____

4. Toma, aquí está el control remoto. _____

5. Es un mensaje de texto. _____

6. Sí, es que tenemos una antena parabólica. _____

CD8, Track 20 **LM 15-2 | La tecnología es cosa de todos los días.** Listen carefully to the definitions. Match the definitions with the corresponding words below by writing the letters in the blanks.

1. el control remoto _____

2. el satélite _____

3. el teléfono celular _____

4. el disco compacto _____

CD8, Track 21 **LM 15-3 | Minia, la piba (chica) digital** First, listen to the description of a young Uruguayan woman. Then, based on the description, complete the sentences below with the appropriate words.

1. Minia es una chica del siglo XXI y sus amigos la llaman _____.

2. Siempre lleva su teléfono celular _____.

3. Cuando conduce va escuchando sus _____ o la radio; por los altavoces sale una música infernal.

4. A Minia le fascina la computadora y siempre está _____ al Internet.

5. Usa su _____ para mandarle fotos a su novio en San Francisco.

6. Por teléfono, los enamorados se mandan besos que recibe el _____.

Making statements in the past: Past (imperfect) subjunctive

LM 15-4 | Los deseos de los padres Many times, children don't do exactly what their parents want them to do. In Alejandra's case, she and her brothers did the opposite of what her parents wanted them to do. Listen as she describes what she and her brothers used to do as children. Then, complete each sentence below with the appropriate verb. Follow the model.

Modelo   Yo nunca hacía la tarea.
           Mis padres querían que yo *hiciera* la tarea.

1. Mi madre prefería que ellos no _____ mensajes de texto a nadie.

2. Mi padre quería que nosotros no _____ el televisor encendido nunca.

3. Mi madre quería que yo no _____ el control remoto de la videocasetera.

4. Mis padres no permitían que él _____ el estéreo después de la medianoche.

5. Mi padre insistia en que yo nunca _____ el contestador automático.

LM 15-5 | La reacción de los hijos Sometimes children react strongly to what their parents do. Listen as Alejandra describes some moments in her childhood. Then, complete the following sentences with the appropriate verb form in order to find out how she and her siblings reacted in each case. Follow the model.

Modelo   Mi madre le compró una computadora a mi hermana.
           Y mi hermana se alegró de que ella le *comprara* una computadora.

1. Y mis hermanos se alegraron mucho de que mi madre les _____ un reproductor de MP3.

2. Y a mi hermano le sorprendió mucho que él _____ su estéro.

3. Y mis hermanos se quejaron de que ellos _____ el servicio de su teléfono celular.

4. Y a mis hermanos y a mí nos gustó que él _____ una antena parabólica en casa.

5. Y a mi hermana le molestó mucho que ella _____ su disco compacto favorito.

LM 15-6 | Clientes de ayer y hoy Federico and Alejandra are talking about some clients that visited their store yesterday, and some that are in the store now. Listen to Federico's questions, and then complete Alejandra's answers by choosing the correct verb tense.

1. Una que tenga / tuviera control remoto.

2. Uno que funcione / funcionara sin enchufarlo.

3. Uno que incluya / incluyera DVDs gratis.

4. Uno que sea / fuera fácil de usar.

5. Uno que pueda / pudiera grabar discos compactos.

VOCABULARIO La computadora

CD8,
Track 25

LM 15-7 | ¿Cuánto sabes de tecnología? How much technological vocabulary do you know? Listen carefully to the vocabulary words and identify them in the illustration below. Write the names in the space provided.

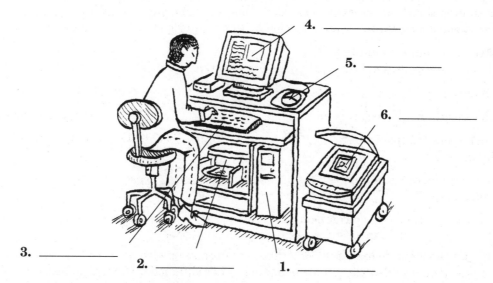

4. _____

5. _____

6. _____

3. _____

2. _____

1. _____

CD8,
Track 26

LM 15-8 | Ciberespacios en la sociedad del siglo XXI First, listen to the scenarios. Then, use the words and expressions below to complete them in a logical manner. **¡OJO!** Don't forget to write the letters that correspond to the appropriate scenario.

1. Internet _____

2. salón de charla _____

3. archivar _____

4. correo electrónico _____

5. navegar la Red _____

6. teletrabajaremos _____

CD8,
Track 27

LM 15-9 | ¿Adicto a la computadora? Federico owns a computer store, but does he use his own computer? Alejandra wants to find out how much he really uses his computer, and so she asks him a few questions. Listen to her questions, and then select the most logical answer.

1. **a.** Sí, cuando necesito contectarme al Internet.
   b. Sí, cuando necesito imprimir documentos.

2. **a.** No, porque no tengo una computadora portatil.
   b. No, porque no tengo los altavoces.

3. **a.** No, porque no tengo el archivo necesario.
   b. No, porque no tengo el programa necesario.

4. **a.** Sí, pero mi pantalla no es muy buena.
   b. Sí, pero mi teclado no es muy bueno.

5. **a.** Sí, tengo mi propia página Web.
   b. Sí, tengo mi propio correo electrónico.

LM 15-10 | Resuelve la hipótesis Listen carefully to each sentence. Then, complete it by selecting one of the three choices.

1. **a.** la buscaba en el Internet
   b. la buscaría en el Internet
   c. la buscaré en el Internet

2. **a.** habría menos accidentes
   b. había menos accidentes
   c. habrá menos accidentes

3. **a.** ahorrarás tiempo y dinero
   b. ahorrarías tiempo y dinero
   c. ahorrabas tiempo y dinero

4. **a.** no habrá suficiente tiempo para hacer otras cosas
   b. no habría suficiente tiempo para hacer otras cosas
   c. no había suficiente tiempo para hacer otras cosas

5. **a.** la comunicación internacional era más difícil
   b. la comunicación internacional sería más difícil
   c. la comunicación internacional será más difícil

6. **a.** tendré que ir a la biblioteca
   b. tuve que ir a la biblioteca
   c. tendría que ir a la biblioteca

LM 15-11 | ¿Probable o improbable? Some hypothetical situations are more likely to occur than others. Listen carefully to the following statements and decide whether they are likely (**probable**) or unlikely (**improbable**) to occur.

1. **a.** probable   **b.** improbable

2. **a.** probable   **b.** improbable

3. **a.** probable   **b.** improbable

4. **a.** probable   **b.** improbable

5. **a.** probable   **b.** improbable

LM 15-12 | Condiciones Munia loves new technology, but she is also very cautious and will only do things under certain conditions. Listen to the questions she's being asked. Then, select the correct answer, according to the context of each question.

1. **a.** Sí, si encuentro una barata.
   b. Sí, si encontrara una barata.
   c. Sí, si encontraría una barata.
   d. Sí, si encontraré una barata.

2. **a.** Sí, si mi jefe lo permitirá.
   b. Sí, si me jefe lo permite.
   c. Sí, si mi jefe lo permitiera.
   d. Sí, si mi jefe lo permitiría.

3. **a.** Sí, si yo sabría cómo crearla.
   b. Sí, si yo sé cómo crearla.
   c. Sí, si yo sabré cómo crearla.
   d. Sí, si yo supiera cómo crearla.

4. **a.** Sí, si la conexión funcionara bien.
   b. Sí, si la conexión funciona bien.
   c. Sí, si la conexión funcionaría bien.
   d. Sí, si la conexión funcionará bien.

5. **a.** Sí, si tengo el dinero para comprarlo.
   b. Sí, si tendría el dinero para comprarlo.
   c. Sí, si tuviera el dinero para comprarlo.
   d. Sí, si tendré el dinero para comprarlo.

RITMOS Y MÚSICA

LM 15-13 | La música Listen to "Mi corazón" by Bajofondo Tango Club. After listening to this song, indicate if each of the following statements about its content is **cierto** *(true)* or **falso** *(false)*.

1. Hay varias voces, masculinas y femeninas.

2. La música es una mezcla de instrumentos clásicos y modernos.

3. El ritmo básico es el de un tango.

4. Es una canción folclórica; no es muy moderna.

5. Se escucha el sonido del bandoneón y el bajo *(bass)*.

LM 15-14 | La letra After listening to "Mi corazón", choose the option that best applies to its lyrics.

1. **a.** La letra es repetitiva.
   b. La letra es variada.

2. **a.** La música es simple; lo importante es la letra.
   b. No hay mucha letra; es mayormente instrumental.

3. **a.** La letra tiene un mensaje importante.
   b. La letra no tiene mucho sentido.

4. **a.** El cantante dice la palabra «bandoeón».
   b. El cantante dice la palabra «acordeón».

5. El cantante dice «mi corazón me lleva / hacia el hondo bajofondo». ¿Cómo pronuncia la *ll* en la palabra *lleva*?
   a. como la *y* de *York*.
   b. como la *sh* de *show*.
   c. casi no la pronuncia.

CD8,
Track 31 **LM 15-15** | **Comprensión** After watching the **¡A ver!** video segment for Chapter 15, answer **cierto** *(true)* or **falso** *(false)* to the following statements.

1. _____

2. _____

3. _____

4. _____

5. _____

6. _____

CD8,
Track 32 **LM 15-16** | **¿Quién lo dijo?** Choose which of the five roommates is responsible for each statement you hear.

1. Sofía   Valeria   Alejandra   Javier   Antonio

2. Sofía   Valeria   Alejandra   Javier   Antonio

3. Sofía   Valeria   Alejandra   Javier   Antonio

4. Sofía   Valeria   Alejandra   Javier   Antonio

5. Sofía   Valeria   Alejandra   Javier   Antonio

6. Sofía   Valeria   Alejandra   Javier   Antonio

Autobruebas Answer Key

CAPÍTULO PRELIMINAR

TOPRUEBA

WB P-12 Una conversación típica

Hola; Qué; estás; gracias; gusto; es mío; dónde; Soy; Adiós,
Adiós; Nos

WB P-13 Números

1. quince / catorce
2. uno / cero
3. treinta / veintinueve
4. diecisiete / dieciséis
5. veinticinco / veinticuatro

WB P-14 Presentaciones

eres; Soy, es; son; somos

WB P-15 ¿Sois de España?

vosotros; nosotros, Yo, él; Ud.; Yo; Ella; tú; Yo; Uds.

CAPÍTULO 1

AUTOPRUEBA

WB 1-18 Los cursos

1. Letras: **b.** matemáticas
2. Lenguas: **c.** historia
3. Ciencias sociales: **a.** biología
4. Arte: **c.** biología

WB 1-19 ¿Qué hora es?

1. Son las tres menos cuarto de la tarde.
2. Es la una y veintidós de la tarde.
3. Es la una menos veintinueve de la tarde.
4. Son las cinco y cuarto de la mañana.
5. Son las nueve y media de la mañana.

WB 1-20 Está muy ocupada.

1. Los martes Nancy estudia alemán a las cuatro menos
   cuarto de la tarde.
2. Los miércoles Nancy estudia chino a la una menos
   cuarto de la tarde.
3. Los jueves Nancy estudia ruso a la una y media
   de la tarde.
4. Los viernes Nancy estudia italiano a las cinco y cuarto
   de la tarde.
5. Los sábados Nancy estudia portugués a las siete
   y media de la noche.
6. Los domingos Nancy estudia japonés a las diez de
   la mañana.

WB 1-21 Los colores

1. amarillo 2. negro 3. rojo 4. marrón 5. blanco 6. verde

WB 1-22 Lupe y Lalo

1. una 2. la 3. una 4. la 5. las 6. el 7. el 8. los 9. el
10. una 11. La 12. las 13. la 14. los 15. la 16. los

WB 1-23 Las actividades del día

1. Ramón trabaja todos los días.
2. Teresa y Evelia estudian matemáticas por la tarde.
3. Yo practico deportes por la mañana.
4. Nosotros descansamos a las cuatro de la tarde.
5. Tú enseñas ejercicios aeróbicos por la noche.
6. Uds. regresan a la casa a las seis de la tarde.

CAPÍTULO 2

AUTOPRUEBA

WB 2-26 Los miembros de la familia

1. esposa
2. primo
3. apellido
4. sobrina
5. nietos

WB 2-27 Descripciones

1. es; mexicana
2. somos; simpáticas
3. son; tontos
4. eres; atlética
5. es; paciente

WB 2-28 Probablemente son...

1. trabajadores
2. inteligente
3. tacaño
4. irresponsable
5. perezosa
6. gordos

WB 2-29 Los números

1. treinta y dos
2. noventa y nueve
3. veinticuatro
4. doce
5. quince
6. diecisiete
7. cuarenta y seis
8. setenta y nueve

WB 2-30 Una conversación

1. Tienes 2. mi 3. tengo 4. tienes 5. mis 6. tienen
7. tienen 8. su 9. Su 10. Tienes 11. tengo 12. Tienes
13. tengo

WB 2-31 En la universidad

1. vives; 2. vivo; 3. vive; 4. escribes; 5. escribes;
6. recibo; 7. debo; 8. tienes; 9. creo

CAPÍTULO 3

AUTOPRUEBA

WB 3-23 Los meses y las estaciones

1. diciembre, el invierno
2. febrero, el invierno
3. enero, el invierno
4. octubre, el otoño
5. mayo, la primavera
6. noviembre, el otoño

WB 3-24 En la ciudad

1. a 2. g 3. b 4. d 5. c 6. f 7. e

WB 3-25 Los pasatiempos

Possible answers:
1. Me gusta ver películas en video.
2. Me gusta sacar fotos.
3. Me gusta jugar al tenis.
4. Me gusta tocar la guitarra.
5. Me gusta bailar con la música rock.
6. Me gusta visitar a mis abuelos.

WB 3-26 Entre amigos

1. vas 2. voy 3. vas 4. vamos 5. va 6. van

WB 3-27 Un joven contento

1. salgo 2. hago 3. voy 4. hago/doy 5. Pongo
6. conozco 7. sé 8. veo 9. estoy

WB 3-28 ¿Qué vas a hacer?

1. Voy a practicar deportes.
2. Voy a jugar al tenis.
3. Voy a nadar en la piscina.
4. Voy a montar a caballo.
5. Voy a levantar pesas.

WB 3-29 ¿Qué tiempo hace?

Possible answers:
A. Hace sol. *or* Hace calor., *or* Hace buen tiempo.
B. Hace sol. *or* Hace buen tiempo.
C. Hace mucho calor.
D. Hace fresco. *or* Está despejado.
E. Hace viento.
F. Hace mucho frío.

CAPÍTULO 4

AUTOPRUEBA

WB 4-30 Los muebles

1. un escritorio 2. un armario 3. mi cama 4. el inodoro
5. el jardín

WB 4-31 Los electrodomésticos

1. una lavadora
2. un horno microondas
3. una aspiradora
4. un despertador
5. la nevera

WB 4-33 Entre novios

1. tienes 2. Tengo 3. quieres 4. quiero 5. Prefiero
6. comienza 7. Comienza 8. queremos 9. preferimos
10. pienso

WB 4-34 La hora del almuerzo

1. almuerzo 2. sirve 3. dice 4. almorzar 5. duermo
6. vuelven 7. vuelvo 8. jugamos 9. juego

WB 4-35 En otras palabras

1. Tengo ganas de bailar.
2. Tengo sueño.
3. Tengo celos.
4. Tengo miedo.

WB 4-36 ¿Qué hago?

1. Haz tu cama todos los días.
2. Quita la mesa después de comer.
3. Saca la basura todos los días.
4. Ve al supermercado todos los sábados.

WB 4-37 ¿Cómo están todos?

1. Lolita está emocionada; Está jugando en el patio.
2. Teresita y Javi están ocupados; Están regando las plantas.
3. Miguelín está aburrido; Está leyendo un libro.
4. Ángel y yo estamos sucios; Estamos preparando un pastel.

WB 4-38 ¿Cuántos son?

1. mil setecientos treinta y ocho
2. mil ciento sesenta
3. mil cuatrocientos dieciséis

CAPÍTULO 5

AUTOPRUEBA

WB 5-24 El cuerpo humano

1. el ojo   6. el estómago
2. el pelo   7. la pierna
3. las orejas   8. el pie
4. la nariz   9. la mano
5. la boca / los dientes   10. el brazo

WB 5-25 Los problemas médicos

1. alergia, estornudo
2. catarro
3. enfermedad

4. congestionado
5. escalofríos, síntomas
6. sano, enfermo
7. examina
8. fiebre, toma la temperatura
9. náuseas, guardar cama

ESTRUCTURAS

WB 5-26 La rutina diaria

1. Se despierta a las seis.
2. Se levanta a las seis y media.
3. Se ducha y se lava.
4. Se seca.
5. Se viste.
6. Se pinta. / Se maquilla.
7. Despierta a su hijo a las siete.
8. Se acuesta a las once.

WB 5-27 ¡Cómo vuela el tiempo!

1. Acaba de despertarse.
2. Acaba de levantarse.
3. Acaba de ducharse y lavarse.
4. Acaba de secarse.
5. Acaba de vestirse.
6. Acaba de pintarse / maquillarse.
7. Acaba de despertar a su hijo.
8. Acaba de acostarse.

WB 5-28 Lorena Bobada

1. es 2. Es 3. está 4. está 5. está 6. está 7. Es
8. es 9. está 10. ser 11. es 12. es

WB 5-29 Gemelos distintos

1. No quiero ésta, prefiero esa medicina.
2. No quiero ver éste, prefiero ver ese médico.
3. No quiero comprar ésta, prefiero comprar esa pastilla.
4. No quiero pedir éstos, prefiero pedir esos jarabes.
5. No prefiero esto, prefiero eso.

CAPÍTULO 6

AUTOPRUEBA

WB 6-24 La comida

CARNES:	jamón, res, pollo, bistec, pavo, chuletas de cerdo
PESCADO/MARISCOS:	calamares, camarones
BEBIDAS:	café, vino, agua mineral, té helado, leche, cerveza, jugo
POSTRES:	helado, flan, queso
FRUTAS:	naranja, manzana, banana
VERDURAS:	lechuga, papas
CONDIMENTOS:	mantequilla, sal, piminenta, vinagre, aceite

WB 6-25 En el restaurante

1. c 2. c 3. a 4. a 5. b 6. a

WB 6-26 ¡Viva la igualdad!

1. Beti come tantas verduras como Martín.
2. Beti almuerza en tantos restaurantes como Martín.
3. Beti pide tantas aprepas como Martín.
4. Beti es tan amable como Martín.
5. Beti toma tanto café como Martín.

WB 6-27 El más...

1. Guillermo es el mayor.
2. Alejandro es el más paciente de los primos.
3. El jugo es la bebida más dulce.
4. Michael Jordan es el mejor jugador.

WB 6-28 Un sábado por la tarde

1. almorzó 2. almorcé 3. comimos 4. tomé 5. bebió
6. terminaste 7. terminé 8. comencé 9. leí 10. leyó
11. busqué 12. compré

WB 6-29 Padre e hijo

1. se divirtieron 2. pidió 3. sirvió 4. se durmió

CAPÍTULO 7

AUTOPRUEBA

WB 7-25 La ropa

1. Para nadar: el traje de baño
2. Para la cabeza: el sombrero
3. Para los pies: los zapatos, los calcetines, las sandalias, las botas
4. Para las mujeres: la blusa, la falda, las medias, el vestido
5. Para los hombres: los pantalones, el traje, la corbata
6. Para la lluvia: el impermeable

WB 7-26 En la tienda

1. En qué puedo servirle 2. probarme 3. talla 4. queda
bien 5. Hace juego 6. moda 7. le debo 8. ganga 9. tarjeta
de crédito

WB 7-27 ¿Son tuyos?

1. ¡El sombrero es tuyo!
2. ¡Los cinturones son suyos!
3. ¡Los zapatos son suyos!
4. ¡Las gafas de sol son mías!
5. ¡El paraguas es suyo!

WB 7-28 Entre amigas

1. fuiste 2. Fui 3. hicieron 4. Tuvimos 5. vinieron
6. trajeron 7. estuvo 8. hiciste 9. fue 10. hice
11. quiso 12. supe

WB 7-29 A La hora de la cena

1. La 2. lo 3. Me, te 4. (compra)las

WB 7-30 La pequeña Elena

1. vivía 2. Tenía 3. sacaba 4. limpiaba 5. íbamos
6. compraba 7. gustaba 8. comíamos

WB 7-31 ¡Y ahora baila!

1. trabajábamos 2. llamó 3. éramos 4. se burlaba 5. invitó 6. bailaba 7. aceptaste 8. acepté

CAPÍTULO 8

AUTOPRUEBA

WB 8-20 Una celebración especial

1. cumplió 2. entremeses 3. invitados 4. disfrazarse
5. máscara 6. disfraz 7. procesión 8. se reunieron
9. celebrar 10. brindis 11. gritaron 12. Felicidades
13. pastel 14. velas 15. recordar 16. regalos
17. llorar 18. lo pasaron 19. anfitriona

WB 8-21 En la playa y en el campo

1. f 2. a 3. d 4. h 5. c 6. g 7. b 8. e

WB 8-22 Más preguntas

1. De dónde 2. Dónde 3. Cuál 4. Adónde
5. Qué 6. Cuántas 7. Qué

WB 8-23 Un viaje inolvidable

1. era 2. hice 3. Fui 4. tenía 5. tenía 6. decidieron
7. vivíamos 8. era 9. había 10. podía 11. sabía 12. fui
13. empezó 14. nadaba 15. mordió 16. sentí 17. grité
18. se metió 19. salvó 20. tuve 21. fue 22. asustó

WB 8-24 Significados especiales

1. tuvimos 2. supo, sabía 3. quise
4. pudo 5. tenía

WB 8-25 En el mercado

1. algo 2. algunos 3. algunas 4. también 5. ninguna
6. algunos 7. tampoco 8. ni… 9. ni 10. nada

WB 8-26 ¿Cuánto tiempo hace?

1. Hace tres meses que Lucía no trabaja.
2. Hace un año que Santi y Silvina no están casados.
3. Hace una semana que nosotros no vamos al centro comercial.
4. Hace demasiado tiempo que yo no tengo novio(a).
5. *Answers will vary.* Period of time. Hace [xx] años que yo no estoy en la secundaria.

CAPÍTULO 9

AUTOPRUEBA

WB 9-22 Viajes

1. c 2. b 3. d 4. a 5. f 6. g 7. e

WB 9-23 En el hotel

1. cuatro estrellas 2. cuartos 3. limpios 4. sucios
5. dobles 6. sencillas 7. privado 8. aire acondicionado
9. ascensor 10. recepción 11. cómodo

WB 9-24 ¿Dónde está todo?

1. al lado 2. detrás 3. a la izquierda 4. entre
5. a la derecha 6. enfrente

WB 9-25 Indicaciones

1. cruce 2. siga 3. Doble 4. suba 5. Siga 6. hacia

WB 9-26 Una carta

1. les 2. les 3. le 4. le 5. les 6. me 7. te
8. me 9. me 10. les

WB 9-27 Elena, la buena

1. Sí, te la presto.
2. Sí, se la preparo.
3. Sí, se lo escribo.
4. Sí, me la pueden pasar. *or* Pueden pasármela.
5. Sí, se lo puedo comprar. *or* Puedo comprárselo.

WB 9-28 Antes de salir del mercado

1. Perdone 2. déme 3. Tome 4. Dígame
5. Salga 6. vaya 7. Tenga 8. Vuelva

CAPÍTULO 10

AUTOPRUEBA

WB 10-21 El noviazgo

1. noviazgo
2. amor
3. nos enamoramos
4. cariño
5. nos llevamos
6. enamorados
7. matrimonio
8. casados

WB 10-22 La boda

1. novios 2. casarse 3. se besan 4. recién casados
5. aplauden 6. recepción 7. tienen lugar 8. banquete
9. brindis 10. felicitan 11. orquesta 12. ramo de flores
13. agarrar 14. luna de miel 15. se separan
16. se divorcian

WB 10-23 ¿Qué han hecho?

1. Pablo ha leído tres libros.
2. Teresa y Ángela han visto una película nueva.
3. Mamá y yo le hemos escrito cartas a la familia.
4. Yo me he divertido con mis amigos.
5. Tú has vuelto de un viaje largo.

WB 10-24 El romance de Ken y Barbie

1. Ken y Barbie se conocieron en Malibú.
2. Ellos se miraron intensamente.
3. Ellos se abrazaron fuertemente.
4. Ellos se enamoraron inmediatamente.
5. Ellos se casaron en junio de ese año.

WB 10-25 Miguel lo hace así

1. Miguel lee el periódico detenidamente.
2. Miguel habla con las chicas nerviosamente.
3. Miguel come rápidamente.
4. Miguel saca buenas notas fácilmente.
5. Miguel va a las fiestas frecuentemente.

WB 10-26 La rutina

1. Todos los días
2. Muchas veces
3. Solamente
4. A veces
5. Una vez
6. Nunca
7. siempre

WB 10-27 ¿Cómo lo hago?

1. Primero te sacas una cuenta electrónica de Internet.
2. Después/Luego/Entonces, te compras software para el email.
3. Luego/Después/Entonces le pides a tu novia su dirección electrónica
4. Entonces/Luego/Después puedes escribir el mensaje que quieres mandar.
5. Finalmente, le envías el mensaje.

WB 10-28 ¿El nuevo novio de Valeria?

1. que 2. que 3. lo que 4. quien

CAPÍTULO 11

AUTOPRUEBA

VOCABULARIO

WB 11-20 ¿Qué debe hacer?

1. arquitecto 2. peluquero 3. contador 4. periodista
5. programador 6. maestro 7. traductor 8. policía
9. siquiatra 10. dentista

WB 11-21 Solicitando trabajo

1. solicitar 2. currículum 3. computadora 4. imprimir
5. impresora 6. fotocopias 7. solicitud 8. llamar
9. entrevista 10. proyectos 11. beneficios 12. empleados
13. sueldo 14. contratar 15. tiempo parcial / tiempo
completo 16. tiempo completo / tiempo parcial
17. jubilarte 18. despedir

WB 11-22 Consejos financieros

1. ahorrar 2. deposites 3. cuenta de ahorros 4. saques
5. cajero automático 6. presupuesto 7. tarjeta de crédito
8. cheques 9. facturas 10. prestar 11. en efectivo
12. a plazos

ESTRUCTURAS

WB 11-23 De vacaciones

1. por 2. por 3. Por 4. para 5. para 6. Para 7. por
8. para 9. por 10. para

WB 11-24 El amor y los negocios

1. escribas 2. llames 3. tengas 4. mire 5. pienses
6. te enamores 7. pierdan 8. mandes 9. vayamos
10. nos divirtamos

WB 11-25 Entre amigos

1. salir 2. venir 3. sigamos 4. trabajemos 5. ir 6. vuelva
7. acompañes

CAPÍTULO 12

AUTOPRUEBA

VOCABULARIO

WB 12-17 La geografía rural y urbana

a. 1. metrópolis 2. acelerado 3. sobrepoblación 4. ruido /
tráfico 5. tráfico / ruido 6. contaminación 7. transporte
público 8. medio ambiente 9. basura 10. recogen 11. bella
b. 1. tranquila 2. campesinos 3. cultivar 4. regar
5. colinas 6. arroyos
c. 1. resolver 2. recursos naturales 3. petróleo
4. reforestar 5. capa de ozono 6. desarrollar 7. explotar
8. energía solar 9. desperdicio 10. destrucción
11. reciclar 12. escasez

WB 12-18 Entre amigos

1. estemos   2. poder
3. venir   4. estén
5. digas   6. acompañen
7. pienses   8. vayan
9. tengan   10. sea

WB 12-19 Hablando del viaje

1. Yo creo que estas vacaciones son excelentes.
   Sí, pero dudo que David quiera venir este año.

2. Gabriela no está segura que el hotel sea bueno.
Yo estoy segura que todos los hoteles van a ser muy buenos.

3. En San José nosotros tenemos que buscar un restaurante que sirva gallo pinto.
Yo conozco un buen restaurante que sirve gallo pinto.

4. Yo quiero visitar una reserva biológica que tenga muchas especies exóticas.
Manuel Antonio es una reserva preciosa que tiene todo tipo de animal exótico.

CAPÍTULO 13

AUTOPRUEBA

VOCABULARIO

WB 13-18 Las películas y los programas

1. e **2.** c **3.** d **4.** f **5.** g **6.** b **7.** h **8.** i **9.** j **10.** a

WB 13-19 El mundo de las bellas artes

1. concierto **2.** fotografía, fotógrafo **3.** director **4.** actriz
5. arquitectura **6.** cuadro **7.** bailarín **8.** danza
9. compositor **10.** cantante

WB 13-20 Consejos para la cita

1. limpie **2.** venga **3.** se asuste **4.** llegue **5.** está **6.** guste
7. vas **8.** invitas **9.** diga **10.** guste **11.** decida

WB 13-21 Pero ¡no fue nuestra culpa!

1. Se nos cayó una escultura.
2. Se le escaparon los niños.
3. Se me olvidó la cita.
4. Se nos acabó el dinero.
5. Se me perdió la llave de mi coche.

WB 13-22 ¿Ya está hecho?

1. Los estudiantes ya están invitados.
Fueron invitados por Jaime y Juan.
2. El entretenimiento ya está confirmado.
Fue confirmado por Analisa.
3. La lista de música ya está organizada.
Fue organizada por Rosa y Eva.
4. La comida ya está preparada. Fue preparada por Marta y Esteban.
5. Las decoraciones ya están colgadas.
Fueron colgadas por Julio.

CAPÍTULO 14

AUTOPRUEBA

VOCABULARIO

WB 14-19 Políticamente hablando

a. **1.** partidos políticos **2.** republicanos **3.** liberales
4. conservadores
b. **1.** candidatos **2.** campaña **3.** debates **4.** ciudadanos
c. **1.** dictadura **2.** democracia **3.** elegimos **4.** deber
5. votar
d. **1.** ejército **2.** paz **3.** defender

WB 14-20 Las preocupaciones cívicas

1. f **2.** i **3.** k **4.** e **5.** a **6.** c **7.** h **8.** l **9.** n **10.** d **11.** j **12.** m
13. o **14.** g **15.** b

WB 14-21 El primer día

1. tendrás **2.** comenzará **3.** será **4.** vendrán **5.** sabrán
6. querrá **7.** dirás **8.** habrá **9.** durará **10.** veré
11. podremos **12.** haré **13.** serás **14.** irá

WB 14-22 Puros sueños.

1. harías
2. viajaría
3. gustaría
4. Podría
5. saldríamos
6. iríamos
7. tomaríamos
8. Pasaríamos
9. querríamos
10. volaríamos
11. tendríamos

WB 14-23 No lo creo.

1. Es imposible que te hayas quedado en hoteles de cuatro estrellas.
2. No creo que tú y tu novia hayan conocido al presidente de los Estados Unidos.
3. Estoy seguro que tu novia lo ha pasado bien en Washington.
4. No dudo que has participado en tres manifestaciones políticas.
5. No pienso que tu novia te haya dicho que no quiere volver a Chile.

CAPÍTULO 15
⬤TOPRUEBA

WB 15-13 Los domingueros modernos

1. cámara digital
2. videocámara digital
3. teléfono celular
4. DVD
5. grabadora de DVD
6. antena parabólica
7. satélite
8. desconectar
9. equipo
10. estéreo
11. enchufado

WB 15-14 ¿Estás al tanto?

1. c 2. b 3. h 4. d 5. i 6. g 7. a 8. f 9. e

WB 15-15 Las instrucciones

1. abrir el programa 2. hacer click 3. pantalla 4. quitar
5. archivar 6. página Web 7. navegar

WB 15-16 Buenas amigas

1. me recordaras 2. hiciéramos 3. nos casáramos
4. fuéramos 5. nos metiéramos 6. dieran 7. pudiera
8. estudiara 9. se graduara

WB 15-17 ¿Qué harían?

1. Si Juan no tuviera que trabajar, pasaría todo su tiempo en la computadora.
2. Si Carlos y Marga compraran una mejor computadora, podrían usar el Internet.
3. Si Tomás no fuera tan tímido, podría conocer a más chicas en los salones de charla.
4. Si Nancy se graduara con un título en informática, ganaría mucho dinero.
5. Si Óscar me ofreciera un trabajo con su compañía, yo cambiaría de carrera.